MARSTON MAGNA

"OUR VILLAGE" IN THE 20TH CENTURY

Researched, Written and Compiled by

Molly Crabb, Elizabeth Crouch, Jenny Dench,
Pam Goodwin, Lyn Pemberton and Edie Robinson

Published by Honeybee Books
Broadoak, Dorset
www.honeybeebooks.co.uk

Printed in the UK using paper from sustainable sources

ISBN: 978-1-910616-41-3

Cover Image: Gray Marden and Jack Noyce. The apple picker was invented by Gray Marden in 1922.

Contents

INTRODUCTION

Mrs Marian Davis delighted the inhabitants of Marston Magna in 1984, when she published her memories of the village at the turn of the 20th century. She also contributed a regular column throughout the first decade of the Parish Magazine and we are indebted to her for inspiring us to record the village life of Marston Magna in the 20th century.

It was our desire to convey the essence of "Our Village" as it fought its way through a century of breath taking change. We have been privileged to tell the stories of some of its inhabitants, as well as recording changes and developments that have taken place.

The greatest change from 1900 to 2000 was the introduction of the motor vehicle and alongside it, mechanisation in the farming industry. These two innovations transformed a quiet backwater village into a noisy busy thoroughfare and provoked a major loss of employment for the men of the village.

It is remarkable to observe that despite this revolution and also the effect of two World Wars, Marston Magna has clung to its supportive community roots and that the sentiments expressed by Marian Davis in her book of childhood memories have survived and are still very evident today.

The countryside has been loved and relished by villagers in the last century. The roads may be busier now, but the fields and trees are still all around us. Wildflowers are coming back in our lanes and hedgerows, the birdsong is still vibrant and beautiful, and we do see rabbits running across the paths!

The year 2015 marks the 100th anniversary of the formation of the National Federation of Women's Institutes and it is also the 90th anniversary of the W.I. formed in our village. Six members of Marston Magna Women's Institute undertook the challenge to compile this story to mark the occasion of this anniversary. It has not, of course, been possible to include all the inhabitants who have taken part throughout this century, but we hope you will enjoy this glimpse into the recent past! We apologise for any errors or omissions and trust that you will enjoy the book as much as we have enjoyed writing it.

Early History

Roman Period

In 1983 Dr Richard Gardner found a Roman coin in his garden at Portelet, Camel Street, and took it to the Heritage Centre, Norton Fitzwarren, for an expert appraisal. The coin is a Nummus, a small coin made of base metal, not of any great value. It is, however, in mint condition and bears the head of Constantus, with the reverse side depicting two goddesses of victory bearing a shield between them. The coin was minted in London and dates from 319-329 A.D. It is the only Roman artefact to be found in the village to date.

Marston Magna Marble

Legend has it that a large slab of charcoal grey stone was found in the church graveyard while a well was being dug. It was used for making headstones and a few tabletops for the large tombs. There is one marker stone left in the Natural History Museum, but unfortunately all the other marble headstones have since been stolen from the churchyard. Retrieving it from where it is located is impossible due to the depth.

Marston Magna marble is made up of a conglomeration of *promicroceras martonensis* and *ziphoceras* ammonites. It is from the Jurassic period, and as such is 190 million years old, found in the lower lias and exceptionally rare. (Obtusum zone).

In a piece of Marston Magna marble the ammonites still retain their original shell, preserved as a white film. Billions of these ammonites were wiped out some 200 million years ago either by a poisonous algal bloom, or possibly by volcanic activity.

**Ammonite = a fossil cephalopod of many kinds, with coiled chambered shell resembling a ram's horn.*
Ammon = the ram headed god of Ancient Egypt, hence "ammonite".

THE CHURCHES

The Church of St.Mary the Virgin

The church at Marston Magna is dedicated to St. Mary the Virgin and consists of a nave, chancel, a Lady Chapel on the north side of the nave and a western tower.

The chancel is Norman with broad clasping buttresses. On the north wall herringbone masonry can be found, together with a Norman window and traces inside of a second window, which was removed in the 15th century to allow more light. The East end has a group of three stepped thirteenth century lancets, which contains modern stained glass, given by Mr Thomas Flooks of Dorset in 1902. The window on the south side contains pieces of old stained glass.

In the Lady Chapel to the left of the east window there is a canopied niche containing a statue of the Madonna with Jesus. Painted on the north wall is an ancient portrayal of the murder of St. Thomas à Becket. The screen to the Lady Chapel is in the Perpendicular style.

The circular Font is Norman with scallop moulding around its sides. Standing on its original stem and base it is lined inside with the original lead.

The pulpit is eighteenth century with an ogee-canopied tester over it.

The tower is a fine one of three stages and entered by a small fourteenth century door. There are six bells. The tower, its masonry, carvings, and pinnacles were all restored in 1998-1999.

At the beginning of the 20th century the incumbent was Canon Coles. He was an invalid and a curate carried out his work.

After Canon Coles died later in 1900, the Reverend J. W. Firth was appointed and came to live in the Rectory. He had a wife and three children - Jack, Cyril and Stella. There were two or three maids in the kitchen and a nursemaid in the nursery.

Queen Victoria died in January 1901, and then village Coronation celebrations had to be organised. The King Lewanika of Barotseland (now part of Zimbabwe) came with his entourage to the coronation of Edward VII in August 1902. The Firth family moved out to stay with the Marden family at Marston House, while the King stayed in the Rectory.

It was Colonel Harding who brought King Lewanika here for the Coronation. Colonel Harding may have known Revd. Firth. At some time before 1901, King Lewanika had sought British protection, and subsequently met the Colonel in Barotseland. Colonel Harding, possibly from Montacute, accompanied the King and his entourage during his stay in England and Scotland, and on the return journey to Barotseland. The Colonel wrote an account of those remote parts of Africa, including an appreciative account of the statesmanlike character of King Lewanika.

In 1902 a great deal of restoration work was carried out on the church. It was in a very bad state of repair and very damp. New roofs were needed on the chancel and nave, the oak gallery was removed from the back of the nave, and pews made with sloping backs from the wood. All the plaster was taken off the nave walls inside the church. Outside the earth was removed from the walls, which were then re-pointed, and a concrete channel installed around the church. Down pipes were attended to in order to drain the rainwater away. The paint was scraped off the font. The chancel was repaved and the floor sealed. Marble was laid down in the sanctuary and new altar steps made. Wood blocks were laid in the chancel, nave, Lady Chapel and below the tower. All the windows in the church and belfry had their lead glazing renewed. A new floor and ceiling was put in the ringing chamber and the heating stove had a new chimney. The cost of these improvements was £1257. The church was re-dedicated on 29th November 1902. In 1905 Revd. Firth left the village.

Mrs Davis wrote about the Parish Clerk at the turn of the century:

Mr John Linthorn, usually called John Lintern. Almost any fine day he was in the churchyard cutting the grass with a scythe, sweeping the many gravel paths, re-erecting the stone slabs of the old wall or digging a grave. On Sundays he put up the hymns and then rang the three bells in the dark base of the tower, emerging just in time to precede the curate up the aisle, where he opened the door of the three-decker pulpit. Then he slipped into the front seat ready to lead the General Confession.

In 1905 Reverend Gerald Francis Codrington Peppin arrived with his wife and family.

The Revd. Peppin was Rector here for 19 years, until 1924. He was here during the Great War 1914-1918, and present when the brass plate was erected in the nave, bearing the names of the nine soldiers killed from this parish during that war.

Lord Bishop Kennion, Bishop of Bath and Wells dedicated the new clock in the tower on the first anniversary of the end of the war, 11th November 1919, to the memory of those who lost their lives. It was hoped everyone could see the two clock faces on the north and west of the tower and hear the Westminster Chimes, as the old clock had only struck the hours.

A further memorial of the Great War is the Marden window, situated on south side of the nave. This window was filled in 1924 by a coloured representation of Victory, St. Gabriel and St. Uriel, and was given by Mr and Mrs E.D. Marden in memory of their son, Arthur Cecil Marden.

Revd. Peppin visited his parishioners on horseback. He spent much of his time at his desk writing letters, sermons and a history of the church, all in longhand. The history was published in a small booklet and dated 1924. It contains a list of priests from 1314-1905.

In 1912 the bells were recast and rehung with the addition of two new bells at a cost of £300. Originally the peal consisted of four bells with the following inscriptions: -

E.D. Marden and Revd. G. Peppin with the recast bells in 1912.

1. Treble WK. EE. F. Edward Pain – I. U. C. W. A.D. 1728.
2, No inscription.
3. T.P. T. K. Nathaniel Barnard A.D. 1707.
4. Tenor Nathaniel Barnard A.D. 1707.
5. New Bell, a gift from Mr. and Mrs. E. D. Marden in memory of their second son, Montague Marden, who died in Australia while reading Holy Orders.
6. This bell was paid for by subscriptions.

The Bishop of Bath and Wells dedicated the bells on 31st October 1912.

Mrs Davis wrote about the sexton ringing the church bells in a letter to John Peppin in 1985:

There were four bells which rang fa, me, re for ten minutes before Morning and Evening Prayer. The old sexton did this with two hands and a foot and then there was five minutes of bong on doh.

In 1924 Reverend Alfred John Bartlett came to the village as priest, and was here for 27 years. He was a single man and had a housekeeper. He had lost his fiancée when the Titanic sank in April 1912. He lived in the

Rectory here, but when Rimpton was united with Marston Magna in 1932 he moved into Rimpton Rectory. He preferred living in Rimpton and his curate, Mr Willmott, probably lived in the Rectory here. However, when the war began in 1939, the Navy, based at Yeovilton, took over the Rimpton Rectory, so Revd. Bartlett moved back to Marston Magna.

The Revd. Bartlett was knowledgeable about aviation matters. He has an entry in Who's Who In Aviation in 1928. As a young man he had experimented with propeller design with regard to man-powered flight.

During the 1939-1945 war he led his congregation through all the hardships such as food rationing, blackouts, shortages of petrol, the barrage balloons and bombing of the Borough in Yeovil, and the machine-gunning of Sherborne by German planes.

A memorial plaque was erected in the church to record the death of two men lost in this war. In 1946 the "Fourteen Stations of the Cross" were erected around the nave by Mr and Mrs Ashworth Hope in memory of their son, Herbert Eldon Hope, who died of war wounds on 2nd February 1946.

Revd. Bartlett died on 26th December 1951 and his grave is near the church entrance.

The Reverend J. W. Blunt became Rector in 1951. He was here for 4 years and liked to be known as Father Blunt. He was Rector here when George VI died and for the Coronation of Queen Elizabeth II in June 1953. Revd. Blunt was very high church. He celebrated Holy Communion every day, helped by Charles Knight from Queen Camel, who was his server and swung the censer.

Revd. Blunt brought the statue of St. Mary with Jesus to this church from a blitzed church in London, where everything had been destroyed except this statue. It was placed in the Lady Chapel, where an earlier statue had no doubt stood before the Reformation. He wanted to process it around the village on a cart festooned with flowers, but this was not encouraged. During his time here he helped to run a Boy Scouts group assisted by Charles Knight. Revd. Blunt left the village in 1954 and joined the Roman Catholic Church.

Many years later, in 1997, Henry Trim wrote a piece on Revd. Blunt in the parish magazine:

It is of some interest to recall that when the late Rev. J.C. Blunt was Rector here for about three years until May 1954 he organised a Tower Appeal and nearly £900 was raised to finance the repointing of the Church Tower. That was a great deal of money in those days. I recall that one of his fund raising events was the hiring of the Odeon Cinema in Yeovil for the showing of a special film. During that period the roof of the Lady Chapel was restored chiefly by his own labour. I believe he gained experience in a family Sheet Metal business. At that time Marston Magna was then known as "Low Church" and the congregation which had initially attended in fair numbers gradually dwindled away with the introduction of incense swinging and the carrying of statues and other matters. However, the Rev. and Mrs Blunt and the two children were a very nice family indeed and the Parish supported their fund raising efforts well in spite of some reluctance to attend services! When they left Marston the fabric of the Church was in pretty good order and there were to be no great problems for the P.C.C. in this respect for a number of years.

The Reverend F. W. Bowler was Rector from May 1955 for three years. He had a wife and three children, Elizabeth, James and Thirza. A cousin came with them, Miss Clarke, who assisted with the family and also with parochial duties.

Henry Trim also wrote about Revd. Bowler in the August 1997 parish magazine:

In May 1955 came the Rev. F. W. Bowler M.B.E. and his family. He started the form of service which we still use to this day and many children came to form a choir. The Rev. Bowler had been a Missionary in Borneo and was awarded the M.B.E. (Military) for services as Chaplain on the Anzio beach head.

The Medieval Painting

In 1957, at the request of the Rector and Mr Caroe FRIBA Miss Eve Baker visited the church to examine the traces of the medieval painting from the 15th century on the north aisle of the Lady Chapel. Under many coats of lime wash, a good painting was found depicting the Martyrdom of St. Thomas à Becket in 1170. Great veneration was once paid to St. Thomas but Henry VIII decreed that pictures of him should be destroyed and all festivals in his honour be abolished. There are very few pictures of Thomas à Becket in this country. The painting is still visible today.

Revd. Bowler left the parish in 1958 to be a priest in Radstock. He died in 1997, the year after the death of his wife, Patricia.

Reverend H. de Jersey Hunt arrived in 1958 and was here for 21 years. He was an ex naval chaplain. His wife, Gladys, known as Gabriella, had been a ballerina, and although she was quite a short woman she had a formidable reputation. She was an excellent needlewoman and made many altar frontals for this church together with chasubles for her husband to wear at Holy Communion. However, when they retired and moved from the village, they took these items with them, and left them in their wills to Wells Cathedral.

Revd. de Jersey Hunt wrote topical letters for the Parish Magazine every month, as all our vicars have done since it began. In 1978, just before the Lambeth Conference of July 1978 was due to discuss the ordination of women, he expressed his views:

> *In one or two overseas diocese some Bishops have already ordained a few women as priests, but in England it is illegal, as well as being out of keeping with the tradition of the Church at large. Our English Bishops have reached the conclusion that, while there appears to be no theological reason for not doing so, to do so will inevitably split the Church of England into two parties, and effectively put a stop to re-union with those much greater parts of the Church, the Roman Catholics and the Orthodox.*
>
> *Both the Orthodox and the Roman Churches have declared their opposition to the ordination of women and will disassociate themselves from those Churches who do so. For many years there has been steady progress towards re-union with the Orthodox and Roman Churches, and with some branches of them we are already in full Communion. To many of us it seems folly to pursue an uncatholic and divisive practice in order to satisfy a minority who reject the corporate nature of the universal Church to which we belong.*
>
> *From the days of the Apostles the ministry has been of men ordained by the laying on of hands and called by the Holy Spirit to the office of Bishop, Priest or Deacon. For one part of the Church to ordain women against the tradition and practice of the rest of Christendom will cause a schism within the Body of Christ and a defiance of Our Lord's expressed will that we should all be one.*

He also expressed his views against the re-marriage of divorced people in church, concluding:

> *At a time when this Nation is being tempted of the devil to a way of living which is pagan or sub-Christian, the Church in England ought to stand firmly for those principles which we believe have been given to us by God, not least of them being the immutability of Holy Orders and the indissolubility of marriage. In these matters to change from the traditional teaching and practice of the whole Church will disrupt the Church of England and create a division which may never be healed.*

Molly Crabb remembers that when she and her family moved to Wickham Farm in 1963, at this time Holy Communion was celebrated every Sunday. The whole service was sung to Merbecke (plainsong). The congregation knew the whole service and prayers by heart and everyone sang. There were no prayer books, only Ancient and Modern Revised Hymnbooks.

When Peter Clarke arrived in the village to help the Rector as a Server, he organised the printing of little blue prayer books, so that newcomers and visitors could take part in the service. David and Richard Crabb were Altar Boys. They helped Revd. Hunt in the celebration of Holy Communion and held candles when he sang the Gospel. When Revd. Peter Clarke was ordained he helped take services as a non-stipendiary priest. His wife, Ann, helped him to start a Sunday school for the children. Ann and helpers would take the children out after the first hymn. They then went to the Clarke's home for their lesson, but would return to church in time for a blessing at the altar rail during Holy Communion. As the children grew older they joined the church choir and helped to lead the singing.

In 1964 the new electric heating system was installed after the oil heaters caused a pew to catch fire. In 1971 a builder, Mr Taylor, paid for a new stone cross to be erected on the apex of the nave. In 1972 all the electrical wiring was renewed and spot lighting placed over the font. New bell ropes were purchased in 1976 and all the elm trees, which had Dutch elm disease, together with a beech tree, were cut down in the churchyard. The nave roof was retiled in 1978 at a cost of £1,600.

A new flagpole was purchased in 1976.

Revd. Hunt and his wife left the village in 1978, when they retired to live in Dinder near Wells. Shortly before they went, Revd. Hunt wrote about the future of the parishes of Marston Magna, Rimpton, Queen Camel and West Camel, as the Archdeacon of Wells was due to discuss the matter of amalgamation with the PCC.

Revd. Hunt acknowledged that there was a greater need for clergy to work in the parishes of the industrial north of England, and that now fewer men were coming forward to be ordained into full time ministry. However, he stated that he would not consider taking on the parishes of Queen and West Camel, should he be asked to do so.

In February 1979, Mr. Jack Batson was presented with an oil painting by Mr. Gerard Leader, commissioned by the Parochial Church Council of St. Mary's Church. This gift was given in recognition of Mr. Batson's faithful work in winding the church clock for 26 years, and as Captain of the Bell Ringers for 50 years.

The Rectory was sold in 1979. In that year, Revd. B. L. Morris was the vicar of Queen Camel. Marston Magna and Rimpton were added to his Benefice, which included West Camel, Corton Denham, and Queen Camel. The Revd. Peter Clarke assisted him.

The Revd. Lyn Morris had already been the Rector of six parishes in Herefordshire, so this experience must have been very useful as he took over his new Benefice. He had also been a Parish Councillor, a British Legion chaplain, and Chaplain and Civilian Instructor for the Air Training Corps in Bristol. His hobbies included photography, caravanning, village electrician and "Do-It-Yourself"!

Mrs Peggy Morris, the vicar's wife, was a very good needlewoman. She started a tapestry-sewing group with the ladies. They met every week and designed the lovely kneelers in St Mary's Church. They made the communion rail kneelers, those in the priest's stall, and cushions for the Bishop's and Priest's chairs.

In 1980 the Highmore family donated green vestments, and in 1981 the Reverend Frank Sargent, in memory of his brother and sister, donated the white vestments. Mrs Chaffy donated the red vestments in memory of her husband. The lightning conductor was installed in 1983, and more choir robes were purchased for £417.50.

During the 1980s the church grass cutters were stolen four times in 1983, 1987, 1989 and in 1990. Although they had been painted pink and police advice was followed, in the last robbery the whole shed had been lifted by someone using a crane from a stationary vehicle parked in Court Garden field. The mower had been stolen without opening the locked shed door!

In 1987 the Deanery was again reorganised and became the Merston Rural Deanery. (The name "Merston" dates from 1291. It is the old name for Marston). Our church is now in the Benefice of Marston Magna, Rimpton, Ashington, Mudford and Chilton Cantelo.

Revd. D. E. White was the vicar of Mudford from 1987-1996. He found it difficult to come to Marston Magna and Rimpton but his wife, Yolanda, helped him a great deal with Mudford, Ashington and Chilton Cantelo. When the Revd. Peter Clarke left the village in 1988 to accept the living at St. Margaret's Tintinhull, retired priests took the services each Sunday, both here and at Rimpton. For eleven years our Benefice was in a vacancy, which was not a vacancy. Revd. White intended to retire at Easter 1996, however he died in February of that year.

In 1988 the Lady Chapel Screen and the wooden railings above were restored. The brass cross and candlesticks were inscribed with a dedication and the village name. In the same year the Tower Clock was converted to electricity in memory of Rear Admiral Philip Illingworth, who had lived in the Manor House.

In the Parish Magazine of October 1987, Henry Trim wrote about the "modernisation" of the church clock:

> *It is now proposed that the present clock be fitted with an automatic electric winding device. Think of all the hours that have been put in by villagers manually winding the clock over all these years! Unsung heroes for the most*

part! That well-loved villager Rear Admiral Phil Illingworth was one who devoted a tremendous amount of time and energy in caring for the clock, and his family and the P.C.C. have agreed that the modernisation of the clock be carried out as a tribute to his memory. The cost is likely to be in the region of £1,500 but the greater part of this sum is already to hand from donations in lieu of floral tributes to Phil's memory. Like many others, Phil sought no acclaim for his voluntary work, but all concerned felt he would have been secretly very pleased over this token of esteem.

The electric heating units were renewed in 1989. In the same year a faculty (permission from the diocese) was obtained to rebuild the organ. Mr. Edward Thompson carried out the work and the organ was returned in 1994. The restored organ was re-dedicated by the Bishop of Bath and Wells, the Rt. Rev. James Thompson on 11th September 1994 at our first Patronal Celebration. The final sum paid for the organ restoration was £8,250.00. At the Patronal Festival, a new stool was dedicated to the memory of the late Mr. Philip Mitchell. After the service, the congregation was able to meet and talk with the Bishop in the new village hall.

It was reported in the Parish Magazine in March 1989 that Mr. Michael Illingworth and Mr. Norman Illingworth had made a new Processional Cross for the church in memory of their late father. This was blessed in the church and used during services.

It is interesting to note that in May 1994, the Parochial Church Council voted in favour of accepting a woman as minister and incumbent. 1994 was the year the first women priests were ordained in England.

On 11th April 1997 a Restoration Appeal was launched to fund repairs to the church, especially the tower, and to bring the building in good order to celebrate the Millennium. By June 1998 the sum of £41,623.40 had been raised.

Work began on the tower in January 1998, to stabilise the pinnacles and repoint the walls and stonework of the tower. The fund received £339 from Somerset County Council to regild the figures on the clock. Safer steps leading to the ringing chamber were made, with a grab rope.

A new Rectory in Camel Street, Marston Magna was purchased for the Benefice in February 1998 at a cost of £160,000. The double garage was altered into a single garage and an office.

The Reverend Peter Thomas Wood became the first vicar to live in the new Rectory in 1998. He arrived from Hereford with his wife Evelyn. They had three adult children. In Peter and Evelyn's earlier years they had been missionaries in Chile, which they had enjoyed very much, and stories regularly appeared in his sermons. Peter Wood organised several concerts held in St Mary's Church, and events such as Chilean evenings, when Chilean food would be served and slides shown. He and Evelyn joined in with village and church events, such as the Fête and Harvest suppers. He also ran an Alpha course, with sessions held in the New Rectory. (Peter and Evelyn retired to Norfolk in September 2006).

The restoration carried on from October 1998. The bells were reconditioned by the firm of Nicholson's at a cost of £9,685.53. The Fund now stood at £42,747.94 and the amount paid out for repairs was £19,323. In January 1999 the original medieval clock pieces were taken by Mr David Mitchell to be restored at Chipping Norton, Oxfordshire. The clock was returned on 29th March, placed in a glass case with an alarm in the gallery to keep it safe, and a lockable iron gate was put in at the foot of the stairs. By 31st August the Restoration Fund stood at £48,699.69. Everything planned had been completed except for the renewal of the two copper roofs on the tower and Lady Chapel. Fortunately, these are still rainproof.

Celebrating the Millennium

In 1999 Lavinia Dolbear originated the idea of floodlighting the church to celebrate the Millennium and to be a memorial to Henry Trim and Bill Marden, both former churchwardens. This was paid for by the village, and the floodlights were switched on at the Christingle Service in December 1999. The cost was £1,950. Millennium mugs depicting the church were distributed free to 75 children of the village. 110 mugs were sold at £5 each and the remainder given to newly baptised babies. The money for the mugs was obtained by having two table-top sales. New bell ropes and sallies were also dedicated at this service.

Visitors Book

The church had a Visitors book for comments after 1951. This book indicates that the church has many visitors to the village, in particular children and young people have entered their names and addresses. They are a reminder of families who lived here but perhaps moved away.

People coming back to the village included Dorothy Ann Ward, née Davis, who noted in 1965 that she was born in Wickham Farm and married in the church in 1923. In the same year Marjorie Greta Wyatt, also born at Wickham Farm, visited and noted that she had married at the church in 1928. "Marston" was the name of the house where she was then living. Norman A. Sabin visiting from Leamington Spa had been stationed here on army service from 1940-42. People mentioned the houses they lived in, their own christenings, childhoods, weddings and their ancestors.

Mrs A McFarlane née Guppy visited in 1964 and commented "Many happy memories of this dear village." On a later visit in 1970 she wrote "So very glad to see the beloved village and church again."

The families of past clergy have revisited the church. The Peppin family were regular visitors. The great, great granddaughter of the Revd. Thomas Fitzherbert visited in 1961 and in June 1977 Kathleen Lansley née Fitzherbert also visited.

Others had childhood memories, or were revisiting the church of their ancestors. The Fooks family had relatives reaching back to 1635. Winifred Good wrote that her father had been a choirboy and confirmed in the church. A former altar boy, Brian Gorringe from Ontario, Canada came with his family in 1991. A visitor from Zimbabwe was a descendant of Cresswell Roberts, who was a curate who moved to Marston Magna from Sheffield in the late nineteenth century.

George Appleton was a choirboy here from 1909-12. Later on he was ordained and became a curate in Stepney, London, and then spent 20 years working in missionary work in Burma. On his return to England he worked in London parishes. In 1962 he became Archdeacon of London and a Canon in St Pauls. He became Archbishop of Perth, Western Australia, before becoming Archbishop of Jerusalem in 1974. It was in the year of his retirement when he revisited the parish church where he had sung as a choirboy.

Henry Trim wrote in the Parish Magazine of January 1981:

> *A welcome visitor during October/November was Charles Miller, returning to visit his father at Townsend. Charles was accompanied by his wife. They emigrated to Australia four years ago. One of the simple pleasures he enjoyed during his visit was to call in on the church, where he was once in the choir, and look at the marks on the choir wardrobe door where he and his fellow choristers had charted their height.*

Visitors to the flower festivals of 1982 and 1987 are recorded. Restoration work completed in 1985 was noted, as was the Quarter Peal of bells rung in 1986 as a tribute to the Queen Mother, to mark the fifty years since her husband's accession.

A visitor from 1992 summed up what many seemed to feel about revisiting the church when she wrote: *Used to live here, good to revisit and remember.*

The Methodist Church

The Methodist Chapel stands in Camel Street, built of rose-red Bridgwater bricks with Ham stone facings. The foundation stone bears the date 1882, together with the initials W.N. (William Nettleton) and J.B. (Josiah Bush). Mrs M I Davis wrote in May 1977:

> *There is not much doubt that the materials for building the Chapel were supplied by the Somerset Trading Company.*

Josiah Bush was Manager of the Somerset Trading Company branch in Marston Magna. Details of the early beginnings of the chapel no longer exist except for the document relating to the early trustees. A plot of land for £10 was paid for a Wesleyan Chapel measuring 30ft by 32ft. The first trustees came from Sherborne, Milborne Port, Stalbridge and Marston Magna. William Nettleton and Josiah Bush both lived close to the Chapel and were active in building up the Chapel in the early days. Initially the Chapel was in the Sherborne circuit, but in 1962 Marston Magna joined the Yeovil circuit.

In the early days the Minister arrived by pony and trap for the Sunday service and would be entertained to dinner by three or four families in turn. There was no set form of service, the prayers were mostly extempore and the Moody and Sankey hymns were sung heartily. The sermon often lasted an hour.

In 1928 Mr and Mrs Dare came to live in Wickham Farm. They were Baptists who attended church at Yeovil taking an active part in its work all their lives. As they settled in Marston, they decided to take care of the running of the Chapel at Marston too. Mrs Dare played the organ and kept the accounts. Mr Dare welcomed folk on arrival, took the collection and was responsible for the general upkeep and administration. For many years they ran the only Sunday School in the village. Flower services were held, when the children sang and recited poems before their parents. There were summer outings to Weymouth when two buses were needed to transport everyone! On that day the village would be empty.

However, by 1970 the membership of the Chapel had fallen to 8 and the average attendance over many years was 9, according to Miss Bicknell and Miss Dennett, the longest serving members. Without the mainstay support of Mr and Mrs Dare it was felt that the Chapel would not have survived as long as it did.

In 1978 Mr Dare died leaving a legacy of £500 to the Chapel. It was decided that this money should be reinvested to provide a continuing source of income for the Chapel, and to place a simple memorial to him in the form of a wooden cross on the pulpit. The Methodist Church reported in April the following year that:

We have recently taken the opportunity to make the interior of the chapel a more worshipful place in which to meet. Mr Ray Cornford has made us a simple oak cross, which has been fixed, in the arched recess behind the pulpit.

In 1978 Mrs Olive Griffin also died. She had cleaned the Chapel for many years and had provided flowers for the altar each week, which she placed in brass vases previously donated by her parents.

A faithful band of members continued to work hard on the upkeep of the Chapel. Mrs Dorothy Taylor took some services. Mrs Dorothy Crowther played the organ. Mr Charles Crowther helped to keep the chapel running immediately after Mr Dare's death, but then Mr Crowther died in 1980. Miss Anne Dennett helped to retain the membership. She was often seen on a Sunday evening driving her Mini, taking people to and from the service when they were no longer able to walk or drive to the Chapel.

The Revd. Peter Clarke was asked to take the Harvest Service in 1980 and all seemed in favour of Church and Chapel members working together. In 1981 Mr Trim auctioned the Harvest goods. In 1982 the average attendance at services was 9.

The members at this time were Mrs Parrott, Mrs. O. Gaylard, Mrs. Pamela Blackwood and Mrs White from Mudford; Miss M. Bicknell, Mrs. Clare Watts, Mrs. Margaret Bartlett, Miss Anne Dennett, Mrs Ellen Price, Mrs Edythe Robinson, Mrs Dorothy Crowther and Mr and Mrs Raymond Rance from Marston Magna.

1982 was memorable as it saw the Centenary of the Chapel. The Chairman of the District, the Revd. Ashman, conducted the centenary service and friends came to the service from all parts of the Circuit. In that year however, there was no Christmas service as there were not enough people to attend. By this time the Revd. Price was in charge of Old Vicarage St, St Marks in Yeovil, Marston Magna and Stoford. His successor in the late 1980s was the Revd. Graham.

In 1977 the Chapel had been given the organ from East Coker Chapel to be used, if it could be repaired! Repairs and improvements to the building were discussed at the Annual General Meetings of the Chapel. In 1976 the interior of the chapel was redecorated. A new carpet was purchased in 1977 at the cost of £80.23

In May 1977 the parish magazine included this entry:

The oil lamps offered for sale, which turned out to be of cut glass, didn't find a new home in the village and so were offered for sale at the Crewkerne auction rooms. They realised £42 and to think they might have been thrown away when they were superseded by electricity or have fallen off the shelf and broken in the years between.

In the late 1970s repairs were made to the Chapel steps. The condition of the roof was discussed in 1981. In 1982 the Chapel was closed for three months when new heaters and plugs were needed. In 1984 pointing and guttering work was undertaken. Boards in the vestry were in need of repair as was the wood in the side room. A crack in the wall over the organ was noted in 1986. A small membership continued to deal with property issues. Unfortunately the membership continued to decline mainly, due to the death of long-term supporters of the Chapel.

Miss Newberry left a legacy and 6 new Hymnbooks were bought in her memory. This legacy left a good balance in 1985 and helped to sustain the finances of the Chapel. Miss Bicknell, who had been a regular attendee and kind friend to all, left a further legacy in 1989.

However, in 1990 income for the first time for some years was reported to be less than expenditure. There was discussion about getting a quote for cracking plasterwork but the quinquennial inspection was due.

A carol service was arranged for December 23rd 1990 and also a Special Church Council Meeting for February 28th 1991. Membership had now fallen to 5, and the quinquennial report revealed that £3,500 would need to be spent to bring the building up to standard requirements. The Chapel would have to draw on its resources in future, as expenditure was now higher than income. The Revd. Graham did not consider it would be the right use of money.

After discussion, some reluctance and sadness there seemed no sensible alternative. It appeared that everyone would be able to get to Yeovil to church. Mr Graham "proposed that Marston Magna Methodist Church cease to be a place of worship as from the end of this quarter (Mar31/91) and that membership be transferred to Vicarage Street Methodist Church, Yeovil." Mrs Robinson seconded the proposal. Mr Graham expressed his thanks for the help he had received in coming to this decision. He agreed to take the final service, which took place on 14th April 1991 when 50 people attended.

The Parish Magazine of June 1991 noted:

The Methodist Chapel have generously offered to the church a gift of their lovely old Bible which has been placed in the Lady Chapel of St Mary's.

The Methodist Church requested planning permission to convert the property to residential use after its closure. An attempt was made to purchase a small plot of ground beside the chapel but this was unsuccessful. The planning permission was not granted. The property was put up for sale and sold privately. Sadly, since that time it has been used only for storage. The Parish Magazine reported in 1994 that permission was granted for Mr. Laxton to use the Methodist Chapel as an Art Gallery where he would be able to sell works of art, subject to conditions, but this did not eventuate.

The Parish Council

The Parochial Church Council originally took responsibility for village affairs. Its function changed over time with the evolution of local government. Poor law unions were founded in the 1830s. Later in the 19th century rural sanitary districts were formed where areas had no town government. These districts were formed using the boundaries of poor law unions. If the area of the union changed so did the sanitary districts. The districts were overseen by a sanitary authority dealing with and responsible for public health matters such as providing clean water supplies, sewers etc.

After the Local Government Act of 1894 the rural sanitary districts were replaced by elected Rural District Councils. Marston Magna, which had been in the Sherborne Poor Law Union since 1835, was transferred to the Yeovil Poor Law Union which covered the Yeovil Rural District Area. The Rural District Councils were abolished in 1974. Marston Magna is now in the non-metropolitan district of South Somerset, which was formed on 1st April 1974 under the Local Government Act 1972.

The first Parish Meeting in Marston Magna was held on 4th December 1894 and Parish Council status was acquired in 1911. The first meeting of the newly elected Parish Council was held on 1st May 1911. The five elected members were Messrs;

Percival Everard Davis - Farmer and Miller residing at Wickham Farm
Charles William Ketley residing at Millbrook House
Walter James Hayward residing at this time at Garston Farm
Joseph Noyce licensee of the Marston Inn
William Florance licensee of the Red Lion

A dedicated team of residents has served on the Parish Council since this early formation, managing the village amenities and the environment according to the prevailing priorities and sentiment. The remit covers Planning, Co-operation with the Police Force, Trees, Highways, Footpaths, Health and Community care, Play Area and Leisure.

In 1978 consideration was given to the review of the Parish boundaries. At that moment in time they extended in the north to the Lambrook and the Parliamentary and former Yeovil-Wincanton Rural District boundaries, to the east to the north-west edge of Rimpton village and the first mile-stone on the Sherborne Road, to the south almost to the Marston Elms Crossroads on the A359 to Yeovil, and to the west to Thorney Lane and the Dorset County boundary. The area of the parish was reputed to be 1,392.410 acres.

The Council decided to make no recommendation for change for the following reasons:-

The Village is roughly in the centre of the parish and most of the population live within half a mile of it; the Church, Village Hall, Post Office, Garage and both shops are close to the centre. To extend the boundaries would add an insignificant number of people and those would be inconveniently placed for these facilities and might well be better served by either Queen Camel or Rimpton. To transfer part of the parish to an adjacent one would benefit nobody and in any event would deprive Marston of some of the rate revenue which support the services to the village.

The Parliamentary and County boundaries to the north and south/west respectively make a natural division and to attempt to alter those would be like David taking on Goliath gratuitously!

Neither Queen Camel nor Rimpton, our neighbours, with whom we have friendly contact, have any desire for territorial aggrandisement and both wish to retain the status quo.

Also in 1978 Parish Council members learnt with gratitude of a legacy of £100 from the estate of the late Mr Stanley Dare to be used for the maintenance of the bus shelter which he and his wife had so kindly presented to the village some years ago.

In 1981 a 'Parish Home Defence Plan' was established, in common with many other Parish Councils, at the request of Central Government. Brigadier Lerwill prepared the Plan which is summarised as follows:

A chain of command would be set up in the event of an emergency. It was likely that all communication would be totally disrupted and at least temporarily, the village would probably be isolated completely. Under such circumstances our village would be entirely responsible for its own survival, that is to say, for its own food supplies and controls, emergency feeding, medical service, security of life and property, maintenance of law and order, until such time as District Control and services could be re-established. Furthermore, the Parish Council would bear responsibility for the continuing survival of the community.

A community organisation headed by an Emergency Committee would need to be established. A building to be used as a Parish Control Centre must be selected. Allocation of responsibility within the Committee might be along the following lines:

A Controller with overall responsibility, co-ordinating and directing volunteer labour. Maintenance of law and order and any instant action required to save life.

A committee member to organise accommodation, billeting. Hygiene and sanitation. Burial of the dead.

A committee member to organise and administer such communications as are feasible, to have control of and use of such radio instruments as are made available.

A committee member to organise and if necessary to ration food supplies, to supervise community feeding if necessary.

(if perchance there is an amateur radio operator in the village, would he kindly make contact with the Clerk, as his services could be invaluable.)

Jim Nowell remembers that he attended about 6 weekly training sessions together with Steve Holland. They took place in the Yeovil Council Offices and were focused on dealing with the threat of nuclear attack. They were advised there would be a four minute warning and the council decided they would muster in this event at The Marston Inn which would be The Parish Control Centre. All Councillors were issued with Geiger counters. In tandem with these arrangements, as Vice Chairman of the District Council, Jim was asked to represent them at a four day training session held at Easingwold about ten miles north of York. The general private opinion expressed at both sets of training was that in the event of nuclear attack, little could be done!

1985 Moat Field in Public Ownership.
(See Chapter on Houses)

Mary Martin reported on the Neigbourhood Watch Scheme in 1988:

The number of Neighbourhood Watch Schemes in England and Wales (excluding London) had reached 35,000. Our Neighbourhood Watch Scheme has taken off with great enthusiasm and the whole village has now been canvassed. If you are without a sticker, please be patient, we are awaiting further supplies.

She subsequently asked the Council if they would agree to purchase two Neighbourhood Watch Scheme signs for either end of the village. This was agreed and permission for their erection was to be sought.

RNAS YEOVILTON 1970-2000

Aircraft noise and disturbance was a popular subject of conversation in the 1970s and 1980s. The Parish Council sent two representatives, Jim Nowell and Philip Gibbs, to meet Captain Williams and his staff in November 1979 and they gleaned the following information:

Yeovilton is to be the Land Base for three Squadrons of Sea Harriers, thirty-six aircraft in all. They will be at Yeovilton only for training and when not at sea. A new breed of aircraft carriers is now being built to take the Harriers. At the present time, there are three Harriers at Yeovilton with another three coming shortly after Christmas, then slowly increasing to their maximum number. Regarding their noise (the main concern of everyone) Marston Magna should NOT be subjected to excessive noise from the Harriers as its circuit does not include us. The farthest east on their landing circuit is some several hundred yards towards Yeovilton.

If any Harriers come low over Marston, and by this it is meant if you can see the plane number with the naked eye, in the Commander's words - "I want to know about it". Should this occur, contact our local Plane-Spotting Councillor Philip Gibbs and NOT telephone the camp. Take a note of the day, time and plane number and report it to Councillor Gibbs so that he may keep a log of complaints and report back to the Captain.

One last point, according to the Yeovilton Village representative at the meeting, four windowpanes were broken in the village and in his front garden a noise reading of 110db recorded.

In October 1980 Philip Gibbs wrote that there were some eight Sea Harriers at Yeovilton, but this would probably increase to thirty-six:

There seem to be considerable low-passes over the village on landing approaches, which will surely get worse. Last week a representative from the Air Station kindly agreed to discuss the current situation. Apparently the Station has made all necessary recommendations, in their eyes, to flight officers and has increased the circuit height to 1500 feet. Unfortunately they do say that occasional overshooting is inevitable, perhaps once or twice a day.

During the one and a half hours the officer spent with him, there were no low passes of aircraft over Marston, although plenty landed. Ten minutes after he left two aircraft almost dropped in for tea!

The Editor of the Parish Magazine invited parishioners to share their point of view as some seemed to want to become more militant on the subject, and even seek a reduction in the rates:

One respondent noted that R.N.A.S. Yeovilton has been in existence for forty years, subjecting the surrounding area to varying noise levels during that time. Those people who have moved here since 1940 must have realised they were within two miles of an airfield and its accompanying racket. By all means let those individuals apply for a rate reduction if they so wish - that is their privilege but I shall continue to sleep soundly trusting that the lads training noisily overhead will never have to use their acquired skills in defence of our country.

Another asked how many jobs have been created in making these aircraft. Can we take a parochial view of occasional noise when much wider problems are the cause of it? Noise is probably a complaint of the older section of the community. Youngsters who can survive a disco are not worried.

Even if a few pounds were taken off our rates, would that really compensate us for the quality of life, which is being destroyed in our village? Would it compensate for the considerable fall in the value of our properties?

A year later, and the topic is still hot news. The Rector, Revd. Lyn Morris, made this moving contribution:

Forty-one years ago a different sound filled the air over this country. The sound of aircraft. German bombers and fighters, and a handful of British fighters. The clear sky was criss-crossed with vapour trails and occasionally the sound of machine gun fire was heard. Where I lived our own aircraft were rarely seen and stray German bombers and fighters seemed to come with complete immunity. On September 20th the country will remember the Battle of Britain, those who gave their lives, those who fought and thus prevented the invasion of this country. However, few people below the age of fifty will remember those days and perhaps this is one of the reasons for the lack of sympathy with low flying aircraft exhibited recently. Personally, having suffered many disturbed days and nights in the blitz when the only sound of engines was the irregular beat of unsynchronised German bombers, followed by whistling bombs and the ground heaving with explosions, I am only too happy to hear and see aircraft flying by day or night, secure in the knowledge that now it is one of ours, and that some young man is following in the great tradition of those who gave their lives that we might have freedom and this his skills, perfected by continual practice will be available should, God forbid, there be any return to war-time conditions in this country.

Eight years later, Mr. Sirrett, the Community Relations Officer from RNAS Yeovilton addressed the Annual Parish Meeting, advising of the proposed increase in flying which was to take place, because the initial training of Sea Harrier pilots was to take place at Yeovilton from 1989. When the initial training was completed, the pilots would be practising take off and landings, which were the most intrusive. The expected increase in aircraft movements would be approximately 20%. There was to be a re-assessment of the noise contour in June of that year, the last one having taken place in 1983. When the noise levels are taken, it would be approximately six months before the results became available.

In January 1990 a new Noise Compensation Scheme was announced and although the noise contour line (within which grants for secondary window glazing may be claimed) does NOT extend to Marston Magna or Rimpton, claims for Injurious Affection Compensation may be submitted. The following is an extract from documents given out at the meeting:

From 1 January 1990, owners of homes and certain small businesses with a rateable value of less than £2250 per annum near to RNAS Yeovilton, may be eligible to claim for compensation if there is evidence that the value of their property has been adversely affected by an increase in noise resulting from the completion of works and the subsequent arrival of the Sea Harrier Basic Training Wing in January 1989.

The September 1996 Parish Magazine warned villagers that the level of flying at night had increased greatly over the last few weeks, as new air crews were being trained. The more complaints that RNAS Yeovilton received would carry weight for action to be taken.

In October 1997 the Parish Magazine reported that the Marston Magna Parish Council were invited to spend the day at the Air Station to learn a little of what happens there. They found the visit very interesting, particularly as they were treated to a helicopter ride to view Marston Magna, Rimpton and Queen Camel.

By the year 2000 RNAS Yeovilton was sending details of their flying schedules to the Parish Council. These were placed on a village notice board at the beginning of each week.

In Michael Ondaatje's novel "The English Patient", Marston Magna is briefly portrayed as the English countryside ideal, yet spoilt by noise on the soldier's return.

Fortunately for us, there is now only noise from the helicopters, and the green fields and the skies are mostly peaceful.

FARMING

The village of Marston Magna is situated on the A359 between the villages of Mudford and Queen Camel. The area is 1,392 acres, the soil is rich loam and stiff clay, and the subsoil is gravel and clay. In 1905 most of the parish was under grass with only 93 acres of arable land. Cheese was made in at least one farm in the 1920s.

The chief crops produced in the first quarter of the century were wheat, grass and dairy produce. The whole population in 1911 was 311 persons. There were 12 farmers reported in Kelly's Directory and these were dairy producers. The "Western Counties Creameries Ltd", utilised the milk produced by the farmers. "Magna Cider, Fruit and Farm Co Ltd" were fruit pulp manufacturers, cider growers, bottlers, merchants and farmers. "Brut" or dry bottled cider was a speciality, with some even exported to Australia. This factory used apples grown in the orchards of the village and neighbourhood.

The farmers at the beginning of the 20th Century were:

Paul Pitman (d.1913) farmed ***Vine Farm*** and his son Samuel continued there until 1927.

Henry Chalker at ***Park Farm,*** followed by Samuel Pitman who moved to farm there, after his farmhouse, Vine House, had been pulled down by Ashworth Hope to obtain stone for the Court.

P. E. Davis lived at ***Wickham Farm*** until 1928, when it was bought by S.W. Dare, who sold it in 1963 to S.E. Crabb.

William R. Hockey farmed ***Cooper's Farm*** until his death in 1916.

Edward Drake then took on the farm until the 1930s. In 1935 Mr Longman's name is noted as the farmer but it was then occupied by Henry Chapman. Charles Hockey farmed from ***Dampier House.***

Ernest Wadman, farmer and hay dealer, farmed at ***White House Farm.***

Rowland Thorn farmed ***Laurel Farm*** and Mr Ralph had ***Westend Farm.***

Albert Norris, and for a while James Hayward farmed ***Garston Farm*** in Rimpton Road until F. Noyce took over the farm.

For many years the Bollens farmed at ***Studleys Farm.***

James Hayward and Reginald Loader were small holders. William Smith was a cattle dealer and later farmer, one time resident at ***Wisteria House.***

Most of the population of Marston Magna found employment within the village. Aplin and Barrett and Magna Cider were employers and many found work there. The farms too needed a great deal of manpower. As most kept cows, which must be milked twice a day, men were needed to milk them by hand. There was a limit to how many cows one man could milk and therefore how many a farmer could own. There were no milking machines!

The main source of power on the farm was the horse. The majority of new machinery introduced in the nineteenth century was horse drawn and it is estimated that by 1913 there were over one million horses working on farms throughout Britain. There were shire horses for heavy work e.g. pulling loads of hay, corn and for ploughing. Lighter horses e.g. cob horses were used for pulling a milk float containing churns, or governess cart for shopping or pleasure. On bigger farms a carter was employed, whose sole occupation was to look after the horses. He fed them with hay, oats, and linseed cake, groomed and watered them, looked after the harness and kept it clean.

All these animals, cows, horses, sheep, calves had to be fed. The main crop was grass. For most of the year grass could be grazed but during the winter cows are kept under cover. Some fields were laid up for haymaking, which was carried out in the summer and used for winter feed. The grass was cut with a scythe or horse drawn mower and left in the field to dry. Many people were employed to toss the grass with picks until it was deemed dry enough to be hauled. Sometimes a horse drawn hay turner was used. The loose hay was pitched onto wagons, which were pulled back to the farmyard, usually by two shire horses. A hayrick was built and later thatched with straw.

In the winter, or on rainy days, spars had to be made in order to attach the straw to ricks when they were thatched. Spars are long fronds cut from the willow or withy trees when they were pollarded every year. Each spar was about four feet in length. It had to be bent and twisted twice in a certain way, so that it was then "V" shaped. These spars were put into bundles and soaked in water to make them pliable. There were many withy trees growing in Marston Magna along Hornsey Brook and they were needed for this purpose.

Some farmers had an arable field or two in order to grow wheat, barley, and oats. Corn was a food supplement for their animals and also generated the by-product of straw. The field would be ploughed using a horse plough pulled by two shire horses, the man walked behind holding the two handles and guiding the horse with two long rope plough lines. In 1914 it was recorded that one man could plough one acre in a day. The land would then be cultivated by more horse drawn machinery. The seeds could be broadcast or scattered by hand, or sown with a "fiddle sower" i.e. a bag full of seeds, which scattered as a long rod was moved up and down, later horse drawn drills were used. When the corn was ripe, it was scythed by the reaper band of workers, or by a horse drawn binder, which cut the corn, tied it into sheaves which fell to the ground, then picked up and put into stooks. These were hauled to the farmyard, built into ricks and thatched.

When the potatoes had been picked up from the field and apples gathered from the orchards, the harvest was complete.

Later in the autumn or spring the corn would be threshed. A steam engine and threshing tackle would arrive at the farm; belts driven by the engine drove the working of the threshing machine. The corn was separated from the ears, and stored in the barn in hired West of England sacks. The straw was built into a rick and thatched. Straw was a valuable resource as it was used for bedding down the horses and cattle. Usually twelve men were needed on threshing day for which they received £1 each for one day's work.

Farmer's wives and daughters were also busily occupied – they fed and looked after chickens, fed milk to the calves, made bread, butter and clotted cream, some for the household and some to sell.

Mrs. Davies remembered:

> *If the spring had been favourable haymaking began. Mr. Higdon especially, whose field was at the end of the garden of Netherton House, generally began as early as he could. I remember this field being cut by two men with scythes, working on parallel lines but far enough apart for the second one to miss the sweeping scythe of the man in front. The hay was both turned and ricked by hand with wide wooden rakes and pitchforks. We liked to play in the hay, making little nests for ourselves and our black cat often joined us on the chance of finding a field mouse that had lost its way now the grass was cut.*

World War 1

In August 1914 the First World War began and agriculture faced unprecedented challenges – produce more or risk being starved into submission. At the outbreak of war 60% of our food was imported. 70% of our wheat was imported, 40% of our meat and all sugar. In December 1914 Lloyd George's Government prioritised milk production and guaranteed prices for oats and wheat for farmers, in an attempt to stimulate arable production. In 1916 compulsory rationing was introduced and by 1918 sugar, tea, margarine, bread, meat and flour were among the rationed foods.

The war led to the loss of one third of the male force, so 98,000 women were given the opportunity to join the Women's Land Army in 1917 to work on farms throughout the country. The Women's Institute (W.I.) movement begun in Canada in 1897 and the war resulted in the formation of the first W.I. in Britain in 1915. The aim was to encourage countrywomen to help revitalise rural communities and become involved in producing food during World War 1.

When the war began, the army owned 25,000 horses, but another half a million were needed to go into battle. Many farming families had to give up their horses to the army, who used them for transport and logistic support through deep mud.

A scheme was set up for the returning men at the end of the war in 1918, whereby they could have a smallholding, run by the County Council, in order to produce milk, eggs and arable products. Most of these holdings were less than 100 acres each. In Marston Magna there was Portway Farm, lately farmed by Norman Holt, Westend Farm, lately farmed by Derrick Tottle and Laurel Farm, farmed by M Gregory.

Between the Wars

Farming carried on much the same as before the war. Horses were still the main source of power, although steam power was used. Steam ploughing was commonly used but needed a skilled operator. It was an indirect method with a plough attached to a cable powered by two steam engines. There were 2 stroke steam engines employed for a variety of uses e.g. pumping water, working the apple pulping machine when making cider, and for making the shears work when shearing sheep.

The cows were still being hand milked on most farms. Fresh milk and cream was sold direct from the farm to the village population. This milk was not pasteurised. Some milk went to the village creamery or was sent from the railway station to London to be sold there.

When the Milk Marketing Board was set up in the 1930s, there was a guaranteed promise that all milk would be collected daily in churns and taken to a central dairy. It would be pasteurised, bottled and distributed, or made into butter or cheese. The farmer would receive the money for his milk paid directly into his bank account each month. These arrangements lasted almost to the end of the century.

The farmers employed a great number of workers to run their businesses. There were from 4 to 12 men per farm depending on the acreage. Women and girls were required in the farmhouses to help the farmers' wives cope with the laundry, making bread, cleaning and looking after the children. There was so much daily work to be done on every farm e.g. milking, cleaning up manure, collecting it by wheelbarrow, putting it in a putt (2 wheeled cart) and in spring getting it to a field and placing it in small heaps. Later, these small heaps would be spread by hand held picks over the whole field. In winter the manure was deposited in a dung heap, growing bigger each day. The hedges had to be cut every year with hand held hooks, and if they had grown high they had to be laid.

Ditches had to be dug and kept free from silt to drain the rainwater away. This job was completed with spades. Root crops e.g. mangolds were grown to feed animals during the winter. The mangold seeds were sown in spring, but as they emerged in clumps it was necessary to single them out. This job was called "striking." They also needed to be hoed to keep them free from weeds. A horse hoe was used for this work. Two men were needed – one to lead the horse, the other to hold the hoe handles and guide it. Later in the year the mangolds were pulled by hand, brought back to the farmyard, deposited in one long heap and covered with straw and soil to keep them frost-free. This heap was called "a mangold cave"

Pulling mangolds at White House Farm.

The dawn of a new era came after the end of the First World War. Although a lot of machinery was used in the fields, it was still horse drawn. The motor tractor was still in its infancy, but in 1916 the Ministry of Munitions became responsible for the supply of agricultural machinery. The United States developed tractors but the models were unsuitable for British conditions. In the 1930s some farmers owned a Titan tractor.

Henry Trim wrote this piece in the Parish Magazine (1979):

Ern Rainey was telling me when a boy in World War I, his father, who was then employed at Park Farm, took him across the fields to Home Farm, Rimpton, where the first tractor to be seen in the locality was being used. It was a "Titan" and was pulling a 2-farrow plough, the driver and the ploughman being members of the Labour Corps.

It was not until the end of the Second World War that owning a tractor was really necessary. At first nearly every farmer owned a "Fordson". These had iron wheels with spade lugs for heavy going, over which a band was put for travelling on the road. It had to be cranked by hand to start it, and it was noted for backfiring and many people had broken arms - never put your thumb over the starting handle! Horses were still used to close furrows on ground being ploughed, because it was thought a tractor driver could not plough a straight furrow. Ferguson tractors were the next make to become a favourite with farmers because they had P.T.O. (Power Take Off), which meant that power was available for the machinery being towed behind the tractor, under the control of the driver.

Dairy was the least mechanised sector with the majority of milking still done by hand until the late 1940s. "Alpha-Laval" and "Fullwood" were popular makes of milking machines. The dairyman put the clusters of four teats on the cow, so that milk went into the bucket beneath the clusters. Milk was tipped into the cooler and ran down a corrugated surface that had cold water inside it, into the churn. Each churn contained 10 gallons. A pipeline installed around the cow stall was an improvement to this system, and the milk was then pumped into a refrigerated bulk tank. Every day the milk would be collected by a milk tanker lorry and transported to the dairy. (Things have moved on from this method - cows are milked in a milking bale or carousel, 10 or 12 at a time - get milked automatically- then leave when they have been milked). The whole of this machinery depends on a supply of electricity.

During the 1920s and 1930s transport methods were changing. An increasing number of bicycles were used throughout the century mainly by those going to and from work. Cars were owned by a few people, mostly professionals and factory owners, but not by the general public. The farmers could have owned a small Austin 7 or Morris 8, which they used for attending market to buy or sell animals.

World War 2

In 1939 World War 2 was declared and all food production was very important. War Agriculture Committees had the power to order farmers to plough up meadows and grassland. They were told to grow more cereals and potatoes. Flax must be grown and pulled by hand (to obtain longer stalks), and later a machine was shared around by the farmers. Sugar beet also had to be produced, pulled and cleaned by hand, and delivered to the railway station, from where it went to Kidderminster to be turned into sugar. Failure to observe the regulations meant the farm could be seized and someone else could farm it.

The rationing of food began in 1940 with the rationing of bacon, ham, sugar, butter, meat, tea, margarine, cooking fat, and cheese. In 1941, jam and marmalade, treacle, syrup, eggs, (1 egg per person per week) became rationed, and in 1942 milk, sweets, clothes and shoes were also rationed and needed coupons. Farmers at this time were in a good position because they had their own eggs, milk, lamb's tails, sweetbreads, rabbits, hares, pheasants, and potatoes. Most farmers kept a pig which ate kitchen waste and was slaughtered for meat and bacon. Farmers' wives made butter and cream. Jam was made from plums, blackberries, gooseberries, strawberries and raspberries. They grew vegetables in their gardens. There were special allocations of rations to farmers during hay making and harvest, so that the workers could be sent food and drink while they were working in the fields – a lot of cider was also drunk. We were on double summer time so the work went on late into the evening. Because we were two hours ahead of G.M.T. there was a lot of dew on the ground, so work in the fields was late beginning in the mornings.

Men were in short supply, so the Women's Land Army was called upon to help on the farms, as they were in the last war. They milked the cows, worked with the horses and were trained to do all the jobs on the farm. Italian and German prisoners of war also helped on farms pulling roots, mangolds, sugar beet, and potatoes. They helped with the harvesting and haymaking. Italian prisoners of war also did a lot of ditching, clearing watercourses and rivers. Indeed, at the end of the war our rivers in Somerset were in really good condition after all their hard work.

Petrol could not be bought. It was strictly rationed and coupons were given to protected industries like farming and used very carefully in the work of the farm, not for holidaying or joyriding! Many of the general public removed the wheels from their cars and laid them up on blocks until the end of the war.

Peace arrived in 1945 but the rationing of food did not end. Most food was taken off the ration by 1953 but at last, in 1954, butter, margarine, lard, cheese and meat all came off the ration and the ration books no longer were needed. In April 1953 cream could at last be bought in the shops legally.

1945 onwards

Just before World War 2, dairy cows were being tested for tuberculosis. After the war, testing was encouraged for all dairy cows. In 1950 farmers had a choice: they could buy cows untested or tested (T.T.). However, from 1951 all dairy cows had to be tested annually. By the end of the century all bovine livestock i.e. dairy cows and beef cattle had to be tested once each year and also before going to market. If an animal is a reactor the farmer is penalised. He may not move any livestock on or off his farm, for 60 days. All cattle must be free from T.B. with a clean T.B. test.

After the war, with the lessening of fuel restrictions and the diminishing use of horses, tractors came into their own. Most farmers owned at least one tractor; there were Fordsons, Fergusons, Gordon Browns, and Internationals. Balers came onto the farms enabling hay, straw and silage to be made into bales and making the job still easier when sledges were invented to collect a number of bales, which were then lifted mechanically onto a trailer pulled by a tractor. Combine Harvesters came into use by the 1960s-1970s, owned at first mainly by contractors. Combines can cut and thresh wheat, barley and oil seed rape in one operation. The corn or rape seeds are blown into a trailer running alongside, the straw is left in lines on the ground later to be baled and hauled to the farmyard and stored in a Dutch barn, with no thatching needed. The fields were ploughed, cultivated and sown with another crop, all by tractor power. Today fields can be sown directly with another crop, thus no ploughing is necessary.

When Mr. & Mrs. Samuel E. Crabb arrived in Marston Magna in 1963, they bought Wickham Farm from Mr. S. W. Dare. In the annual farm returns, the farm is reported thus:

1965 - Wickham Farm with over 100 acres was mainly laid to grass but produced 11 acres of barley and smaller acreages of wheat, potatoes, mangolds and kale. Livestock comprised 76 Friesian cows and calves, 15 Landrace sows and 1 boar, 335 deep litter poultry and 115 cockerels, ducks and turkeys. Annual produce included 49,128 gallons of milk, 250 bacon pigs for slaughter and 300 dozen eggs. The farm was self sufficient in fruit and vegetables.

Hay is still made by some farmers, but our climate, with a significant rainfall in the summer months, makes the job difficult. Farmers prefer to make silage instead. Grass is cut, left for a day to wither, then gathered and put into large round bales covered in plastic. It can also be hauled loose in large silage wagons, deposited in a covered barn, where the cattle can feed in winter, as they need it. Maize is another crop grown today. It is harvested, chopped up and becomes silage, which is fed to animals in winter to supplement their diet. Mangolds are no longer grown, neither is kale, although it was grown for stock feeding in the 1960s and 1970s.

Cutting hedges and digging ditches are now all controlled by using correct machinery.

Agricultural Wages

The wage for a farm worker at the beginning of the 20th century was 10 shillings per week (50p) for a six-day week. Saturday was a working day. In the 1930s wages were £1/12/6 per week (£1.65p) and Saturday was a working half-day. By the 1950s wages had risen to £7/10/- (£7.50p) and Saturday was a day off with Sunday. In the 1970s wages doubled to £14 - £16 per week.

At the close of the 20th century, wages rose until in 2013 the Agricultural Wages Board was abolished. A farm worker would negotiate with the farmer as to the amount of wage he/she would receive, depending on the nature of the work he/she was expected to do. There were perks for a farm worker. Perhaps he lived in a cottage belonging to the farm, rent free, and most workers received free milk if they worked on a dairy farm. They were also given potatoes. Holidays increased from only bank holidays to up to a month per year, all with pay.

By tradition part of the farm labourer's wage was cider. Most farms including Park Farm and White House Farm made cider. It is alleged that until the middle of the twentieth century the quality of a farm's cider would entice casual labourers to work at farms where the cider was good. Two quarts was the day's ration for a man and one quart a day for a boy. Drinking cider was also to combat any risk of labourers drinking polluted water when labour was so vital to farms at very busy times like harvest and in turn labourers could not risk being laid off work as a result of illness.

Breeds of Cattle

The cattle seen in our fields during and before the 1939 war were mainly Shorthorns, the breed preferred for milk production. Hereford and Aberdeen breeds were reserved for beef. As soon as the war ended Friesian cattle were imported from Holland. Friesian semen was also imported from the best bulls. Cows were artificially inseminated with this semen. So we see mainly black and white Friesian or Holstein cows around the village farms. The amount of milk they produced dramatically increased. Channel Island breeds arrived – the Jerseys and Guernseys, which give less, but much richer milk, with more butter fat. Next to arrive were Charolais, Blonde d'Aquitaine, Limousin from

France, Simmentals from Germany and Switzerland. All these breeds are excellent beef animals.

Diseases

There are two diseases in farming which all farmers dread. The first is Tuberculosis in cattle. This disease is controlled by annual T.B. testing for all bovine animals. Movement Book records have to be kept by every farmer. These records provide traceability for all cattle leaving or coming on to every farm in the country.

The most dreaded is Foot and Mouth disease. If this disease is found to be on a farm, the whole herd is slaughtered and their carcasses burnt. For pedigree herd farmers this can be a catastrophe, because overnight they have lost their life's work in improving their herd by selective breeding.

The years for the worst outbreaks of Foot and Mouth disease in Somerset were 1916, 1933, 1967, and 2001.

The EU and the Common Agricultural policy

In 1972 Great Britain became a member of the European Community. Joining Europe has been beneficial for farmers in many ways. There are more customers for our products. Farmers receive help in the form of subsidies based on what they produced in the past, what they grow now, and the acreage of their farm. There are schemes to improve the environment of their farm, e.g. create ponds for wildlife, and to encourage the growth of hedges and trees. For a starter environmental scheme a farmer could receive almost £2000 per year.

In 1984 Milk Quotas were introduced because the European Community Milk "lake" had become too big. If a farmer produced more milk than their quota allowed they were penalised. Many small milk producers sold out their dairy herds and also sold their milk quotas to other farmers for a great price.

At Wickham Farm, the dairy herd of pedigree Friesians was sold out in 1983 and no compensation for any quota was given. Beef production started with a herd of Simmental pedigree suckler cows, the calves of which would be sold for beef when they were two and a half years old. Since 1983 the farm has produced beef and more recently has grown wheat, barley and oil seed rape.

By the end of the 20th Century, farming had changed a great deal in Marston Magna. There are fewer farms now than there were in 1900.

Norman Holt was a tenant farmer in 1957 at Portway Farm. Norman recollects that there were still 14 farmers or smallholders who were actively working the land in that period. Portway Farm was a council owned farm. They had 16 cows, mainly Ayshires, and a Ferguson tractor on 50 acres. This is a reminder of how the scale of farming has changed since that time.

The farmhouses of Cooper's Farm, White House Farm, Villa Farm, Park Farm, Portway Farm, Westend Farm, and Laurel Farm have been sold away from the land once farmed by them. Their land has been sold to the remaining farmers. The farmyards and barns of Cooper's Farm, White House Farm, and Park Farm have been utilised and built on with new houses. Most land is owned privately, and either farmed directly or "let" on an annual basis. Some land is, however, still owned by Somerset County Council under their "County Farm" programme, brought in after World War 1 to find farms for returning soldiers, as large Estates were broken up.

In the Parish Magazine of September 1980 Henry Trim wrote about the closure of the livestock market in Yeovil. He wrote:

> *It is a little sad to see the whole site cleared – presumably yet another car park in the offing? To us "Old Uns" it appears that Yeovil will eventually be all car parks with nothing for people to come to Yeovil in order to park!*

In 1991 Henry Trim also noted the fact that there were only three farmers in the village at that time. He mentioned Derek Tottle at West End Farm, Jim Nowell at Easton Farm on the Rimpton Road, and Norman Holt at Portway Farm:

> *Going back in time, the Red Lion and the Marston Inn were also small-holdings. Bert Florance was the last landlord of the Red Lion to keep milking cows and when he retired he tenanted Parkway Farm on the Sherborne Road. Jack Giles, who was my step grandfather, used to milk about 20 or so at the Marston Inn and the old cow stalls are still in existence there although not many tiles left! I can still picture him coming through the archway carrying two buckets of milk on a shoulder yoke to the "milk house" which was on the site of the present dining room. Usually he was accompanied by a few farm cats which nobody else could get near to! As a young lad he used to put me on the back of one of the cows, a very gentle animal, who gave me a ride down the Yeovil Road when the little herd was being returned to pasture.*
>
> *Cooper's Farm was once occupied by Henry Chapman. He supplied milk direct from farm to London by lorry. Also in Camel Street was White House*

Farm, run by Mr. Ern Wadham and later his sons, Selwyn and Aubrey.

On School Corner was Villa Farm owned by the Moore brothers, with land off Garston Lane. In Rimpton Road there was Studleys Farm owned by Bill Bollen, a staunch churchman. Opposite the Red Lion was Garston Farm, owned by Fred Noyce. Fred was a keen horseman and was always available to encourage youngsters leaning to ride.

The working force is very much smaller than in 1900. The number of workers has decreased from at least 4 – 8 for each farm, and more at busy times, to 1 or 2 at the end of the century. Machines do the tasks once done by men and horses – tractors are the main source of power – they need fuel only when they are working!

However, the farm workers today are experienced engineers and experts able to cope with complicated farm machinery, such as milking machines, hedge cutters, ditch diggers, silage cutters, balers, sledges, combines, drills and loaders. They are the guardians and gardeners of the landscape. The countryside looks as it does because it has been looked after for many centuries.

Rabbits

Tony Penn wrote the following:

The Influence of Wild Rabbits on Village Life in Marston Magna 1945-1955.

Wild rabbits were a huge resource in the village in the 1940s and 50s. They formed an important part of virtually every household diet. The rabbit skins were also important because they were sold to specialist dealers who processed the skins for fashion clothing of the time.

Rabbits were common and widespread in every farmer's fields and orchards and although they damaged all types of crops grown on the farms they were not heavily persecuted at the time, because of their value for meat and skins. As a result of this inherent value, farmers carefully protected their rabbit population by allowing only certain favoured people shooting and trapping rights.

Wild rabbits live in burrows that are usually dug beneath the roots of small trees and bushes and at that time virtually every field in the village that was surrounded by hedges were full of rabbit burrows. Farmers, landowners and their guests generally hunted the fields and hedgerows with shotguns and dogs were used to flush rabbits into the open to provide shooting opportunities.

It was possible to hunt in this fashion because rabbits spend a large amount of time in the open feeding on grass and other vegetation. When the rabbits become aware of the danger they rapidly return to their burrow. A method of forcing the rabbits out of the burrow was to use a ferret, which was introduced into the burrow driving the rabbits back into the open. Using a ferret in this way also provided the opportunity to cover the burrow exit holes with small nets, so that when the rabbits came out they became entangled in the nets. Once the rabbit became entangled in the net the hunter would pick it up and quickly and humanely despatch it by 'pulling its neck out'. The use of a ferret was not always an easy method, because on occasions the ferret would decide to 'make a meal' of a rabbit and refuse to come out of the burrow. This meant that the ferret had to be 'dug out' and digging out under a hedge meant cutting through hedge and small tree roots. Some ferret owners used what was called a 'liner' where the ferret wore a collar with a line attached. This approach could also lead to problems, because the burrow is a labyrinth, and it was quite possible for the line to be wrapped around a 'U' turn or a root.

In addition to shooting and netting rabbits, dogs were also used to chase and catch the rabbits once they had been flushed into the open. Broadly speaking there were two types of dog, the hunter, usually a rough mongrel type with a 'good nose' and the chaser, a whippet or small greyhound.

The only time that the people of the village were encouraged to kill rabbits was during the harvest. When the wheat and cereal crops ripen the rabbits like to feed and sleep inside the tall strands. When the harvest began using a 'binder', a machine that cut and bundled the stalks, a tractor was used to pull the binder beginning around the outside of the crop and gradually progressing toward the middle. The combined noise of the tractor and the binder drove the rabbits to the middle of the crop, with some breaking from the crop and attempting to escape into the surrounding hedge. As the rabbits increasingly left the shelter of the crop they were either shot by people with shotguns on one side of the field, or caught by villagers with sticks and dogs on the other three sides of the field.

One particular farmer's son in the village, affectionately known as 'Moonshine' because of his liking for cider and his very red complexion, used to sit on the seat of the binder with his shotgun by his side. When he judged it safe he would take a 'pot-shot' at a rabbit as it came out of the corn, rarely hitting the rabbit by effectively putting on a 'wild west' show.

The farmer/ landowner always instructed the rabbit catchers to put the dead rabbits in a pile, and at the completion of the harvest each person would be allowed to take one rabbit for themselves, with the remainder being left for sale by the field owner. However, there were also those villagers who caught significant numbers of rabbits and used the well known sharing principle of 'two for him and one for me' to create their own cache of rabbits.

The farmers and landowners often sold the rabbit catching rights to professionals, mostly people from outside the village, who used a variety of methods to catch the rabbits including the methods mentioned above. These people also used spring loaded gin traps at burrow exits and rabbit wires set along a run where rabbits had trampled a favourite route. A rabbit wire is a device made using strands of thin brass wire that is used to form a noose. The noose is set vertically by a small wooden peg and is tethered at the other end to secure the rabbit once its head is in the noose and it begins to struggle. Although both gins and wires were extensively used they caused the rabbits a great deal of stress and pain.

In addition to the official rabbit catchers there were a few clever and resourceful village people who regarded catching rabbits as a vital source of food supply and also as an exciting recreational activity. These people were often totally misunderstood and were labelled as 'poachers'. The so-called 'poachers' believed that the rabbits, pheasants, partridges and wild ducks were all part of 'nature's rich bounty' to be shared by all and never regarded as being 'taken illegally'. These poaching activities were a small but important part of the legacy handed down from father to son, and were a closely guarded secret, kept in order to maximise the 'haul' whilst at the same time remaining anonymous.

The poachers used the same methods of rabbit catching techniques as the farmers and landowners, but because they had carefully studied the life and habits of rabbits they were able to use additional methods needed to operate undetected. Poachers rarely used shotguns because of the noise. Instead, they were very effective stalkers, and used small airguns at very close range. The poachers generally had well trained rough dogs, typically spaniel/fox terrier cross breed used for 'flushing' the rabbit and a whippet or small greyhound to catch the rabbit once it came into the open. They carried ferrets in a special pocket and where there was a rabbit burrow unobstructed by roots or vegetation they 'netted' the rabbit holes and used the ferret to flush the rabbits.

When the weather began to warm up in the spring, rabbits often dug a single tunnel up to about six feet in length out in the field, and after feeding would retire to such a short hole to sleep. Because of the earth that had been dug out these burrows could easily be spotted, the practised eye of the poacher rarely missed such a hole. Because these holes had only one entry, which was also the exit, a ferret could not be used to flush the rabbit and so a long 'bramble' was used for catching the rabbit. The bramble was carefully trimmed with the maximum numbers of thorns at one end and a smoothly trimmed handle at the other. The thorny end of the bramble was used firstly to detect the presence of a rabbit in the hole by twisting it and withdrawing and inspecting it for any sign of rabbit fur. If a significant amount of rabbit fur was present, and at the right time of year there nearly always was, the bramble was reinserted into the hole and twisted, snagging the rabbit via its fur coat. The bramble was then withdrawn, pulling the rabbit with it.

Toward the end of the summer into early autumn, when the grass was beginning to change colour from green to yellowy brown and the sun still had a little warmth, the rabbits tended not to dig short holes in the open but instead to create a 'squat' in the grass. The rabbit would arrange the grass around its curled body creating a comfortable space being warmed by the sun. The poacher knew exactly the type of field that provided the ideal situation for rabbits to create a squat and with his practiced eye he would walk through such a field and quickly identify the position of a rabbit in a squat. Once the squat had been identified, the poacher would approach the squat in a steady ever-decreasing circular walk around it, which confused the rabbit, and finally the poacher came close enough to use his stick to stun the rabbit before despatching it.

Finally, when the rabbits had been caught they needed to be 'paunched' and skinned!

Paunching was the term used to remove the rabbit's intestines, and for this purpose a very sharp knife was used. The rabbit was hung by its neck, preferably as soon as possible after it had been caught; the sharp knife was then used to shave an area of the rabbit's stomach, which was then carefully opened to reveal the intestines. The bladder was first very carefully removed to avoid possible bursting and contaminating the flesh. Once the bladder had been removed the remainder of the intestines were withdrawn and the liver was generally given to the poachers dogs as a reward for their contribution.

Once the rabbit has been paunched, the skinning becomes straightforward. The back legs of the rabbit can be bent at the knee joint and pushed through the skin and into the stomach opening whilst holding the cavity open. When the back legs have been skinned the whole skin can then be removed by pulling it up and over the rabbit's head completing the operation.

The two preferred methods for cooking rabbits were to roast or stew them; both of these methods provided a delicious meal of delightfully flavoured tender meat.

During the years 1945 to 1955 not a single poacher was ever caught, although several farmers and landowners claimed to have 'strong' suspicions, and the amusing thing was that if any farmer or landowner had a problem with a fox taking any of his free range chicken they knew who to ask for help!

By 1955 the introduction of myxomatosis decimated the rabbit population around the village and rabbit catching became a thing of the past.

SOCIAL LIFE

In the early part of the century, entertainment was largely ' home based' and ranged from singing round the piano at home, to belonging to the Glee Society which gave madrigal concerts in the School. Mrs. Davis recounts many occasions when she went 'out to tea' with various village matrons. She also remarked:

> *The one really bright spot in November was of course, the fifth and how we hoped for a fine dry evening. We didn't dare to set off any noisy fireworks near home but we were allowed to have a box or two of Bengal Matches (a penny each) and there was a bonfire on a vacant space in the garden. We dressed in old clothes with paper masks and orange peel teeth and when the night came we all had a lovely time dancing round the fire, finishing with a mug of sweet cocoa.*

There were 'Parish Teas' when farmers' wives 'took a tray' of food along. A Fête in 1901 was held in the Glebe Field and included dancing round the maypole. The Mothers' Union met in the early years of the century and was still running when Kath Chainey was a young housewife. She remembers meetings at the Rectory in the room that abuts the road. There were no more than a dozen at each meeting and sometimes they would take the children.

John Peppin recalls:

> *In the first decade, with no wireless or telly, no buses, and just the odd train to Yeovil - our shopping centre - villagers were very much thrown on their own resources for entertainment. Very occasionally some travelling entertainers would take the schoolroom for a performance, which certainly enthralled me, but which was probably very bad. I remember one occasion when a man and a woman came and gave an exhibition of 'mind-reading', which has puzzled me to this day. The man was blindfolded on the platform, while the woman moved amongst the rustics, taking articles out of their pockets and asking the man what she had in her hand. It would not be difficult to devise a code whereby watches, note-books etc could be identified, but how the man on the platform was able to read what was written inside the covers of watches, for example, is beyond my comprehension.*
>
> *All amusements were homemade and about once a year, the rectory and one or two of the 'big houses' organised a revue at which the gentry unwound*

a little for the benefit of the rustics. The rectory was not very good at this sort of thing, but there were one or two gifted people living in a largish house near the station that could come up with some songs of their own composition, which had an element of humour about them.

Apart from the clerics and the few middle-class people from the country round about who called, our most frequent visitors were tramps, who used to walk from place to place begging. Sometimes they would have some means of attracting folks from their houses, such as a barrel organ or one of those pianos that played about six tunes at the turn of a handle. Mostly they were down and outs dressed in rags, worn out shoes etc. and they wanted bread, a pair of shoes, or anything to keep them going for another day.

The **Ancient Order of Foresters** were active in the village from the beginning of the century and there is photographic evidence of them parading through the village on horseback around the year 1912. We also have the following account from Mrs Davis:

Mr Charles Hockey, a farmer, lived at the end of the lane off Camel Street in Dampier House. Further up Camel Street lived his brother William, also a farmer. These two belonged to the Ancient Order of Foresters and on occasions they appeared on horseback wearing green velvet suits and plumed hats, riding before the Banner of the Order carried by other stalwart members, in a grand procession. This would be followed by a Fête held in the field opposite Marston House.

The Ancient Order of Foresters parading at school corner for the Fête, 1913.

The Order started in 1834 although its beginnings hail from an older society called the Royal Foresters, formed around 1745. Members acknowledged that it was necessary to assist other men who were in need and in 1892 women were also granted membership of the organisation. Membership was not granted to all, as health declarations were necessary. Members paid money into a common fund. When the main breadwinner was unable to work through illness, or died, then sick pay or a funeral grant was awarded.

At some stage a decision was taken to erect a hall in Marston Magna for the use of The Ancient Order of Foresters, but we have found no record of how the money was raised or of a benefactor. Before this hall was built, village gatherings were sometimes held at the school, or in the Marston Inn skittle alley.

The Hall was officially opened on 23rd September 1926 and Brenda Darch recorded the opening ceremony:

> *It began at 4.45 pm with members outside the hall. 'Brother' Marden turned the key in the lock and declared the hall open. The Chairman (Bro. Webber) gave an address with Bro. Marden responding. Bro. Bryant also gave an address, followed by a prayer by Rev. Bartlett. Major Goodford proposed a vote of thanks to the officers of the District and the assembly ended with the National Anthem.*

A committee of ladies was formed to arrange a Whist Drive and Dance on the evening of the opening and they arranged catering and social events for the next three years. The original committee was comprised of: Mesdames Bishop, Bollen, Grant, Bugby, Hatcher, Pitman, Brine, Rose, Noyce and Webber.

That first evening on September 23rd 1926 the committee decided to provide refreshments for 150 people. There were a variety of cakes including jam and cream buns, ham and tongue sandwiches made with butter, coffee made from bottled liquid, tea made with loose tea, and home made lemonade using vast amounts of sugar. 6lbs of sugar was also purchased for the tea and coffee and it is certain that most people would have sweetened their hot drinks. The event was a huge success. 108 people sat down to whist and about 200 people attended the dance. The Cheerio Band was in attendance. During the autumn of 1926 a series of social evenings took place. A smoking concert on December 2nd attracted 120 people and was considered a great success. In the same week on December 8th there was a sixpenny dance with 90 people present and a profit of 5/10d (29p) was made. The profits from these functions were used to purchase new equipment for the hall.

The records show an extensive shopping list which was systematically reduced, including tumblers, teacloths, trays, jugs, a small tub for washing up, crockery, paper doilies, a 6 pint tin kettle, a clock, a mirror for the dressing room and a cupboard. Baize too, was often bought, presumably for the card and games tables. The most usual fundraising format was a whist drive followed by a dance. The music would be provided by a pianist but sometimes by the Farthings Band or Harry Virgins band. Skittles matches also took place. The proceeds from one such evening raised enough funds for a children's Christmas party for 70 children. They all went home with a gift, an orange and a bag of sweets.

Money was raised by the Order in 1927 for the District Nursing Fund, which the Women's Institute also supported around the same time. This was a very important service to rural communities and did not come under the NHS until 1948.

Events were not held during the summer months, which would have been a busy part of the agricultural year.

The 1939 Kelly's Directory notes that for Marston Magna the Secretary for The Ancient Order of Foresters (Court Jubilee No 7608) was Ernest Frederick Rose of Portway Farm. People in employment took money to Mr Rose to pay their contributions towards sick pay, which would be distributed if they were unable to work. This was after the National Insurance Act of 1911, when Foresters became an 'Approved Society', and involved in the state system of National Insurance.

With the advent of World War 2, the Hall was taken over by the military and during the American occupation of the village a stage was built and other improvements made.

A few years after the end of the war, the Hall was purchased from the Ancient Order of Foresters by the Village Hall Management Committee on 1st January 1948. The sum of £434 was paid for the building and furniture, which generously represented no more than the original cost. The money was kindly advanced by Mr Stanley Dare in the form of an interest free loan, the final instalment of which was repaid on 31st December 1953.

Following the purchase of the hall there was a Whist Drive held on Wednesday evenings in aid of Hall funds. These lasted without a break for 45 years. Doris Sharp and Phyllis Bartlett arranged the prizes, Archie Sharp and Dulcie Pitman provided transport for supporters from neighbouring villages and Henry Trim was M.C. from the start. Ill health and advancing years amongst the helpers drew it to a close on 25th September 1991. Thanks were expressed to all who had helped and supported the event over so many years and especially the friends from outside the village without whom it would have expired much earlier.

In order to raise funds for the Village Hall, a concert party called The Marstonaires was formed. The Rehearsals took place in a cottage in Church Path. Not only did they involve many villagers in their productions but they also went "on tour" to neighbouring villages, even travelling as far as Barrington. Village children also trod the boards, performing in pantomimes for several years.

A Marstonaires Production.

Les Dewey, an evacuee who returned to the village after the war, was working at Lambrook Farm and has this memory of The Marstonaires:

I went into Yeovil in about 1949 to purchase a new 350cc BSA motorbike. I remember it cost £150. I went into the Post Office in Yeovil (Barclays Bank now) took the money out of my account and went down to the BSA Motor Mart just into the Hendford Road. All paid for and duly delivered. I had never ridden one before but I quickly learned. I then started to meet some other young lads outside on the steps by Tommy Aplin's Garage at Marston Magna on a Saturday night. We would all go off on our bikes wherever we fancied, Weymouth or West Bay were favourites on a summer's evening. All this led to me meeting more lads from Marston Magna including Jim Trim. Winter came on and we were both roped into the Marstonnaires. I can't remember much

Henry Trim with supporting cast!

about it but we performed in the Hall and a lady was the organiser. I think I was the Fairy Godmother!

By 1980 maintenance work on the Hall had been identified and help arrived in the shape of Young Offenders. The following appeared in the Parish Magazine of April that year:

The work being done by young offenders who have been ordered by the Court to undergo Community Service on our Village Hall is now nearing completion. Nobody who has seen their excellent work under the direction of their Works Supervisor can deny how hard they have worked. It makes one shudder to think what it would have cost if the work had been done professionally, but as it is, all we have had to pay for is the materials.

Any sentence passed by a court of law must include an element of reparation. A Community Service is normally imposed as an alternative to a custodial sentence. We would like to thank these young people and the Probation Service for their hard work and for the marvellous results.

The New Village Hall

The old Village Hall was a corrugated iron and timber building. It was well used and much loved for a number of activities and social events, but its worn and splintered floors were becoming unsafe for young children, and it was so poorly heated and insulated, causing severe condensation at times, that it was practically unfit for use during cold weather. The equipment was also showing signs of wear and as early as 1977 the caretaker Phyllis Bartlett mentioned the piano, firmly embedded on the stage, was showing signs of age and senility and needed "putting down". The Hall Committee asked if anybody had any idea how the deathblow could be administered e.g. a piano-smashing competition, or a good bonfire for November 5th? "*Please do take it away someone, we haven't the heart or the courage to do it ourselves and we don't really know what to do.*"

The kitchen needed to be extended. Government requirements meant spending many thousands of pounds to bring this up to date. Philip Mitchell, the Village Hall Committee Chairman, called a meeting to explain that it was felt that rather than spending a large amount of money on a new kitchen, it would be better to put it towards a new hall. As there was some reluctance expressed, it was decided to have a village referendum, which resulted in a majority interest in a new hall.

In April 1988 the WI meeting was dominated by the Village Hall improvement proposals as the members confined themselves to the end of the hall - cut off from the main hall by an 'imaginary folding screen'. It gave an idea of the space available in the various proposals, which were discussed at great length.

The Hall Management Committee, at its A.G.M. in January 1990, voted unanimously to start planning for a new hall and to start fund-raising for this purpose.

As there were no current funds for a new hall, many fund raising ideas were put into action: a Silent Auction, Duck Races, a tea party, a horse racing night, and a 50/50 auction were among the events organised.

By January 1994, the accumulated funds amounted to £29,513.68 after having spent some £5,400 on Architects' fees, Planning Application, building regulations and legal fees. The lowest tender from builders amounted to £82,000 and Council grants of 50% of building costs (subject to a maximum total cost of £120,000) had been agreed by Somerset County and South Somerset District Councils. The original estimate allowed for single glazing and timber window frames.

Early in 1994, a possible loan of up to £10,000 repayable over five years was agreed with The Community Council in case it was needed. This gave the Committee the confidence to make the crucial decision to go ahead and build the new hall.

A good number of local residents in this small community, with a population below 400 people, made Deeds of Covenant for the benefit of the Hall, a registered charity. Finances were further improved by grants of £7,150 from the Council for Sport and Arts and £2,500 from Gaymer Group, who then operated the Winery in Marston Magna. These gifts enabled the Committee to opt for double-glazing throughout. PVC window frames and suspended ceilings were also installed for improved thermal efficiency and reduced maintenance costs.

Mr. Raymont, a local farmer, generously gave a strip of land to enable the new hall to be set back from the main road, alongside the children's playground.

The builders, F.J. Reeves & Sons of Sparkford, started building the new hall on 1st March 1994, scheduled to complete in six months. The Building Inspector visited the site and requested that the foundations at the front of the building be 2 metres deep (this resulted in an extra charge of £900 being due to the builders). The inspector also stipulated that no trees must be planted within 6 metres of the new hall.

The new hall was completed ahead of schedule in August 1994, in time for a planned Village Open Weekend. This afforded villagers a visit to both halls - one for the first and the other perhaps for the last time. Henry Trim describes first class and eye-catching exhibits on display in the Hall including David Nelson's model houses, the icing skills of Pam Millichip, Rachel Holt's Corn Dollies and Stan Gardner's photographic studies. Visitors were also able to draw on Les Sayers' extensive knowledge of Marston Past.

An auction was held in September to sell off items from the old Hall. A large portion of the wood and almost all fittings including windows, doors etc. were sold and removed prior to demolition. The space under the floor revealed an interesting collection of items - mummified cats, long forgotten brands of cigarettes, a newspaper from 1941, US Army vehicle forms, old bottles etc!

Messrs Reeves finally demolished the old hall on Monday 12th September and the site was cleared very rapidly.

The Rt. Hon Paddy Ashdown MP officially opened the new hall on 29th October 1994. After speeches by County, local officials and Paddy Ashdown, a plaque was unveiled commemorating the event. The Opening was attended by many villagers and reported in the Western Gazette.

The new hall was completed and paid for without borrowing any money, with funds remaining for future use.

Henry Trim later admitted to having his feathers ruffled when one of the visiting speakers referred to the old building, which holds so many fond memories, as "the old tin hut".

A report of this project was prepared and entered in the 1995 " Somerset Community Council Best Run Village Halls Award." The judges awarded Marston Magna Village Hall First Prize for the South Somerset Area, and Second Prize for the whole of Somerset.

Phyllis Bartlett had been Caretaker of the old village hall, and continued as the first Caretaker of the new hall in 1994. She ran a second hand Shop or Community Jumble in both halls for many years from 1984 until after 2000. It was reported in the Village Magazine of March 1997 that the Hall Shop raised an amazing £8,216 for Village Hall funds.

The Women's Institute

A regular user of both halls has been the Women's Institute although the first discussion meeting in November 1925 was held in the Schoolroom with the Revd. Bartlett presiding. The inaugural meeting took place the following month and by the end of the first year there were 56 members. The meetings took place at The Foresters Hall from 1927 as the schoolroom had become too small to accommodate all the members.

Outings were a feature of the early WI in the village with charabanc trips to Bournemouth, Southampton, Torquay, Weston-super-Mare and other destinations as well as more local outings when the whole Institute took a charabanc for a picnic on Cadbury Hill. Visits from Taunton were made by Voluntary County Officers to offer advice on conduct at meetings, educational opportunities and pep talks on "Duties, loyalties and morals". Marston Magna WI benefited from a grant towards dressmaking classes, which were popular as were all classes offered. Demonstrations and talks took place, cricket teams played matches, choirs entered County competitions, parties were held and the village fête was supported.

Donations were made on occasion to other local causes. In 1928 a donation was made to the rebuilding of Sandford Orcas hut after it was burnt down. Donations were made to the school and to the District Nurses Association.

From 1933-1944 Mrs Ashworth Hope was President of the WI. She made her house and garden available for numerous events for members and their families and friends. She worked hard and began every meeting with a motto on which she spoke. These included "Good cooks waste nothing", "A time for everything and everything in time" and "If there is a smile on your lips, those around you will smile too". When she handed over to a new president she presented the WI with a silver cup to be awarded to the member who accumulates the most competition points throughout the year. This is still in use today.

In 1938 Rimpton joined Marston Magna with a vote of twenty for and twelve against and then in 1955 formed its own institute again and so was deleted from the "Marston Magna and Rimpton WI" by a byelaw. There was a very large WI contribution to the war effort which is recounted elsewhere. In 1946 the 21st birthday of the WI was celebrated with a buffet supper of rabbit pie and apple tart.

Transport was easier after the war and coach outings resumed; summer picnics were taken at Ham Hill and Batcombe Down. Food rationing continued and deserving causes made appeals. By 1950 the WI decided to concentrate on two charities: the British Empire Cancer Campaign and St. Dunstan's. The Sunshine fund was started in 1949 to provide cards and gifts for those who were elderly, housebound or hospitalised. A year or so later new mothers were included in the list to receive cards and flowers on the birth of their babies.

The annual whist drive for 1952 in aid of the British Empire Cancer Campaign was cancelled following the sudden death of King George V1. 1953 saw preparations for Coronation celebrations. The WI had a members only evening with refreshments of cold rabbit pie, sausage rolls, salad and then trifle, cheese and biscuits. The toast to Queen Elizabeth II could be made with cider from the Magna Cider factory, cordial or the tea provided. The Children's Coronation Tea Party was arranged jointly with the village hall committee.

Members stood up and took their turn at speaking on chosen mottos at meetings. Roll calls continued; over the years an amazing selection of subjects was chosen. How to use stale bread, my favourite quotation, how to get rid of slugs, your worst cookery blunder, my favourite song, Somerset Dialect sentences, the best cure for a bad temper, a treasured possession and Granny's favourite remedy are just a few. The responses occasionally caused hilarity to break out amongst the members. Competitions called upon skills; a refooted sock may cause problems today!

The round of activities continued through the 1950s and 1960s. 1963 was a long, very cold winter and the Children's Party was delayed until Easter. An evening outing was arranged for the first time that year and a coach outing to Stourhead and Longleat was enjoyed for 5 shillings (25p). The Golden Jubilee of The National WI was celebrated in 1965 with a week of celebrations in the village. The President went to a garden party at Buckingham Palace given by Her Majesty the Queen.

In 1970 the annual children's party took place, the under fives had games in the hall, the over fives went to the cinema, with 2 shillings (10p) to spend on sweets, whilst the older children went to another cinema and were treated to fish and chips. This was a great success but a few years later only two parties were held in the hall for the under fives and their mothers and then a 2-hour party for primary school children. This was the last children's party and so a long tradition ended. Pancake races held with Mudford was another annual event that ceased in the mid-1970s. The Golden Jubilee of the village WI was marked by providing the seat on the village green in 1975.

The rise in the cost of living in the 1970s caused many charities to appeal for help. As a charity itself the National WI headquarters reminded the Institute that donations could not be made from funds.

Members of the WI were very involved in the Queen's Silver Jubilee celebrations of 1977, and more of this occasion is recorded below under National Celebrations!

Subscriptions rose, membership wavered and on occasion in the early 1980s there was some question of the Institute surviving in the village when a new secretary could not be found. The day was saved however when a loyal member stepped up to the plate.

President Rachael Holt and Yvonne Lawrence holding the WI Diamond Jubilee celebration cake in 1985.

The WI continued and 1985 marked the 60th year of the Women's Institute in Marston Magna, so on December 9th a special Diamond Jubilee party was held in the village hall to celebrate this milestone. The colour scheme for the decorations was pale blue, white and silver and the only diamonds were of pale blue card covered with glitter because they could not afford the real thing! The beautiful cake was made by Miss Agneta Hickley (Rimpton) but iced by Mr Harold Lawrence (West Camel). He had portrayed the river of time flowing across the cake, crossed by two freestanding bridges spanning the years 1925-1985 and with the WI emblem as a centrepiece. A Silent Auction continued throughout the evening raising just over £70 for the Denman College repair fund.

At this time too a poem was read at each meeting, but mottos seemed to have ceased. A wide range of poetry was read. Well known poems, reflective poems and humorous poems, which at times caused tears of laughter to fall.

Delegates from the Institute have attended the WI AGM where they have debated a wide range of issues relating to the welfare of people and their environment. This is an opportunity to meet members from across the country as well as attending local County and District events. Friends from neighbouring WIs have attended functions at the village hall. Financing the WI has had its ups and downs. Jumble sales were a good source of income in the 1980s. The competition entries were made easier and fewer home-made entries were required. The use of Christian names instead of a more formal means of address caused some discussion in the 1980s, but the use of first names is now familiar practice!

The 1990s brought an innovation; if the speaker was deemed appropriate then men could be invited to the meetings. For a time too there were three vice-presidents and one president so that no member took more than three meetings in the year. This too was the decade when Anne

Dennett became Secretary, and her sense of humour and turn of phrase meant that the minutes of the meeting were positively anticipated!

1995 brought the WI's 70th birthday. A good party, but for once the cake was not home-made. The Millennium approached and some members worked to produce the sampler that currently hangs on the hall wall and depicts village features of 2000.

The pattern of meetings over the years has varied slightly but there has been continuity so a fairly similar pattern is followed as it did when it started in the 1920s. A speaker, demonstration or activity usually takes place at every meeting and a competition is held. The Sunshine fund continues. Groups with similar interests meet to share their interests. Links with other local WIs are maintained, as is the link with the National Federation. Outings are arranged, fund-raising activities take place. National events are supported and celebrated in the village. Perhaps of most importance are the friendships which are formed, alongside learning new skills and information.

The Village Pubs

The two village pubs, the Marston Inn, on the corner of Sherborne and Yeovil Roads and the Red Lion in Rimpton Road were always at the centre of village social life. They are mentioned in several chapters, but a little further information is included here, with a few anecdotes.

The Marston Inn is the longest established and has been owned by various brewers over the years. It used to be called The Old Angel and was renamed in 1805. It has a skittle alley and the main building used to have a Public Bar with a Lounge but this has since been made into one large room and much of the space is given over to dining. The longest serving tenants were Mrs Noyce at the beginning of the century and George Barnes who in 1988 celebrated 20 years service. Both landlords performed many acts of kindness in the community, especially to the elderly and the children including free transport, meals and Christmas dinners, all provided unheralded and unsung.

The Marston Inn

The Blackmore Vale Hunt met outside the Marston Inn, and during Edwardian times the schoolchildren were given time out of school to see the hunt.

Around 1920 the Marston Inn was the last stop at night for the fish man. He used to sell bloaters to the customers at the pub at one penny each and they would cook them on a fork over the bar fire!

During the war when beer and spirit supplies were restricted it was a very difficult time for the Landlords. They used to keep their customers happy with cider, which could be purchased, from local farms and The Cider Factory. It was amazing how many soldiers, British and American, were fooled at the strength of "Somerset Apple Juice"! Probably many of them woke up with hangovers, which they did not expect!

Brenda Darch remembers as a child having to go for a walk on Sunday evenings with her parents:

> *My Dad would go in the Pub and get me a bottle of Vimto and a packet of crisps to consume when we got home. I was certainly not allowed to eat in the street - how times have changed!*
>
> *Many times the water flooded into the pubs. Over the years the Landlords got to expect it and always had a supply of sandbags to go up to the doors. On one occasion when the floods were bad the water was running down the Rimpton Road like a river and it looked like the sort of Riverside Pubs you see in Magazines.*
>
> *At one time there used to be a man living in the Village who had a horse he used to ride, and almost every day he would call at the Marston Inn, where the Landlord would give the horse a drink of the beer, which had been left over from the previous evening. I cannot remember the man's name but I do remember him saying that the horse got so used to it that he would stop, without being asked, at the Inn.*

Henry Trim pointed out:

> *There was one big advantage which the horse had over the motor car... if its owner had partaken a little too liberally at the Marston Inn, he would only have to be loaded up into the cart and the horse could be guaranteed to transport him safely back home, often a distance of some miles.*

The Red Lion came into being in 1859 and was built in direct response to the promising trade generated by the Railway Station, which had opened three years earlier. Eldridge Pope of Dorchester owned it and it too had a skittle alley out the back. The longest serving landlord is thought to be Reg Millard. William Florance was landlord from at least 1910 until 1935. Word of mouth tells that children were sent to the back door of the pub with a container, and coins to pay for a drink to take home for their father on his return from work after a day working in the fields.

Over the years there have been many characters who came into the Inn. One used to walk round with a stick and after being primed up with the right amount of cider would show people how he had a gun that would shoot round corners. Many is the time that we came across him lying in the hedge sleeping off the cider. It's a jolly good job that he didn't have a car. This character lived in Rimpton and one day he came down the road laughing to himself. When asked why he was laughing he said, "I've been up the road pruning some apple trees, and I cut off the branch I was standing on."

The Royal British Legion

Marston Magna and District Branch of the Royal British Legion was originally formed when Sparkford branch became too large. Its formal inauguration took place on December 5th 1955. It was one of the 172 Royal British Legion Branches in Somerset at that time. In 1967 there were 1½ million ex-service people in the Legion nationally but 7½ million ex-service personnel who were not members. Benevolent work of the Legion was to support all ex-service personnel and in fact in 1955 80% of its work was with non-members.

Bert Webber was referred to by Henry Trim as 'Father' of the Marston & District Branch. He had been the village representative when Marston was in the Sparkford & District Branch. Henry related this story about Mr Webber in the Parish Magazine of March 1977:

It was an occasion when, as a member of the Sparkford & District he had attended a big Legion Parade at Weston-super-Mare. Mrs. Webber, herself a keen and active Legionnaire, had ensured that Bert would be immaculate 'on parade' by touching up his bowler with blacking in places where it had shown some signs of wear. All went well until midway through the parade when it began to rain heavily. Credit had to be given to Bert who nobly stood his ground as the blacking commenced to roll down his features and turned him into a Black and White Minstrel!

The Men's Section of the Branch had more members than attended the regular meetings. A core of people was active in promoting the aims of The Royal British Legion. Donations were made to local and national causes. The Branch funded many activities over the years both for the elderly and the young people of Marston Magna, Rimpton and Chilton Cantello. Much of the fundraising was through Bingo and in later years by the collection of waste paper in addition to other fundraising activities. Donations were made to both local Legion causes and to those in need further afield.

The concern for local care of ex-servicemen was ongoing with visits to sick members. Small gifts e.g. cigarettes and Lucozade etc. were taken to those unwell or hospitalized. Some people were offered and took convalescence at the county Legion House in Weston-super-Mare.

The local organisation had both good and difficult spells, and the recruitment of members was not easy at times. Each village had a representative to call on if members were in need of help or were unwell and needed visiting.

Comment was recorded in the minutes concerning the need to gain sufficient war pensions for ex-service men. Opposition to the closure of the Social Security offices at Yeovil was made as well as opposition to the Post Office no longer paying pensions. These moves would have caused difficulty to many ex-service men and women who needed support and local facilities. In 1958 the Branch was in support of a Boot Factory that wished to come to Yeovil if they were prepared to accept the usual % of disabled people. (County Planning rejected the scheme.)

Meetings of the Branch took place on the first Monday of the month. Each meeting commenced with the Act of Remembrance. There were various committees including the Service Committee, the Executive Committee and the Entertainments Committee. At the end of the main meeting there was a social time with varying activities.

On Boxing Day of 1955 a football match took place between The Royal British Legion and Young Marston. The Legion team lost but £1-3-6d was taken on gate takings. This was the start of many fundraising activities in the years to come. Jumble Sales, Skittles weeks, Whist Drives and fortnightly Bingo sessions constantly called upon the generosity of villagers to support the following impressive list of the charitable work undertaken by the branch -

The purchase of a branch standard
Poppy Day Appeal
The Royal British Legion Fund
The Fund for Village Hall Tables
Refugee Fund
Winston Churchill Memorial Fund
Ghurka Fund
British Legion Lifeboat Appeal
Branch Benevolent Fund
British Legion House

A donation towards the repair of the War Memorial Church Clock
2 trips to Bristol Zoo for 100 children each time paying all railway fares and entrance money
A children's outing to Exmouth and another to Weston-super-Mare
Manpower from the branch helped clear Marston Churchyard

Older people were also recipients of the Branch's generosity. Grocery parcels of 10 shillings (50pence) were distributed to all men over 65 and all women over 60 in the three villages. 87 parcels were made up in 1959 and 98 parcels were given out in 1961. In 1962 a supper and concert party was arranged instead of the gift of parcels.

Mr Ern March worked hard for the Royal British Legion visiting the sick, preparing the parcels for the elderly and helping in the organisation of the bingo sessions.

A new source of income was found in waste paper collection in the late 1970s, which was organised by Mr Louis Martin. It was a lot of work for the organiser. This fundraising continued until the price for waste paper fell in 1981. After that time coffee mornings, sponsored walks, 50/50 sales and jumble sales were sources of income. Support for pensioners continued over the years until it was suspended in 1982, due to the work the Legion was involved in as a result of The Falklands War. In 1983 however there was again a Senior Citizens Party and £79 was distributed in vouchers.

Throughout the years members of the Branch enjoyed summer outings and dinners arranged at local pubs. In 1970 there was an outing to Torquay and Paignton and in 1973 a trip to Bristol to see to the Black and White Minstrels Show. However, many visits reflected the causes and concerns of the Royal British Legion itself. There were visits to the Legion House, which was at Weston-super–Mare. In 1978 a visit to the Poppy Factory was arranged, and in 1979 there was a visit to the Royal Chelsea Hospital.

Attendance at ceremonial events was regularly reported. In 1959 a coach collected people from Rimpton and Marston Magna to attend the Bristol Remembrance Service. In 1978 the Reunion of Standard Bearers took place at Longleat where 200 standard bearers were present. In 1981 one member attended the Festival of Remembrance at the Albert Hall and there was a Diamond Jubilee celebration of the Legion at Yeovilton. On June 7th 1984 members attended the D-Day commemoration celebrations at Yeovilton, while 1985 was an important year for the Royal British Legion as it was the 40th Anniversary of both VE and VJ day.

In 1955 there were a small number of ladies on the membership list who at a later date joined The Women's Royal British Legion Group, which met in Marston Magna Village Hall on a monthly basis. Ladies from Rimpton, Marston Magna and Mudford attended the meetings. The lady members had not all been ex-service personnel, but very often their husbands had been in the Services. The meetings were friendly and well attended. In the 1980s there were about 30 people who attended the local meetings. The Ladies also attended the Women's Conference at Weston-super-Mare.

Mr H.Trim was the organiser of The Poppy Appeal for many years and made great efforts to raise money each year. Poppies were sold in Rimpton and Marston Magna and The Remembrance Service was held on alternate years between Rimpton and Marston Magna. Winnie Dole was the Standard Bearer at one time for the Women's Section. Mr Trim's tireless work for this cause was recognised by an invitation for him and his wife Grace to attend a Royal Garden Party at Buckingham Palace on July 17th 1979. The Parish Magazine stated "Our warmest congratulations go to them both - an honour richly deserved."

Our Henry's column reported on their visit in August:

Grace and I really appreciated the many kind comments on our invitation to a Royal Garden Party at Buckingham Palace on July 17th. The day was particularly fine and warm. We entered the Palace grounds through the main gate – one could enter from other gates but as this was a 'once in a lifetime', it obviously had to be the main one for us! We then entered the inner courtyard past the red-coated Guardsmen sentries, who I am sure would have welcomed a pint. We then went through the main entrance of the Palace, up the grand steps inside at the top of which a smartly dressed uniformed footman collected our invitation cards and didn't try to sell us any raffle tickets. ... we progressed through a room full of probably priceless china - not - 'white elephant' stuff. I said to Grace, "That reminds me, I must get the whist prizes tomorrow." We then emerged on to the steps leading down to the lawns. Two bands were playing alternately. We were very fortunate that after the Royal Party appeared we were within a few yards of Her Majesty the Queen at one stage, not far from Prince Philip. We also saw, but not close, that grand lady, the Queen Mother, for whom most of our generation have a very warm spot. Someone in the village enquired about autographs. I cannot lie, no one asked us! Space forbids me to tell more. We left through the main gate and walked the Mall, and got on the Underground in Trafalgar Square, and threw off any possible shadowers by going the wrong way for one station. As usual, London seemed to be full of people dashing about, but I don't know what they do, as we never saw a load of hay all day! Although my report of the event is in rather light-hearted vein, we really did appreciate the honour of being invited.

After 1988, membership fell due to the ageing of the membership, as indicated by the June 1994 Parish Magazine entry:

The May meeting at the Red Lion was abandoned without a word being fired in anger as only the Chairman, Treasurer and one other member turned up!

Meetings continued but attendance dwindled during the last decade of the century.

On 31st July 2000 the Marston Magna Branch of the Royal British Legion became a sub branch to Sparkford. This in turn joined with the Yeovil Branch.

The **Marston Magna Friendly Circle** was meeting fortnightly in the Village Hall when the first Parish Magazine was published in September 1976. Mrs Dorothy Taylor states simply:

We give our friendship to one another. Usually we play games, the most popular one being progressive whist. We do not take our games too seriously and most weeks have a good laugh when we get muddled about which table we should go to next. Dominoes and Ludo are also played and we have a box full of other games which we may try one day.

Mrs Yvonne Lawrence brings a carload of members from West Camel and we have no upper or lower age limit. Each member pays 10p per meeting which covers the cost of tea and biscuits and a ticket for a little raffle prize. Occasionally we hold a Bring and Buy Sale amongst ourselves and we are proud that we are always able to pay our own way. Each year our funds have been sufficient to cover the cost of an outing to the seaside. We have been to Weymouth, Seaton and Sidmouth. We usually go in small groups to explore the town or sit by the sea in the morning and in the afternoon our coach takes us to a nearby village hall where we have tea together. We take cakes and sandwiches and have a lovely tea party to complete a happy day out.

Each year at Christmas, Mr and Mrs Barnes have given us a truly splendid Christmas dinner at the Marston Inn. Their kindness is very much appreciated.

Each month we are pleased to receive "Yours" a newspaper published by "Help the Aged" and full of helpful and amusing articles as well as interesting letters. Some of our ladies knit blanket squares, which we have been sending to a Mission Hospital in Africa. When we read the thank you letters from the missionaries we are glad that we are able to help in this small way and we realise how very fortunate we are to live in this country at this time and we thank God for all His blessings.

In March 1980 it was announced with sadness that the Friendly Circle was now closed and the funds were distributed in equal shares to the members.

A Scout troop has featured from time to time during the 20th century. The first was started by Cecil Marden (son of ED Marden at Marston House) before WW1. Sadly, Cecil Marden died of his war wounds in 1915, but the Scouts were resumed at some time after the war.

Ralph Bartlett was a member of the "Peewit" Patrol in the 1930s to early 1940s. The Scoutmaster then was Mr Eustace Hope, a son of Mr Herbert Ashworth Hope who lived at Marston Court. They met at one time in a room over a garage in the grounds of Marston Court. He remembers causing quite a stir by arriving at a Jamboree at Bridgwater in a Rolls Royce driven by Captain Frere who lived at the Manor House. On another occasion the patrol was assembled in the Music Room at Marston Court and Mr Ashworth Hope issued them all with a cigar!

Tony Penn reports that Revd. James Blunt started a new troop known as 1st Marston Magna and Rimpton and that he was an outstanding Scout Master who trained and organized the scouts in an impressive manner:

Scout Camp on the banks of the River Cherwell, Oxford

In the 1950s the church clock winding duties were carried out by the scout troop and between 1952 and 1954 Keith Commins and I wound the clock. A photograph of the two of us winding the clock appeared in the Western Gazette at that time. Over that period the scout troop also cleaned the whole of the bell tower where over many, many years Jackdaws nesting materials had slowly built up and a complete clean and redecoration of the area was carried out. These activities were the forerunner to the Rev. James Eric Blunt raising the funds to refurbish the whole of the church roof. The Rev. Blunt was not a particularly popular man in the village but during his tenure he achieved significantly more benefits for the church and the village than many of those who followed him.

Village Youth Club 1986

Prospective leaders for a new Youth Club were interviewed by a small group of villagers led by Peter Clarke. Mike Jagelman was appointed.

The Village Hall was unable to guarantee availability every week and so the offer of free use of the skittle alley at The Red Lion was gratefully accepted:

> *Following a public meeting at the Red Lion on 3rd Dec 1986 attended by approximately 30 people, a decision was taken to proceed with the formation of a Youth Club. A committee was formed of both young and old with Mike Jagelman as Voluntary Youth Leader. It will take place every Wednesday commencing Jan 14th, with both a junior and a senior section covering the ages 8-17. Meetings will take place in the Red Lion Skittle Alley, which has been offered by the landlord Mr John Hartshorn without charge.*

It was subsequently reported that 24 young people attended the first session.

There was always a tuck shop on offer and the modest profits, coupled with very low overheads, meant that two trips could be provided to Bristol Ice Skating Rink. The Red Lion was not a perfect venue as the toilets had awkward access inside the pub and young boys in particular can be tricky to supervise. After about two years, with insufficient extra adult assistance, Mike Jagelman took the difficult decision to close the group.

Young Marstons/Merlin Youth Group 1999

In the summer of 1999, Jack Crouch invited the youth of the village to form a Youth Group, and interested children and adults were urged to attend an Open Meeting in June of that year. An activity group called Young Marstons was formed, and were quickly immersed in Bowling, Bell Ringing and Short Tennis.

Jill Martin took on the appointment of Youth Leader. After 12 weeks she was able to report that 17 youngsters were regularly attending, aged between 11-16. Additional activities were introduced including skittles, fun and games evenings, pop lacrosse and even a karaoke machine. Outings were also organised to Taunton for 10-pin bowling. There were swimming pool sessions and they had two skittles teams entered in the Young Somerset League. At the end of August 2000, a day at Mill on the Brue took place, where the youngsters enjoyed grass tobogganing, zip wire, raft making and crossing the River Brue.

Having run successfully for 12 months, it was felt that an expansion of membership would be beneficial and that more voluntary supervisors and helpers would be helpful. To this end another Open Evening was held and an amalgamation was formed with the young people of

Queen Camel. They chose the name of Merlin Youth Group and quickly attracted an average attendance of 22 young people between the ages of 12-15. The venue switched from week to week between the two villages.

Sport

Sport has not played a huge part in village life, although before W.W.I there was a flourishing Cricket Team in Marston. Douglas Marden was Captain and his brother Cecil was Secretary.

There was no cricket during the war but it started again afterwards and carried on until 1925.

Brigadier Henry Marden of Rimpton wrote the following story concerning Arthur Grant:

He was my uncle's gardener and also his coachman until my uncle replaced his horse with a motorcar – a Panhard - and the first motorcar in Marston, I believe. Grant was then, albeit with some difficulty, persuaded to "groom" the car. In due course – no driving test being required in those days – he learned to drive and was very smart in green jacket, breeches and high boots. He turned out to be a slow but safe driver – in fact a better chauffeur than a cricketer. He was, in fact, the "last reserve", both as a cricketer and umpire. As it was usually not until the eleventh hour that he was called upon either to play or to umpire, he was wise not to invest in flannels. On the whole it was safer for him to play, notwithstanding the fact that he rarely scored a run. But if called upon to umpire he was apt to be an embarrassment to his side. It was against his principles to give any of his own side OUT, whereas he had no such compunction when the opponents were batting, especially if the batsman got his leg in the way of the ball; according to Grant he was always adjudged "LAG AFORE".

John Peppin wrote a memoir of cricket in Marston Magna:

There was a cricket team which we used to watch when they were playing at home. My father (Rev.Peppin) used to umpire, and his decisions though possibly at times rather arbitrary, were always accepted because he was the rector. There was a fast bowler named Webber who was often loud and acclamatory in his appeals for l.b.w. And after two unsuccessful appeals from successive balls, his indignation at my father's refusal of them reached boiling point, and the next ball, which was almost a wide on the off-side, but which the batsman still managed to reach by walking across his wicket, Mr. Webber turned furiously round to my father and bellowed "Ow's that, then?" His indignation at my father's quiet "Not Out" was boundless, and from that moment his bowling deteriorated.

There was another character named Bert Bugby – a general handyman about the village – a man of huge bulk and colossal strength. Bert had only one stroke when batting, and this he employed for every kind of bowler against any kind of ball. It can only be described as a cow-shot.

If successful, the ball would land over the boundary, somewhere in the area between the long-arm and deep mid-wicket. Bert's performances were erratic and usually consisted of sixes obtained with his cow-shot. The first straight ball was usually fatal, and his survival depended on his set receiving one. I remember his coming into bat at number 7, when Marston (as was commonly the position) was facing defeat. The first ball he received disappeared high into the blue in the general direction of long on. There was a stream bordering the ground but it was a long way from the pitch and though it was reckoned to be the boundary on that side it was seldom that anyone managed to hit even a four in that direction. In any case, the state of the outfield almost precluded fours all along the carpet. Bert's bash, however, cleared the brook with yards to spare, and the ball disappeared in a field of long grass and buttercups, ripe for the haymaking, and was never seen again.

Another ball having been ferreted out from our scanty reserves, Bert tried a repeat shot – but the next delivery happened to be the straightest one of the over. There were no questions about it. Bert was out, his stumps spread-eagled at crazy angles. However, he probably remains the only man who ever actually cleared the brook – and by a large margin.

Marston's cricketing fortunes varied sometimes according to the time of year. At haymaking and harvest, it was sometimes difficult to raise a team, but, at least during the harvest it was sometimes possible to draw in visitors who occasionally strengthened the team. Uncle Syd, who often came to stay during the actual summer holidays, was a cricketer of considerable ability, and always ready for a game. As he could both bat and bowl his value to the side was immense, and the locals, who were not used to seeing a batsman treating each ball on its merits, held his prowess in great awe.

When Marston was playing away, we did not follow them. They hired a brake, and there was not room for youngsters. We always knew, in a general sort of way, the result of the away fixtures by the song being sung as the brake bowled into the village. If the song was "Poor Cock Robin" we knew that Marston had lost; any other song meant that at least they had not been defeated.

With the advent of a TV in all households cricket was still followed closely later in the century but usually from the comfort of an armchair!

This amusing piece on cricket was published in the Parish Magazine in 1976:

Cricket – as explained to a foreign visitor:

You have two sides, one out in the field and one in. Each man that's in the side that's in goes out and when he's out he comes in and the next man goes in until he's out.

When they are all out, the side that's out comes in and the side that's been in goes out and tries to get those coming in out. Sometimes you get men still in and not out. When both sides have been in and out, including the not outs THAT'S THE END OF THE GAME!

Tony Penn records some football being played during his childhood, including the annual football match against West Camel, and Henry Trim tells the following tale from yesteryear:

Yeovil Town once played a football match at Marston! This was back in the 1920s when they played a combined Marston/Sparkford side in one of the fields on the Yeovil Road now farmed by Derek Tottle. The reason for the match was that Yeovil were interested in two local players.

He also remembers listening to a football match on the newly acquired one-valve wireless set which sported two sets of earphones. He and his friend got over excited at one point, accidentally loosening a connection and causing a series of blue sparks. The one-valve was quite an advance on the crystal set, when to pick up the programme one had to do something like sticking a needle in a Brillo pad and probing around until the right spot was found!

The women were not to be left out of the sporting life. Mary Milverton (a District Nurse in the area for many years) came to Marston in 1932 having played a lot of sport:

I wondered what I was going to do with myself in what seemed a sleepy little village. I wrote to a few girls inviting them to a meeting to see if we could start a hockey team. Some had never seen a hockey stick before. It was all a case of trial and error but we went from strength to strength doing quite well in tournaments at Weston and Bristol. Some of the originals were Mrs Birch, Dulcie Pitman, Doris Bollen (now Sharp) and Ruby Hatcher (now Rideout). One or two of us even played football for Yeovil Town Ladies.

Gardening

Gardening has always had a strong following throughout the century, although the focus may have changed a little over the years. In 1911 there were 32 Allotment plots, which were let at 7/6d per plot per annum. From 25th March 1912 the rent was increased by 6d per plot.

When the original Marston Council Estate was built in the 1920s, the houses had very large tracts of garden. At that time the tenants were mostly agricultural and railway workers and they really needed the big gardens to help feed their families, for their incomes were very low. There was no social security to fall back on during hard times. If an Estate were being planned on a similar area of land later in the century many more houses would be put into the same space. Even in 1990, when a new arrival moved in from Yeovil, the central green area was a fabulous display of vegetables and flowers. She had never seen anything like it.

The first Annual Flower Show took place on 12th July 1975. A local newspaper reported:

> *Drought affected entries and the rain affected the attendance at Marston Magna's first flower show. Even so there were 162 exhibits entered in the 37 classes. Mrs W.Tofts of Marston Magna opened the show, which included entries from Rimpton and Little Marston. Miss Hickley won the Terry Kimpton Rose Bowl for the best specimen rose, which was presented by Brig. H. Marden of Rimpton.*

The show was held at Rimpton Village hall for the first time in September 1978. The organizers were rewarded with an increased entry of 250. A sunny afternoon brought a steady flow of exhibitors and visitors through the hall, and the ladies of the committee did a good trade in teas. It even brought out the poet in one keen gardener:

THE FLOWER SHOW 1978

Only one month more to go,
Come and enter the Flower Show.
Young or old it doesn't matter,
Come along and have a natter.
Give your veg. their final touches,
With fertilizer, feed or mulches.
Then you may achieve a prize,
Thoughts of failure won't arise.

Have you made your Preserves yet?
Raspberry jam the judge will vet,
Wine buffs try to send a sample,
One from your stock will be ample.

Remember now, September Two,
Rimpton Hall the place for you.
Entries in by 10 at latest,
Come along and be 'the Greatest'.

The Show took turns to be held in both villages in the following years and in 1995 it was held in the new Marston Magna Village Hall for the first time. The entries had climbed to 317 on this occasion.

Mrs Eileen Newell was asked to present the prizes in the year 2000 in recognition of the value of her contribution to the committee over the years.

An immaculate record was kept of the Flower Show, which took place every year with the exception of 1990 when the secretary, Commander Eric Tonkin, was unavailable due to pressure of work, and there was also difficulty in appointing judges. Commander Tonkin featured prominently on the committee throughout the 25 years to the end of the century, and indeed by 2014, when he stood down from the committee, he had served without a break for 40 years.

Other groups enjoying the facilities of the new Village Hall included an Art Group led by Phillip Bachrach, a variety of exercise classes including Yoga, the Advanced School of Motoring Group, Short Mat Bowls and The Buggy Brigade.

Harvest Supper is one of the most popular events of the year in the village. In 1976 villagers enjoyed a meal provided by ladies from the various village organizations and the Fête Committee, then chaired by Mrs. Sallie Brown. In the 1970s, the traditional meal always featured apple pie and cream and cider poured from jugs. In later years wine replaced the cider and more exotic desserts became popular!

Entertainment would include sketches or musical items, or typically a 'take off' of The Generation Game, with well known local faces (courtesy of the Parochial Church Council) taking part as the parents and children, ending with the winner acquiring a redundant Refreshment Stall sign and a bottle of 'life-giving' Marston Brook Water! A sketch by the WI was always well received and talent from the villagers was also included. Henry Trim, a natural comedian, would act as the linkman, telling many jokes, dressed in his smock, red kerchief and stick and keep the audience in fits of laughter. He also acted as auctioneer for the produce donated for the church Harvest Festival service, which with his persuasion fetched ridiculously high prices!

The Village Fête, in support of St Mary's Church, has been an annual highlight for many years, and has variously taken place in the field opposite Marston House, at Marston Court, Wisteria Cottage, in the field behind the Village Hall, and most recently, in the gardens of The Manor House.

At one stage there was a parade through the village by the British Legion Silver Band, which ended up at the village hall, whereupon the fête was opened.

Ern March leading the British Legion Silver Band past the Post Office before the opening of a Fête.

National Celebrations

• 1904 Village celebrations were held in the village on Empire Day, which was marked nationally on 24th May. This originated in 1904 in remembrance of Queen Victoria in whose reign the empire spread around the world.

• 1905 Nov 9th the school celebrated the King's birthday by singing the National Anthem and flag flying.

• 1911 The Coronation of King George V was commemorated in the village by the creation of a raised firm wide path across the field to Rimpton.

The school was closed on June 29th due to the festivities to mark the Coronation of George V. The actual Coronation took place on June 22nd 1911.

• 1921 A School Holiday was declared by wish of the King for the wedding of Princess Mary.

• 1927 A Village Fête was held in aid of the School Upkeep Fund. This was opened by the wife of the sitting MP, Major G.F. Davies. The afternoon included a children's fancy dress parade, maypole dancing and a baby show.

• 1934 A School Holiday was given by wish of the King on the marriage of Duke of Kent with Princess Marina.

• 1935 King George V's Silver Jubilee was celebrated by the nation. Celebrations were held in Mr. W. H. Smith's field adjoining the Foresters' Hall on 6th June and Wingfield Digby opened the event at 3 pm. There were Children's Sports, Side shows (including skittling for 2 pigs!), Adult Sports at 4 pm then a Dance in the Foresters' Hall at 9 pm to music by the "Selmo Trio". Tickets 1/- each. The Yeovil Fire Brigade also gave a display during the evening. (Programme from Bernard Darch) The proceeds went to a Children's Fund, the King George's Trust and the Yeovil and Sherborne Hospitals.

• 1935 A School Holiday was declared by wish of the King on the marriage of HRH Prince Henry of Gloucester.

• 1937 A 3-day School Holiday was granted on the occasion of the Coronation of King George VI.

• 1953 Coronation of Queen Elizabeth II. According to Sally Liddle, (née Rideout), there was a party in the village hall and the street outside. The year before, the Parish Council had decided to present each child in the village with a coronation mug. These were made by the Honiton China Company and cost just under £8 for 84 Coronation Souvenir mugs. There were Coronation Sports and Tea, and a Social in the evening. A television set was hired for the hall, with amplifier, at a cost of £7. 10s.

Mr Hockey, residing at Standlemead in Camel Street, had one of the few television sets in the village and invited people to come and watch the coronation ceremony. Jim Nowell was detailed to specially mow the garden lawn for the occasion!

• 1977 The Queen's Silver Jubilee was celebrated with a Jubilee Service in the church and then an "It's a Knockout" programme in the field adjoining the Sherborne Road, loaned by Mr. and Mrs. Healing for the day.

Proceedings began with a procession led by Boadicea, travelling in a 'chariot' pulled by Jim Nowell on a Ferguson tractor. The "It's a Knockout" event was organized with teams led by Phil Illingworth and Jim Nowell. The games, many of which had an element of water, ended with a tug of war. For the deciding "tug" the original team of 10 had somehow increased to 39! The Morris Men entertained during the interval, Jubilee mugs made by Michael Illingworth were distributed to the children and a barbecue and disco followed in the evening.

Henry Trim's column in the magazine of July 1977 expressed the willing teamwork and enjoyment of this occasion:

First light on the Big Day, Tuesday, saw motorised columns of the WI advancing on the Village Hall, and meeting with no resistance – there being no Jumble Sale for once – they quickly occupied the kitchen and other strong points. Thus entrenched they prepared 400 boxes of refreshments which were to be used to counter the expected offensive by hungry villagers in the afternoon. Patrols occupied a marquee in the Fête field in Sherborne Road, and this position was consolidated by the main body in good time. Luckily the defences had been strongly organised by Generals Rachel Holt, Janet Redmond, Mary Innes and their troops, for when the attack came, it was in overwhelming numbers. The 400 boxes of refreshments were quickly expended, but a second line of defence had busily prepared more, and eventually a well-filled and contented crowd gave up the attack and retreated to watch an entertaining show by the Wessex Morris Men....

I thought that the "It's a Knock-Out" event was superbly organised. What a tremendous amount of work must have been put in to stage this...it was very pleasing to see that most of the young people of the village had been drafted into the two teams captained by Jim Nowell and Phil Illingworth respectively. The highlight, as far as the kiddies were concerned, was the item in which they were called upon to assist by hurling water-filled balloons at the competitors, one of whom was riding a delivery cycle (of ancient vintage).... with a team mate in the basket!

The final event, the tug-of-war, was a spectacle not be missed...Jim Nowell's team were adjudged winners of the competition and the captain was presented with a "gold" cup. Phil Illingworth received a plastic replica for the worthy runners-up, and both captains received the traditional ducking!

• 1981 There was a disco in the village hall on the occasion of the Wedding of Prince Charles and Lady Diana Spencer in September, and the residents of Townsend and West End arranged a street party. Fun and games were enjoyed and there was plenty of food, including a special cake. A month or so later many villagers went on an outing to the Royal Wedding Exhibition at St. James' Palace to see the wedding dress and presents.

• 2000 The Millennium. All children in the village were presented with a mug to mark the event and there was additionally a remarkable degree of co-operation, which resulted in the magnificent floodlighting of the church. A New Year's Eve party was held which catered very successfully for six year olds to ninety year olds.

The Parish Magazine of January 2000 reported:

At our Christingle service Mrs Henry Trim and Mrs Bill Marden switched on the floodlighting for the first time – or almost! Someone had switched the main switch off! Henry Trim's brother-in-law was heard to say, "It's the Millennium Bug, Rector!"

The final result is a stunning tribute to men who served our community with grace and distinction.

The floodlighting has been admired and commented on by those who live in other villages. When we started the project we promised that the lights would not be switched on night after night, but on "high days and holidays." After the New Year begins, this policy will come into play....there will be a £5 charge towards maintenance and lighting costs. We invite you to take full advantage of this exciting offer.

A group of WI members designed, and created a sampler with fifteen views of the village, embroidered in cross-stitch. The sampler was presented to the Village Hall Committee and hung in the village hall at the Harvest Supper later in the year.

Millennium Day saw a large congregation in church before the mid-day peal. This was followed by a Bring and Share lunch and to complete the festivities Hugh and Jane Privett kindly organised a sing-along version of Handel's Messiah dedicated to the greater glory of the God of all Ages.

Employment

In the early part of the century employment continued to be centred on agriculture and associated trades, up until the beginning of WW2. Many village residents were also employed in the service of other villagers.

In 1901 William Garrett was a Groom and his daughter a domestic servant. The Rectory, Marston House and Marston Court consistently employed staff. A cook's job was sought after. The table showing the employment in the village in 1901 makes interesting reading. (See end of chapter).

In 1914 Harry Goodyear was the gardener and Edwin Knight the stud groom to William Chatterton of Marston Court. They were still in employment there after the end of World War 1. The Gardener's and the Groom's cottages were along Garston Lane.

The Bakers

The 1901 census listed 8 people in the village as Bread makers. Albert Foote of Sherborne (known as the Midnight Baker) was one of them in 1902, as was Charles Marks. Wrefords, Deacons, Lanes, Co-op, and Treasures of Sherborne have all provided bread to the village during the 20th century.

The Blacksmith

The Blacksmith's shop is described in Les Sayers' memories, and in M.I Davis' book. (It was replaced by a house built in the 1960s but is still called The Old Forge).

In the 1920s, children would sometimes visit the forge after school to see if they could see a horse being shod. Andrew Newberry was the blacksmith and farrier. He would also mend household items for villagers.

Mrs Davis wrote this in the Parish Magazine in August 1977:

Pitman's Lane joins the Yeovil Road opposite the almshouses and here was the forge, with Mr. Newbery in his leather apron. He shod the horses, mended farm implements, sharpened scythes, repaired wagon wheels and also did smaller jobs such as soldering leaks in tin kettles or nailing new heads on mops for 'swilling-down' the backyard. He was a very useful man. The story is told that one day someone called to see Mrs Newbery and was told by her husband that she'd 'gone to they there Wimmins Substitutes'!

Ern Rainey tells the story of when, back in 1920, he lived with his parents and brothers at Parkway cottage and they worked at Park Farm, owned then by Farmer Bill Chalker. The farm was alive with rabbits and the Rainey boys used to poach them by placing wires down at night and picking up their catch early in the morning. Mr Newberry, the village blacksmith, had permission from Farmer Chalker to shoot over the Park Farm land. Blacksmith Newberry usually came for the shooting on Wednesday evenings. On one occasion, he found some of the Rainey boys' wires and reported to Mr Chalker, which resulted them being in hot water.

The boys decided that they must get their own back. They found an old rabbit that had been partially eaten by a fox, but the head was fairly intact. With the aid of a forked stick, they arranged the rabbit skin in a run in a field in which the blacksmith used to walk, and from shooting distance it looked very lifelike. Sure enough, Blacksmith Newberry saw the Raineys' rabbit and bang! He hit his target all right but was very disgusted when he picked it up!

The Butcher

Walter Hatcher had a butcher's shop in Camel Street in the 1920s in the house adjoining Wyndhams. Most butchers managed their own slaughtering and the slaughterhouse was situated further down the street close by the School.

Butchers received regular visits from the police, who inspected a book, which showed a record of where animals were sourced. The local sanitary inspector from Wincanton came once or twice a year at the very most. He would look around the shop, perhaps instruct the butcher to re-lime-wash the walls, but there were no professional inspections regarding fitness for human consumption.

In approximately 1930 Walter moved to a property which became available next to the slaughterhouse. It had been a petrol pump service and was operated by the wife while her husband worked elsewhere. The pumps were removed and a shop was erected in their place.

Meat was sourced locally before the war. Farmers would be willing to sell suitable livestock and animals were also purchased at the local livestock market held at the Sparkford Inn. Animals would be purchased and then fasted for a couple of days in order to vacate the stomach contents.

Jimmy Noyce was a local itinerant farm labourer in Marston Magna and Queen Camel (and anywhere else where he was requested), but also a freelance slaughter man. He would drop the children off at school in the morning, receive lunch wherever he was working and then collect the children at the end of school. The slaughtering licence was refused at some stage due to the proximity of the school. Children could hear the process taking place and often blood could be seen running in the gutter.

Electricity was introduced in the winter of 1930 and gradually cold rooms were created by the butchers. So before that with no refrigeration, particularly in the summer, the beast had to be slaughtered early enough to rest at least one day before you could joint it, but not too early as it wouldn't be delivered to the customers until Friday or Saturday. The animals were slaughtered with a poleaxe, which was a strong wooden shaft with a point on one end. The animal was brought in and tethered so its head was on the block and the slaughter man drove the point into the forehead and straight into the brain. With a skilled man it was as humane as it could get. Humane killing was introduced in the 1930s.

In approximately 1940, in order to demonstrate equality throughout the country, the distribution of meat was centralised, and slaughtering was transferred to Yeovil. There was a big slaughterhouse where the football pitch now stands. All the butchers were allocated a quota, which was judged very low. A farmer in the area decided to by-pass the central market and was convicted of killing calves and selling them on the black market. On one occasion he was offering the meat for sale in the pub when the local policeman came in the front door. The farmer beat a hasty retreat out of the back door, but he was eventually caught and convicted and went to prison. The then manager of the butcher shop was also convicted of receiving. He regretfully committed suicide by hanging himself in the slaughterhouse.

Paradoxically there was even less meat available after the war as Argentinean beef prices started to rocket and in fact got priced out of the market.

The usual practice was to spend Friday and Saturday delivering the meat direct to customers, but as the years went by the delivery surcharge became greater than the price of a bus fare into town and the local shops could not compete with the ever-growing supermarkets.

Bob Rideout, who married Walter Hatcher's daughter, eventually became butcher and his son Robin carried on when his father retired. The shop was closed in the late 1970s and Robin emigrated.

In March 1990, an application to build an extension to form a cold store at Sunnyside, Camel Street was made to the Parish Council. The

Hatcher's butchers shop in the 1950s.

Council welcomed the extension to what they described as an "essential village amenity".

Two years later, in May 1992, the Parish Council decided to nominate Marston Meats in the "Best Village Shop in Somerset" competition, and in December they congratulated Tim and Polly Hooper for receiving a Commendation, adding that the Hoopers gave a great service to the village.

In August 1996, the Hoopers announced the closure of Marston Meats.

Archie Sharp

Archie Sharp was married to Doris née Bollen. Doris and her sister, Violet, were the daughters of William and Mabel Bollen. Mr. Bollen is listed as a farmer in Kelly's Directory 1914. The family lived at Studley's Farm, Station Road (now Rimpton Road).

Archie Sharp was a butcher in the shop at S.J. Hayne, 85 Princes Street, Yeovil. Not everyone in Marston Magna bought their meat from the butcher's shop in the village during wartime. Some villagers were registered with Haynes and Archie Sharp, who had a van, would take the orders, which he delivered on a Friday.

At the beginning of the war, 1939-40, Archibald C.C. Sharp and Doris Melina Sharp were living at 5 West End Villas. However, by 1960 they were living at Fir Villa, Camel Street according to the electoral register (Qualifying date: 10th October 1960).

In the 1970s they moved to "Sunnybank", which Mr. Sharp had built for his retirement.

Archie always had a word of greeting for everyone he met. He was a member of the Parochial Church Council and a Sidesman at church. He attended church regularly and was always there as a quiet, gentle presence, and spoke to the members of the congregation as they were leaving the service. However, when he retired he resigned from the P.C.C. The vicar, Revd. de Jersey Hunt was very annoyed and said that no one should resign from the P.C.C.!

Archie was also a Trustee of the old village hall. In 1977 Molly and Sam Crabb celebrated their Silver Wedding anniversary, so Archie planted a Silver Atlantic Cedar tree, which they were given as a present, in the churchyard, to replace the deceased elm tree.

The Carpenter

Gilbert Bugby is listed in Kelly's Directory as a carpenter in the village from 1923.

Bert Bugby was married to one of Mrs. Noyce's daughters. He ran his workshop in outbuildings at the Marston Inn. He was carpenter, undertaker and chimney sweep. When there was a funeral, local men would act as bearers.

The Doctors

Prior to the introduction of the National Health Service in July 1948 many families would have used home remedies to deal with illness. The cost of the Doctor's bills would be out of reach for many people on a low income, including those who received an agricultural wage. When treatment by a Doctor was absolutely necessary, payment for treatment would have been an anxiety. The Doctors sent out a periodic bill and when this arrived sometimes several members of a family would have been called upon to try to meet the costs.

The people in Marston Magna received treatment from the Doctors at Queen Camel. Before the advent of buses through the village, walking or cycling to Queen Camel would have been the option, as most people did not have their own transport. A child who had an accident at school was sent home with an older child, as most people did not have telephones at home. A distraught parent asked the person at the garage to take her daughter to the Doctor at Queen Camel, following the accident when she had fallen against the school railings. Dr McCrorie gave her three stitches and a sixpence or shilling for not crying.

The Doctors from Queen Camel did visit patients in Marston Magna. If a prescription was required it would have to be collected from the surgery later in the day. In the early 1940s there were shelves in the waiting room at the surgery. The villages had their own shelf space and so if a person went to collect a prescription they would pick up prescriptions for anyone else and bring them back to the village. Everyone knew everyone and so they helped each other out.

There was a District nurse in Marston Magna, who was also the midwife, but the Doctor's surgery has always been based in Queen

Camel. The surgery at the beginning of the century was in a building opposite England Lane. The rather nice house next to the surgery was where the doctor lived.

In the 1980s the surgery was at Cleaveside Close. Various clinics were held at the surgery, including a baby clinic, parent craft and postnatal classes.

In the 1990s there was a luncheon club on Mondays and Thursdays and a Day Centre on Wednesdays.

Doctors of the Twentieth Century

1884 James Hurley M.D M.Ch surgeon and Medical officer and public vaccinator Queen Camel District. Wincanton Union.

James Hurley was listed up until 1910 in Kelly's Directories.

1914 Edward Percy Hasluck LR CP and S.Edin, surgeon and Medical officer and public vaccinator Queen Camel District. Wincanton Union.

1918 J.Bolton was listed in 1923 Kelly's Directory. LSA London. Surgeon and Medical officer and public vaccinator Queen Camel District. Wincanton Union.

1927 Hugh McCrorie M.B.CH.B Glas. Surgeon and Medical officer and public vaccinator Queen Camel District. Wincanton Union. By 1931 Dr McCrorie is listed as being on the Wells Area Guardians Committee not the Wincanton Union. The telephone number was now listed as Marston Magna 25.

In 1935 the telephone number had altered to Marston Magna 225. The telephone number is now 850225.

1935-1961 John Barlow, Senior
1935-1961 Louise Barlow
1940-1956 John Lowe
1956-1966 John Barlow, Junior
1957- Robert Scott
1960- Raymond Winstone
1966- Kenneth Nicolson

Dr Scott, Dr Winstone, Dr Nicolson and Dr Ketley were at the practice in the 1980s.

Dr Hart joined the practice about the time that Dr Scott retired, and then Dr Taylor and later Dr Huins joined the practice, following the retirement of the other partners. Dr Duffy was also at the practice.

Fir Villa

In 1972, Mr. and Mrs. Pearce opened a Rest Home for Gentlefolk at Fir Villa, having bought the house from a Mr. Sharp. They offered places for 3 residents. Fir Villa was taken over by Pam and Don Ross in the 1980s, with places made available for 8 residents.

Peter Clarke began visiting Fir Villa when Mr. and Mrs. Pearce first owned it:

My role was to be their chaplain, visiting regularly, on call in emergencies and doing pastoral work for both residents and the staff. I got to know them very well.

After Pam and Don Ross retired in 1988, Mrs. Ann Williams took over the home and the 3 staff working there. Ann Williams extended the business further by employing extra staff and in 1990 she had extra rooms built, increasing the number of residents to 13. Fir Villa offered care on a long or short stay respite basis.

Peter Clarke wrote:

I continued to celebrate Holy Communion with the residents on a monthly basis (and Ann and her mother always attended). I officiated at funerals and generally cared for all who lived and worked there.

Ann remarried a man from Rimpton at which wedding I officiated and even when I left Marston to become Rector of Tintinhull I kept up my visits, particularly when my own mother Ena Clarke became a resident, living there for 2-3 years and dying there.

Mrs. Williams created further accommodation by rebuilding the detached stable (at one time a slaughterhouse) and named this the Owl House.

Pam Goodwin remembers:

A warm welcome was always extended whenever I visited a former elderly neighbour who had moved into the home in the 1990s even though young children always accompanied me. I was always impressed by the care of the residents whose needs were always considered.

Outings and activities are organized for residents, and village events have always been well supported by the owners of the home. The monthly communion service continues to this day. From 1992-2002 a "care in your own home" service was provided, but ceased due to changes in the law. Meals on wheels continued until well beyond the end of the 20th century.

Peter Clarke sums up his feelings towards the home with the words:

So Fir Villa has always had a special place in my heart, as I know it did for several members of the community who came to live there and some who enjoyed respite care. I always considered Fir Villa to be a very warm, caring and loving community and a tremendous asset to village life.

Fir Villa is now run by Marston Care Ltd., employing 26 staff, catering for 22 residents and offering full day respite care to the wider community.

Fish and Chips

Terry Batson and Delia Hunt in front of the mobile Fish and Chip Van.

Nigel Penn remembers:

My mother, Rosa Penn, set up this business with her friend and neighbour Greta Hunt in the late 1940s and ran it for several years. The operation was based from a building behind the old village hall, which had been the cookhouse for a small US Army Ordnance installation that covered that whole field (and included the old village hall).

The function of the US personnel was to manage the huge collection of shells and other munitions that were stored between the trees in the many apple orchards of the time. The majority of the ordnance arrived and left via an extensive railway marshalling yard on the site now occupied by the agricultural technicians, just over the railway bridge on the Rimpton Road.

As well as serving fish and chips from the shop, my mother and her friend also offered a mobile service and toured all the local villages most evenings, ranging from Corton Denham to Ilchester and Montacute and most places in between.

As a complementary business, they raised a few pigs, which were partly fed on the potato peelings etc. from the chip shop (an early example of recycling).

The vehicle they used was a 3-ton Morris Commercial truck that they had specially adapted with deep fat fryers powered by Calor gas. Before starting this business my mother did not drive. She learned to drive on an old Lanchester car that was lying in the building behind the village hall, and drove it around the field. I often wonder how a small (barely 5 ft tall) lady managed to drive a 3-ton truck (no power steering, no hydraulic clutch etc.) around the narrow lanes at night. In winter they were sometimes stuck in floods and had to get out and wade to the nearest phone box to call for help.

My mother was very much encouraged in the business by Clifford Hockey who was then the General Manager of the Magna Cider factory at Marston. He was an accountant and helped them to keep their accounts in good order.

The field at the rear of the village hall was owned by Mr. Smith who lived at Wisteria cottage (his daughter later married Clifford Hockey). When I was young there were still a number of Nissen huts around the perimeter of the field as well as the old village hall and the cookhouse installations at the back. Other buildings on the field had been removed, but the concrete foundations remained. I recall that these had been broken up, and sometimes my brother and I would work for the farmer by picking up stones and pieces of concrete to clear the ground. We were paid a few pence for each bucket full that we collected.

How times have changed since then!

The Garages

Les Sayers wrote that the garage was first started by Mr.Williams:

The original garage was in Camel Street and had the first petrol pump to sell petrol. It was wound by hand, one gallon at a time. The petrol was called R.O.P. and cost 1 shilling 1 penny a gallon. There was a taxi service but you were never sure of getting there, and a small shop run by Mr. and Mrs. Woof.

Marston garage was located on the corner of Little Marston Road and Yeovil Road.

Brenda Darch wrote:

During the war the garage was owned by Mr. Tom Aplin who had come to Marston in the mid 1930s. He had a couple of employees, but most of the repair work done there during the war was to tractors, as there were very few cars on the road during that time. There were four petrol pumps, three of which were taken over by the army for the lorries. They had a man who stayed in a little hut on the forecourt ready to serve the fuel for the lorries and motorcycles. There was nearly always a queue of lorries waiting to be served. Paraffin was sold for people with cookers and heaters. Mr. Aplin also had a Mobile shop, which used to go round the local villages selling paraffin, soap, brushes and other cleaning equipment.

In the early sixties Mr. Aplin sold the garage to a Mr. Stainer from Sherborne. Mr. Stainer had several sons who ran the garage. They did a lot of work modernizing the garage and within a few years, sold it to Peter Jones.

The garage was burnt to the ground in 1968/1969 and had to be rebuilt.

In the early 70s the garage was sold again to Terry Kimpton, who stayed there for several years until it was sold to Olds, who had the garage completely modernized but did away with the petrol pumps which was a great loss to the village, as we then had to go at least a couple of miles to get fuel.

The house by the garage (now Rosewell) was lived in by the people who owned the garage at that time until Olds bought it. They let it to employees for a while. Where Olds have their parking area now, it used to be a small orchard, which went with the property.

At the end of the century, the garage was demolished to make way for the building of a small housing estate.

Gibbs Yard

Ricky Gibbs writes:

In 1949, my father Bernard Gibbs wanted to expand his agricultural engineering business based in Crewkerne. He formed a partnership with Harold Woods and set up a company called Gibbs Bros & Woods, operating from rented buildings in Over Compton. Harold Woods had been the workshop foreman for Percy Windsor, an agricultural engineering business with a Ferguson Tractor franchise in Yeovil.

They wanted some better premises and identified a site at Marston Magna which belonged to the Magna Cider business as suitable. The site near the railway line and station had been hard cored to a high standard during the war and used as an ammunition dump by the American Army.

This site was purchased in the early 50s from Mr. Hockey who was the owner of Magna Cider. The existing workshop and one bungalow were built on the site and operated from 1954. Initially they had an International Tractor agency, but this was later changed to David Brown.

After the death of Harold Woods, his son Michael ran the company. In somewhat controversial circumstances, Michael Wood with all the staff left the company during December 1971, having set up a new company at Henstridge. My father sent myself, Brian James and Michael Prescott from the parent company at Crewkerne to run the company. The company name was changed to Gibbs Bros (Marston Magna) Ltd and two new bungalows for staff were built in 1973.

I ran the company until I retired at the end of 1999. The business was sold to a consortium of Colin Hawkins, a farmer from Ashington, and Francis Bugler Ltd, agricultural engineers from Beaminster. They started a new company trading as Marston Tractors. Subsequently the Hawkins share was bought by Buglers.

Glove Making

In 1851 there were fourteen Glovers recorded in Marston Magna, but by 1861 that had reduced to three and there was still some glove making recorded in 1871.

The size of the industry, based in Yeovil, continued to ebb and flow throughout the twentieth century and for all of the early part was the biggest industry in the town. It started a terminal decline after the Second World War, when the emergent aircraft industry offered more attractive pay to workers and gloves started to go out of fashion.

Fownes Gloves, who held an excellent reputation for quality glove making, employed Dilys Jagelman as a machinist in the late 1960s. (They originated in London but moved the manufacturing to Worcester and opened a fine new factory there in 1887. It produced gloves in all fabrics and at its peak employed over 1,000 on the site).

Fownes Gloves established a smaller operation at Mill Lane Trading Estate, Yeovil, which is listed in directories between 1968 and 1974. Dilys took up employment there making a variety of fabric gloves. She was paid on a piecework basis of 5 shillings per dozen and she remembers making 3 or 4 dozen a day.

Different people, starting with the men who cut the fabric, operated each stage of the production. After the sewing, someone else inspected the work, and if satisfactory, turned the gloves inside out before the final pressing and then packing. If the sewing was not up to standard a pin would be placed at the weak point and the error would have to be rectified.

Dilys remembers the sewers walking out in protest at treatment from the supervisor and also a fellow worker having a needle through her finger.

A highlight for Dilys was the invitation to demonstrate her work at the Ideal Home Exhibition in London. She spent a month there and thoroughly enjoyed staying in a hotel with all meals supplied. HRH The Princess Royal visited the stand and Dilys remembers members of the public asking her not to work so fast, as they could not see what she was doing!

Her final time with the company came during pregnancy and child rearing years when she worked from home. Fownes supplied her with a sewing machine and all the materials were delivered and the gloves collected on a regular basis.

Pittards, the leather manufacturer in Yeovil, still use the name Fownes as a brand partner.

Perrys Site

Mr. Edwin Down Marden, or EDM as he was commonly known, was the patriarch of a large and influential family in the village. He started life as a tenant dairy farmer at Home Farm Rimpton on the Genge-Andrews Estate. He made his money by producing butter and cream and by 1891 he had built Western Counties Creamery in Marston Magna, close by the railway. The business amalgamated with Sparkford creamery, which was situated on the site now occupied by Haynes Publishing. Later they were both absorbed by Aplin and Barrett Ltd.

The farmers would bring their milk in by horse and cart. The horses and carts would be backed up to the platform of the factory. They would all tip their milk in turn to get it measured. Marston had about fourteen dairy farms in those days and all the cows were milked by hand. Milk from the factory went by train to London and surplus milk would be made into powdered milk. The big boiler house, with its tall chimney, supplied hot water and steam for the factory.

Production of cream moved to Yeovil around 1925 and then the adjoining cider factory used the buildings. However, milk powder continued to be made in Marston until just before the war and Jim Nowell remembers, as a child, eating scrapings of milk powder when he visited the factory.

At the Cider Factory.

EDM also produced cider on the site and in 1901 established the Magna Cider Co. Ltd. He had a farm in Rimpton Road, which turned some of its land over to soft fruits and culinary apples. In addition the site produced patented Magna Strawmats and Fruit Cages.

Magna Apples

Apples for the factory came from local farms with large orchards. Cider was the main drink in public houses in this area during the 1920s, only replaced by beer at a later date. The cider would go by train to London and seaside towns. Horses and carts transported the apples with 2 horses per cart. Sparks would fly as the carters applied drag shoes coming down the slope from the railway bridge and onto the weighbridge.

By 1924 the factory supplied several types of cider, notably "Magna-Medium Sweet", which was exported to Australia. The company also produced apple chutney, apple pulp and boxed apples.

Blackcurrant pickers in Rimpton Road 1930.

Preserves were also made at the cider factory. There were two blackcurrant fields along the Rimpton Road where local women picked fruit. They were sometimes accompanied by their young children, and took their own stool to sit on whilst picking. The fruit was collected in metal handled containers, which held 6lbs. These were taken to the galvanised shed to be weighed by Ern March. Money earned from fruit picking could go towards a special treat for the children, such as a seaside trip to Weymouth.

The Army requisitioned the Creamery, which was lying empty, during the war until just before D-Day when it passed into the hands of the American Army. The cider factory continued to operate throughout the war.

Clifford Hockey was the Company Secretary of the Cider Factory. His father farmed Cooper's Farm and Clifford married Dorothy Smith of Wisteria Farm. He joined the company as a lad of sixteen in 1922. He affected a management buy-out of the factory along with two others in 1947 and the two managing Marden brothers took retirement. Clifford Hockey built Standlemead, situated in Camel Street in 1952 for himself and Dorothy. He also owned the 4 cottages on the opposite side of the road in front of Dampier House. They may have been reserved for Cider Factory workers. Showerings bought the factory in 1959 and cider production was then moved to Nailsea.

In 1961 a winery was built on the site employing 32 people by 1965. An article in the Western Gazette dated 2nd February 1962 states:

Sherry and port - the words conjure up visions of sun-drenched vineyards in Spain and Portugal, not of a modern winery in the Somerset countryside at Marston Magna. Yet a formidable amount of the wine drunk in Britain this Christmas was produced 'at home' in this rural setting. The company manufacturing sherry and port at Marston, James Duval & Co. Ltd, look back at their first year's business. Before the company took over, the premises near the railway had been used to produce a more English beverage - cider.

But last January the presses of Magna Cider Company gave way to the highly complex machinery used in British Wine manufacture. Mr. C.W.Hockey stayed on as director. There was no redundancy when the take-over was completed. Along with Mr. Hockey, all members of the cider company's staff were absorbed. And now, with plans going ahead for further extension of the Marston Winery, which already covers over three acres, there is a possibility of the company taking on more staff. 'All labour will be recruited locally' Mr. Hockey commented. 'At present the company produce here only sherry and port, which sell at almost half the price of continental counterparts. But when the extensions are complete other wines may be made.'

In 1976 the Winery was granted a licence to abstract water from Mill Stream.

By 1981 the winery had a capacity to produce 2.5 million gallons a year and averaged close to that with some two million gallons of storage. In brief, the Winery's role was to take in concentrated juice, ferment and process it to the various wine types, filter it, render it duty paid and then send it for bottling. It was noted in the in-house magazine at this time that there were no women working in the Winery itself. No woman had ever applied, but the factory manager assured that any female applicants would get their chance.

There were discussions at the Parish Council meeting in March 1990 concerning pollution of the stream, and the National Rivers Authority confirmed that the cause of the pollution was due to seepage from the Winery lagoons. It was reported that the Winery had ceased pumping and had emptied the lagoons.

In July 1990, Vine Products & Whiteways Ltd sent an invitation to the Parish Council requesting the pleasure of the company of the Residents of Marston Magna and Rimpton at an Open Afternoon at Magna Winery on July 14th.

In 1992 Magna Winery became part of the Gaymer group. The grape juice was brought in by tanker and after processing was taken away by tanker to be bottled. A small field at the back of Netherton House was hollowed out (close to the brook) and used to dump the waste from the fermentation process. Clifford Hockey was a key player in this new project and Phillip Bachrach was recruited to act as chemist by Vine Products. Phillip lived with his wife Joan in the rear half of Marston House, which was owned by the company. In 1994 Gaymer was taken over by Matthew Clark and the winery in Marston Magna was closed. The Parish Council noted that the Winery had been a much needed and valued employer for several generations, with a skilled and loyal workforce.

The buildings lay empty for two years, until, in 1996, Perrys Recycling Head Office was relocated to Marston Magna. They took the site with its buildings and amenities, as it is a designated industrial site with no planning restrictions. It also had an enhanced electricity and water supply, which suited their requirement. Perrys told the Parish Council that they wished to be good neighbours and to conduct their business in a manner as little disturbing to residents as possible.

Perrys is a family business with Brian Perry as Chairman. His son Christopher is Managing Director, nephew Nick is Depot Director, son Matthew is Transport Director and daughter Samantha is Company Secretary and Sales Director. They operate a fleet of 20 lorries and employ approximately 50 people. The business processes in excess of 70,000 tonnes per year, recycling over 40 grades of paper, cardboard, polythene, plastics, metal, cans, wood and glass to mills in the UK, Europe and Asia. The majority of the recycling materials are industrial waste rather than domestic. They also provide a Mobile Shredding Service and are fully approved and vetted to deal with High Security shredding, some of which can arrive under police escort.

The Policemen

Marston Magna had its own Police Station at the beginning of the century. It was at No 4, an end of terrace cottage in Camel Street, joined to Camelot and next door to White House Farm.

All the local Policemen enjoyed their own intelligence network and on their bike round would stop off and chat. In that way they gathered information regarding crime in the area.

The Western Gazette, reporting on the retirement of PC Dennett in 1960, stated that 22 village police officers preceded him. Mrs. M.Davis tells us that it was PC Robert Hellyar in 1900 and he appears in Kelly's Directory in 1902 and 1906. The following men served the village in this capacity as follows:

1910 PC Sidney Bartlett

1914 PC William Hillman (He had twin children Ciss and Ern. They were often presented at village functions along with Rev. Peppin's twin daughters.)

1923 PC Charles Norris

1926 Herbert William Baker and Edith Rose Baker lived in the Police House.

PC King is thought to have preceded PC Dennett and probably served 4 or 5 years in the village up to 1937. He might have been fond of a drop of cider!

"Bobby Dennett" is very well remembered. He too liked a taste of cider; it seemed to go with the job! The following extract has been taken from a copy of The Western Gazette published in 1960.

Village Policeman Retires.

A village "bobby" cycling along his beat on a sunny spring morning might give the impression of a rather easy and relaxed life to a visitor used to the hustle and bustle of town life. But that is not so.

For PC Walter Reginald Dennett who retires today (Friday) after 30 years in the force, the last 23 of them at Marston Magna, it has been far from relaxing. To cover his beat he has had to cycle 120 miles every week, something like 139,000 miles during the time he has spent there.

He sets off from his station at Marston Magna twice a day to call at West Camel, Queen Camel, Rimpton, Sparkford, Sutton Montis, South Cadbury and Compton Pauncefoot.

The Police Station moved directly opposite, to a purpose built house and Public Room, in 1954. Mrs. Dennett was particularly pleased to be moving to somewhere that had a flushing toilet. Ron Chainey who lived opposite remembers the blue Police sign and panda cars at the front door.

The Western Gazette also recorded:

One incident, which is still a source of amusement among some local farmers, occurred when Mrs. Dennett answered the telephone. A farmer asked for a permit to remove two sows in a trailer, but she thought he wanted to "move cows to Australia."

The Rev Ralph-Bowman of West Camel said, "His build, his weather beaten face and his good humour typified the ideal country "Bobby" and there must be many a boy in this district who is grateful that the constable had a "word with his father" instead of hauling him off before the "beak".

Another anecdote tells of the evening when the newly installed PC Dennett spotted a parked car without lights in Rimpton Road close by the church and cautioned the owner, Mr. Doug Marden, who was attending a meeting in the school room. Mr. Marden was very displeased and summoned the Police Constable to the Cider Factory and roundly ticked him off.

PC Dennett booked Wyndham Arthur Hewlett of Eyewell early in the 1940s for riding a bike without lights. Wyndham never revealed this misdemeanor to his father. His girlfriend arranged for the vicar

P.C. Dennett

to write a letter to the court explaining that Wyndham was unable to attend due to work commitments and that he wished to plead guilty. He was fined 7/6d for each light making a total of 15 shillings or 75p, which was quite a sum to be out of pocket in those days. Wyndham also recalls that "Bobby Dennett" would turn up when you least expected him but he has seen him inspect his watch and remark that he would have to make tracks for the Telephone Box in the village as he was expecting a call from his superior. On another occasion he caught another lad red-handed bird nesting. It cost the father of the lad several pints in the local to smooth over that misdemeanor.

Henry Trim writes in the Parish Magazine that:

> *The late P.C.Reg Dennett, our respected and loved village constable for over twenty years, always evaded all attempts to 'motorise' him. He maintained that you could hear a motorbike coming miles away, whereas on his trusty pushbike he was silently 'on the scene' before his presence was detected. Certainly Reg didn't miss much that happened on his 'patch' and I have a feeling that on many occasions 'instant justice' and 'admonitions' prevented the magistrates from being over worked.*
>
> *He also took his sergeant's exams but didn't want to move away for promotion. When he retired from the Police Force aged 53 he briefly took work at the milk factory at Sparkford and then went on to become the boiler man at the newly established Winery. It was a coal boiler that needed strong arms to keep it stoked. When he retired he was presented with a set of bowls by the Winery so he had no intention of putting his feet up!*

PC Dennett's daughter Anne trained as a Prison Officer and then progressed to Probation Officer. Towards the end of her life she became a leading light in the village Women's Institute.

PC Partington is the next remembered and he served the village for 10 years from 1960-1970 approximately. He did his rounds on a motorbike and retired to the village of North Cadbury.

The final four policemen living in the police house and serving as area policemen are less well remembered by villagers. PC Malcolm Baker, who is described as tall, good looking and cheeky was promoted and left the area. PC Alex McCartney was in the post in 1974 and the 1977 Parish Magazine reports that he is to be congratulated on receiving a Royal Humane Society Award for breaking into a cottage to revive an unconscious man in Yeovil. He was followed by PC Robert (Bob) Woods, who lived in Marston with his wife Brenda for about 10 years.

Finally PC Adams was welcomed to the village at the Parish Council Meeting on 3rd September 1990, when he said his job was to patrol the village and surrounding areas and he hoped that people would make good use of having a local policeman once more.

However, in June 1993 the village was made aware that the Police Station at Marston Magna would be closing as a police office. PC Adams would be operating from Wincanton, still policing local villages as well. He ended up buying the Police House when it was placed on the open market not long after.

It is certain that these officers were the designated Area Police Officers but with the advent of panda/police cars replacing pushbikes and latterly motorbikes, their presence on the ground was less noticeable and no doubt their responsibilities were flung wider.

The Post Office

A memory from Mrs. Davis on the Christmas Day Post:

In 1900 letters were delivered twice a day in the week and once on a Sunday and a letter posted on Christmas Eve would be sure to arrive next morning. In fact we always hurried home from church on Christmas Day, because that was when the bulk of the cards came - and all for a penny stamp.

At the beginning of the 20th century two sisters ran the Post Office and shop. Mrs Davis wrote of this shop:

On the many shelves ranged on the wall behind the counter were things seldom seen now, Monkey Brand soap and Mazawattee tea, Globe polish, Rising Sun blacklead, Epps cocoa and Red, White and Blue French coffee. There was cheese and candles, soda and salt-petre, pins and needles – it was a very handy shop.

When one of the sisters left to get married their relations Ada and Edgar Barnes moved to take on the post office and grocery shop in 1901.

Letters from Bath arrived at 7.20 a.m. and 3 p.m. Letters were dispatched at 10.55a.m.and 6.05p.m. Postal orders were issued but not cashed at Marston Magna Post Office. A fee known as "poundage" was paid for this service. It was introduced in 1881 and much in use in the days before the majority of people held a bank account. Money orders could be cashed at Rimpton. Marston Magna was not originally a telegraph office and the nearest telegraph office was at Rimpton.

By 1906 Mrs. Hannah Bugby was in charge of the grocers and Post Office and by 1914 it was a telegraph office. The post office was then at The Laurels in Camel Street. In 1919 Mrs. Alice Thorne was sub-postmistress whilst Mr. Frederick Thorne is listed as a shopkeeper at Laurel Farm, now known as Laurel Cottage. Mrs. Alice Thorne was still shopkeeper and postmistress in 1939. She died aged 90 in February 1960. Their son Hubert Thorne also farmed at Laurel Farm during his mother's lifetime. His wife Mrs. Beatrice Thorne became sub-postmistress.

The Post Office in Camel Street early in the century.

Mr. and Mrs. Hubert Thorne were listed at the Post Office, Yeovil Road in the early 1960s. On the death of Mr. Thorne the council tenancy on Laurel Farm had to be given up. Mrs. Thorne moved into 3, Church Path, where she ran the Post Office. (3 Church Path, was lately known as 3 Rectory Cottages and now Church Cottage). The Parish magazine of May 1988 included this tribute from Peter Clarke and Henry Trim:

Sad news during the month was the passing of Mrs. Beatrice Thorne...a very popular figure in the village...

She had been associated with the Village Post Office from the days when it was combined with a grocer's shop run by her mother-in-law in the house adjoining Home Lea. She was a quiet and efficient person and gave much help to many people.

William Milverton was postman in the village for some years early in the century. He lived with his wife Annie and young family in Marston Magna, but died suddenly in the village in 1917.

Mr. Bert Webber was postman in the village and for a while, after he had delivered the post each day in Marston Magna, he went to Chilton Cantelo where he worked for Mr. Goodford.

Brenda Darch commented that:

During the war and some years after our post was delivered by Charlie Pomeroy from Queen Camel, followed by Frank Card from Queen Camel, and Bert Webber (an old Marstonian) who did not give up until around the age of 80.

Postman Bert Webber.

Bert Webber died in 1969.

Then Mrs. Winnie Dole was post lady in the village for many years. Apart from delivering the mail she would deliver goods from the shop on occasion too. The following tribute was made to Winnie in February 1979, a year that began with particularly challenging weather conditions:

We all tend to take for granted that during all types of weather, be it torrential rain, thick fog, ice and snow etc. our letters will be delivered to individual homes. Come hail, come shine, Winnie our Post lady has got through with our mail and it is felt all the village would like to say our most sincere "thank you" to a brave and conscientious Post lady.

Mrs. Dole continued to deliver the post until she retired in the early 1980s.

Mrs. Cynthia Rance was the last postmistress in the village and arrived in the 1980s. Her husband, Mr. Raymond Rance, used to deliver the post in his own inimitable style. Once he was seen by carol singers, delivering the second post at 9pm!

In the Parish Magazine of February 1993 a notice was posted:

> *Notice has been given to the Parish Council that the Post Office will be closing as from 5th April 1993 due to the resignation of Mrs. Rance, unless a replacement can be found. Post Office counter facilities will have to be withdrawn if no suitable candidate is found. It is a well used Post Office and a valuable amenity. Mrs. Rance is to be thanked for the service she has given to the village, which certainly extended beyond the counter.*

In June of that year, Cynthia and Raymond Rance thanked everyone for their kind gifts given to them at the village hall. They had arrived more than 10 years earlier, newcomers to Somerset and never having run a Post Office before:

> *...We have especially appreciated your friendship...and the countless thoughtful acts of kindness you have shown to us...our warmest thanks to you all.*

Visiting the Post Office then was a reminder of the gentler, slower pace of life. Marston Magna Post Office closed in 1993.

Collections and Deliveries

Early in the twentieth century letters arrived from Bath sorting office twice a day and post was dispatched from the village twice a day, although the letterbox at Marston House was cleared on weekdays only.

From 1927 letters arrived via Yeovil. Until the mid-1980s two postal deliveries from Marston Magna post office were made each day except for Sundays. Letters were delivered direct from Yeovil after the Post Office closed in the village. Mr. Philip Hatcher was the postman (coming from Yeovil) after Mr. and Mrs. Rance left. Mr. Hatcher always exchanged a friendly word and delivered the post in Marston Magna until his retirement.

The Potters

Michael Illingworth, the son of Rear Admiral Illingworth, spent his boyhood in the Manor House and eventually worked in the village as a potter during the period 1975-1996. His studio was in the old garage of the Manor House in Garston Lane.

He specialised in white china, designed to commission for occasions such as weddings and commemorative items for the local villages, and he also completed a great deal of work for the Forces. The German forces, Chelsea Pensioners and the Navy commissioned pieces and he also made sculptural copies of helicopters for Westlands, Yeovil.

The business employed two people, one being the daughter of Mrs. Williams who lived in the Court House, and the other employee commuted from outside the village.

In October 1978 the Parish Council reported that a planning application by Mr. Michael Illingworth was approved for the renewal of the permission for the use of the pottery studio at the Manor House. The view was expressed that his was a useful small craft industry and therefore had a place in a village like Marston.

Dennis Healing moved to Marston with his wife Pat in 1965, but commuted to Camberwell College of Art on a weekly basis until he retired. He was an Independent Adviser for exams around the country. He started the pottery, oxidized stoneware, during the holidays. There are many examples of his work in homes in the village and he also sold to London Stores. He made tea sets, coffee sets, goblets, punch bowls, etc. and, for the Lady Chapel in St. Mary's Church, he designed and made two candle holders and a cross which replaced items which had been stolen. Dennis Healing took examples of his work to various Art Fairs etc.

Dennis was Chairman of the Parish Council and the Village Hall Committee for some time and was very active in the village. He died in 1996.

Here is the 1985 Birchfield School Domesday Project entry:

Mr. Healing has been a potter for ten years. He works five full days and two half days at the weekend. He makes such things as clocks, pots, bowls, dishes, cups and mugs. He works in two old garages and has two kilns and three electric pottery wheels. On average he uses one and a half tonnes of clay a year. It takes about three weeks to produce a piece of pottery although he is not working on it for the whole time. First he shapes the article on a Wheel and then leaves it a few days to dry until it is leather hard. He then cuts patterns into it or gives it the final shaping. Next it is fired. This takes from 18 to 20 hours. After this it is coloured with purple, brown, blue/grey or white glaze. Finally it is fired again. The finished article is now ready to be sold.

Employment data from Census of 1901

Date	Job title	Name	Employer (if given)
1901	Agricultural Smith	Andrew Newberry	
1901	Baker	Albert Foote	
1901	Baker	Charles Marks	
1901	Baker	William Thorn	
1901	Blacksmith	F. W. Chick	
1901	Bread Baker	Henry Toop	
1901	Bread Baker, employee	John Toop	
1901	Bread Maker	Charles Sanson	
1901	Brew/Cider works	William Marden	
1901	Carpenter	John Saunders	
1901	Carpenter	Herbert Biddiscombe	
1901	Carpenter	Samuel Laver	
1901	Carpenter	Bertie Bugby	
1901	Carter	George Foote	Somerset Trading Co.
1901	Carter	William Sibley	Portway
1901	Cattle Man	John Sanson	
1901	Cattleman on Farm	Samuel Abbot	
1901	Clergyman	Rev Joseph Firth	
1901	Coal Yard Foreman	Herbert Lamb	GWR
1901	Commission Agent	Albert Tanner	
1901	Companion	Evelyn Saunders	
1901	Confectioner assistant	Kate Turner	
1901	Cook/Domestic	Bernice Middleton	
1901	Cooper	Thomas Davis	
1901	Cream Maker	Sarah Miller	
1901	Dairyman Manager	Job Milverton	
1901	Director of Creameries	E D Marden	
1901	Domestic Help	Sarah Davis	Wickham House
1901	Domestic Help	Emma Davis	Wickham House
1901	Domestic servant	Mary Gillard	
1901	Domestic servant	Beatrice Watts	
1901	Domestic Servant	Rose Garrett	
1901	Domestic Servant	Eliza Cottle	
1901	Draper	John Sheppard	
1901	Employer	George Lock	Garston Farm
1901	Farm labourer	William Hodder	
1901	Farm labourer	William Herridge	

1901	Farm labourer	George Foot	
1901	Farm labourer	Harold Foley	Wickham House
1901	Farm labourer	Robert Foster	
1901	Farm labourer	John March	
1901	Farm labourer	Fredrick Highmore	Portway
1901	Farm labourer	John Linthorne	Portway
1901	Farm labourer	John Pryor	
1901	Farm labourer	Henry Gillard	
1901	Farm labourer	M. Gillard	
1901	Farm labourer	Robert Foot	
1901	Farm labourer	Isaac Cottle	
1901	Farm labourer	George Laver	
1901	Farm labourer	Francis Cannon	
1901	Farmer	Paul Pitman	
1901	Farmer	Henry Chalker	Marston Park
1901	Farmer	Henry Chalker Jnr.	Marston Park
1901	Farmer	Percival E. Davis	Wickham House
1901	Farmer	William Hockey	
1901	Farmer	Alfred Lane	Church Farm(Manor)
1901	Farmer	Elizabeth Whatley	
1901	Gardener Domestic	Arthur Gaskin	
1901	General Labourer	Frederick Watts	
1901	General Servant	Kate Sanson	
1901	Groom	William Garrett	
1901	Hay Dealer	Robert Wadman	
1901	Housemaid	Alice Garrett	
1901	Innkeeper & farmer	Joseph Noyce	Marston Inn
1901	Innkeeper & farmer	David Salmon	Red Lion
1901	Journeyman Breadmaker	William March	
1901	Journeyman Breadmaker	William March (nephew)	
1901	Laundress	Charlotte Biddiscombe	
1901	Light Nurse Monthly	Emily Langdon	
1901	Manager coal & timber yard	William Tom Bush	
1901	Manager of Creamery	Walter Marden	
1901	Mason & Farmer	Alfred Loader	
1901	Mason Labourer	Lawson Barnes	
1901	Mason Labourer	Herbert Cottle	
1901	Mason Labourer	Sydney Cottle	

1901	Nurse Domestic	Alice Herridge	
1901	Parish Clerk	John March	
1901	Police Constable	Robert Hellyar	
1901	Postmaster & grocer	Edgar Barnes	
1901	Railway Labourer	William Whittle	GWR
1901	Railway packer	George Sherring	GWR
1901	Railway packer	George Brine	GWR
1901	Railway packer	George Sherring	GWR
1901	Railway Plate Layer	Charles Miller	GWR
1901	Railway Plate Layer	William Elley	GWR
1901	Railway Plate Layer	Frank Hanham	GWR
1901	Railway Porter	Thomas Collins	GWR
1901	Railway signalman	Fred White	GWR
1901	Railway Station Master	Charles Gilbey	GWR
1901	Retired Super Police	George Holland	
1901	Road Labourer	Arthur Brine	
1901	School Master	Frank Genge	
1901	School Pupil Teacher	Kate Annie Sherring	
1901	School Teacher	Tryphena Genge	
1901	Timber Woodman Labourer	Arthur Vowles	

The School

Educational provision has been made in Marston Magna as far back as the 17th century. Some schooling took place in the 18th century when a charity was founded in memory of Sir John St. Barbe to educate poor boys in the parishes in which he held land: Ashington, Marston Magna and the tithing of Draycott in the parish of Limington. There was a Sunday school established in Marston Magna in 1802 and two cottages on glebe land were used as a day school in the early 19th century.

The School building, still standing in the village, was built in 1841, in the same year of the Schools Sites Act; this gave permission for landowners to sell or donate up to an acre of land to charities for the provision of schooling 'poor persons'. It was through the Sir John St Barbe Foundation that the school was built in Marston Magna. This was well before the Elementary Education Act of 1870; the first of a number of Parliamentary Acts passed between 1870 and 1893 to provide compulsory education in England and Wales for children aged 5 to13 years old. Schooling for all children was not free until fees were abolished in 1891.

Before 1870 National Schools had been set up in many parishes. These schools were set up to promote the education of the poor in the principles and practices of the Church of England. Marston Magna School was unusual, as it was built on land granted to the vicar and his successors by the Sir John St. Barbe charity. The values of the Church of England were adhered to in school life. Non-denominational Board schools were set up through the Education Act of 1870 and were funded by local taxation. The Church of England funded National schools. These two systems then existed side by side. The government did however grant money towards the building of church and non-conformist schools. Quite early in the 19th century government money was increasingly given to these denominational schools and so tensions arose into how much influence each party could wield.

At the beginning of the 20th century schools like that of Marston Magna had come under financial pressure to meet the costs of running the schools, paying the teachers, meeting the expectations for standards and training as well as maintaining the buildings.

Henry Trim recorded in the Parish Magazine of September 1997 that in 1897 a Parish Meeting decided after much discussion that the school was to be treated as Voluntary School and not by the formation of a School Board.

The 1902 Education Act brought both Board and Voluntary schools under Local Education Authorities Secular instruction and the qualifications of the teaching staff were now to come under the direction of the L.E.A. This meant that the running cost of Voluntary schools was now met by public funds, whilst the responsibility of building maintenance remained with the voluntary societies. Each school had to have a Board of Managers. Marston Magna School now had Her Majesty's Inspectorate, as well as Church Diocesan Inspections, following the 1902 Education Act. However, it was not until 1904 that the vicar of Marston Magna and the Board of Education formalised the arrangements with regard to its position. A school log was recorded as from 1904 and the responsibility for building repairs and improvements remained with the Church. This had consequences for the survival of the school.

Mrs Davis recounted some school memories of 1900:

In 1900 the School was full with about fifty children aged between three and thirteen or fourteen. Mr Genge taught the bigger children from 7 years old upwards while Mrs Genge taught the infants, the schoolroom being divided by sliding doors. The girls and little ones played in the playground at the side of the school and the boys played in the road.

Another row of cottages stood at the back of the School House and beyond them the remains of the Old Tithe Barn but all these have long disappeared.

First week in September - back to school again, with the thought that on our performances between now and Christmas depended our places in class next year. The top boys and girls in each standard sat at opposite ends of the eight-seater desks with the less gifted in the centre. At the end of each lesson the slates and pencils, copy-books and pens, readers and arithmetic cards were passed along to the girls at the end who were responsible for packing them into their proper places and distributing whatever was necessary for the next lesson.

In our school the last few days before Christmas were always very exciting. Little work was done for this was the time for turning out cupboards, washing the inkwells, sorting and re-arranging the few library books and generally tidying up everywhere, ready for beginning again in January.

Cracked and broken slates were thrown away together with short pieces of slate pencil, crossed pen-nibs pulled out and new ones pushed into the wooden handles and best of all, those who had drawn a fairly recognisable map of England and Wales or who had reasonably unspotted exercise books, were allowed to take them home.

For at that time the school year began in January and that was when we 'moved up'. Needless to say, we all expected to move up and we usually did.

We usually broke up two or three days before Christmas for two weeks and while he was alive Mr Nettleton came in on the last day with a huge jar of sweets enough for two or three for each of us. A certain amount of swapping took place after the distribution while each flavour of lemon, peppermint, aniseed or liquorice found an acceptable mouth, sometimes after it has been sampled, but no matter.

We left school early on that last afternoon, in fact going home at playtime. In any case, no one could have settled down to work. Quick farewells to those who would not be coming back after the holidays and who had probably been spoken for on somebody's farm or in someone's kitchen or nursery, a shout of Happy Christmas Sir, to our beloved schoolmaster and then we were in the lobbies, scrambling into hats and coats, jamming caps on small boys heads, tying scarves on little girls, and we were away. Along the pavement in front of School House, down those stone steps into Camel Street, fearing no more than a bicycle or a farm wagon, on our joyous way.

In a letter to John Peppin in 1985, Mrs Davis remembered how King Lewanika came to stay in the village while he went to London for the coronation of Edward VII in 1902:

The black king came for the Coronation of Edward VII in the summer...it was a "Royal Occasion". He came into school to see us drill, he wanted to know why we grew all those buttercups. One of his staff had too much cider in the new factory – it was really a wonderful time and I remember it well.

In 1902 Marston Magna School had an average attendance of 48. This dropped later in the century, apart from during the years of World War 2. It became a junior school in 1926. After then children over the age of eleven attended school at Queen Camel, to which many children walked. A succession of Head teachers resided at the schoolhouse, but towards the end of the school's life the teachers were travelling to school by public transport, which did not always prove reliable!

The schoolhouse has small diamond panes of glass, but in 1904 an HMI recommended replacing the diamond paned windows in the schoolrooms with large, clear panes to allow more light. There was a big hedge around school corner and the parish notice board was in the middle of it. In the 1980s this board was still in use on the wall of the schoolhouse.

Even before the NHS, medical inspections and dental checks were made at the school, in addition to visits by a nurse. The school dentist used to visit the school and the pupils were sometimes seen in the schoolhouse when 6d (2½p) was paid to see the dentist but if no treatment was necessary the 6d was returned. Prompt action was taken when there was an outbreak of an infectious disease and the school was closed for periods when there were illnesses such as measles, diphtheria, or whooping cough. Diptheria resulted in the deaths of some school pupils. It was a much-feared illness, but in 1941 children at the school were inoculated against diphtheria. Children with ringworm, impetigo, TB and scarlet fever were excluded from school. Early in 1914, the village saw an outbreak of diptheria and so the school was closed for 2 weeks and the illness caused further closures in May and June. After the Summer holiday the opening of the school was postponed until September 13th because of diphtheria. It was during this Summer holiday period that Great Britain became involved in the conflict now known as World War I .

World War 1

In September 1914 the Geography and History syllabus at the school was adapted to include lessons dealing with the European War and the countries involved. In October 1914 a little time was given to the study of current war news following the morning scripture lesson. In December of that year flags of the Allied Nations were given to the school and fixed in place. The children then sang The National Anthem. In May 1915 the Canadian Emigration Branch sent a Map of Canada to the school, perhaps encouraging people to contemplate emigration. Patriotic songs and renditions were given following an Empire Day Address in June 1915.

Mrs Davis remembered Empire Day celebrations:

The twenty fourth of May was the birthday of Queen Victoria. She died in 1901 and a movement was begun in 1902 to have some kind of annual remembrance of her long and glorious reign. This was established in 1904 as a Day of National Celebration, on 24th May to be known as Empire Day. Marston school was not slow to respond. The headmaster gave cards and pencils to the more responsible scholars and from our friends and relatives, in pennies and twopences, we collected £5. This was used to buy a flag and flagpole, which was duly erected at the southern end of the building. On Empire Day the whole school assembled outside, and to Cromwell Bugby was given the honour of breaking the flag at the masthead.

As the bright colours floated out on that sunny day we raised three cheers for the Union Jack and sang the National Anthem for the late Queen and of her Empire. We were patriotic in those days - in the best of all possible worlds... or so it seemed at the time.

Empire Day certificates from the overseas clubs were given to children who had made a contribution to the Empire Day Fund. The money raised was to help provide gifts to soldiers and sailors at the front. The following month three children were given permission to help with haymaking, an indication that children were needed on the land. Trafalgar Day in October concentrated on work of the navy in the conflict.

In 1916 Somerset County Council withheld all school prizes for the duration of the war although the Managers of the school kindly donated prizes. The Whitsun Holiday was postponed by the Government. A Diocesan Inspection took place on June 20th and then the school closed until July 4th, as the boys were required to help with haymaking on the farms. On their return the school was presented with a framed picture of Lord Kitchener who had drowned on June 5th in the North Sea when the cruiser Hampshire struck a German mine and sank off the Orkney Islands. Lord Kitchener had been the face on the well-known 1914 recruiting poster.

In mid-July 1916 seven boys were absent due to haymaking as there was scarcity of labour available. In the following year of 1917 the HMI commented that several of the older pupils were undertaking manual work before and after school and no haymaking holiday was given that year. In July 1918 only two children were haymaking but on September 16th the Managers allowed the older children to have 3 half-day holidays per week to gather blackberries. The end of the war in November 1918 again saw the closure of the school for 2 weeks because of influenza, part of the pandemic that saw so many deaths across the world. There was an extra day of holiday granted in July 1919 to celebrate peace.

The school was also used for village social events until the opening of the Foresters Hall in 1926. Occasionally this meant that school was closed a little early to accommodate these events. Sometimes a half-day holiday was taken. In 1919 the school was closed for the whole day when there was a concert in aid of blind sailors. In August 1923 the children did maypole dancing for the fête and the school was closed. Funds from the fête were raised for Yeovil Hospital. In 1927 the fête was on a Thursday. It was well-supported and held in order to raise funds for the repair of the school.

All clergy visited the school on a regular basis, some taking regular RE sessions. Children attended services at the church during Revd. Firth's incumbency, such as for All Saints Day on November 1st 1904. The Revd. Firth left in 1905 and then Revd. Peppin joined the parish. He took the children to church for religious instruction.

The School was sometimes closed for activities related to the Church, for example choir outings, confirmation services and days of note in the Church Calendar such as Ascension Day. When a Diocesan Inspection took place and was completed, the children were often given the rest of the day off school. On July 27th 1905 school was closed for a Sunday School Treat. On October 12th that year there was no school as there was a children's fruit service in the church. In 1907 the children were taken to Church for Lady Day. In 1915 Ash Wednesday was too wet for the children to go to church so the vicar went to the school. On Apr 23rd 1918 the children went to church on St George's Day. The school was closed on May 19th 1919 to allow time for confirmation candidates. At the beginning of 1920 the vicar gave a tea and entertainment for the children. On October 9th 1923 some choirboys were absent as they were singing at a wedding. In January 1924 there was a Sunday School Tea at the schoolroom. The elder children attended the Armistice Service in November of that year.

The Revd. Peppin left at the end of 1924. Both he and his wife were regular visitors to the school during their time in the village, which gives an indication of close association of Church and School.

There was quite a high turnover of staff at the school. The HMI inspectorate makes comment on the quality of teaching. In 1904 instruction was noted as good. At this time the curriculum was largely based on the countryside and the agricultural year. The Three Rs were taught alongside Grammar and Recitation, Geography and History, Common Things, Drawing, Needlework and Drill. The boys did drawing and the girls learned needlecraft skills including knitting, sewing, patching, darning, gathering, hemming, pleating etc. The County Needlework Instructress was a regular visitor to the school.

In 1906 there was complaint that drawing skills were being neglected. These skills were important as clerical employment could rely on such technical skills long before the days of computer aided technology. In 1909 the Inspector comments:

> *Children's attitude in the desks and the holding of pens leaves something to be desired.*

The 1911 report states progress as being entirely unsatisfactory, with children being listless and indifferent, producing scribbled written work.

Cookery lessons were given to girls after 1918. They walked to these lessons at Queen Camel, which had facilities for this. However, on one afternoon in September 1922 the children walked all the way back to Marston Magna as there was no one at Queen Camel to teach them cooking!

Children at the village school early in the century.

Over the decades staff came and went at Marston Magna. In the 1920s the HMI felt that the syllabus should be extended for those over the age of 11 years by taking advantage of the Senior school now established in Queen Camel. By the 1930s the school was a Junior school, when the Diocesan Inspection found the work of the Head teacher to be very thorough and painstaking. The Inspector asked the School Managers if the children could have a day's holiday. The HMI too was impressed by the remarkable improvement. County Scholarship exams to enter Yeovil Schools were taken each year and some years there was success for the candidates.

In 1924 the Revd. Bartlett became vicar of the parish. In the years before his arrival there had been comment about the repair and maintenance of the school. In the first decade of the century there was redecoration, replacement windows and doors to the porch fitted. New floors were laid. Fireguards were provided. School lavatory facilities always needed to be cleaned and maintained. The playground needed re-gravelling.

In 1924-5 the Government attempted to improve school buildings across the country as many were no longer fit for purpose and only met the standards demanded by previous administrations. In 1924 the Board of Education introduced more building regulations and tough measures were taken in an attempt to implement changes. Many church schools struggled to finance these new measures. The Church wished to continue to provide the ethos of Christian values in education. Over the decades much negotiation about the provision of suitable buildings and the continuing place of Religious Instruction in schools ensued.

In the 1930s, during the Revd. Bartlett's time, there was a new playground, but the stove went out of action and needed repair. In 1942 parts of the ceiling fell in and the County Authorities gave instruction to send the children home until the roof was repaired.

Recollections of time spent at Marston Magna School include how the children could hear the animals being killed in the slaughterhouse next door and see the blood running into the stream. Anne Dennett related that she used to think that branches from the trees in the churchyard would fall on to the playground. In the 1930s, a verger lived in Bridge Cottages and scared the children because he always wore black. He would not allow thoroughfare through the churchyard unless you were actually going to the church! At this time there was a big dog at the garage on the corner, and so walking past was reported to be frightening!

Brenda Darch (1930-2002) spent her early years in Marston Magna and her memories of school life are included here:

> *I remember well going to Marston School. The teacher's name was Miss Otridge, but she moved not long after I started and then we had Mrs. Jones who lodged in the village but went home most weekends to Cardiff. Miss Bugby taught the infants. Mrs. Jones was very keen on us learning the three "R"s and part of each day was taken up in these three subjects, usually the mornings, and other subjects were fitted around these. The juniors were in the large room and the infants in the small one. We all went to Queen Camel or the Grammar Schools in Yeovil at the age of 11. The children who went to Queen Camel used to cycle whilst the ones who went to Yeovil used to have to go to the station and catch the train to Yeovil Pen Mill. Before the war, the ones who went to QC used to be taken in a horse and cart by Jimmy Noyce. The school was closed in the early fifties and all the children went to Queen Camel as they do now.*

Les Sayers, who was born in 1919, related that his mother left school at the age of 10 years and was put out to work in service. He himself was sometimes kept home from school to pick up potatoes or other jobs. If the hunt was out at dinner time, the children would follow and miss school. He also recalled that:

> *When we filed out of school we would drop a knob of carbide in the inkwell. It would froth up and make a mess all over the desk.*

World War 2 and Post War

When the Evacuees first arrived in the village, there was an outbreak of whooping cough. Numbers at the school were at their height during World War 2. Throughout war time the school nurse continued to visit, and dental and medical examinations of all children took place. In September 1939 24 children from St Albans School, Camberwell, London were billeted in the village. Initially, they worked independently of Marston Magna School, using the spare room there. By June of 1940 there were just 14 LCC children at the school. They were now taught under the direction of the Head teacher of Marston Magna. Following a visit by the Investigation Officer for the London County Council, their own teacher was told to return to London.

In October 1941 there were 64 children at the school which included 20 children from Camberwell. In 1941 22 scholars from Camberwell School were transferred to Rimpton School owing to the overcrowding of Marston Magna School.

The number of evacuees fluctuated during the war, reflecting events in different parts of the country. Some children returned home during 1940-1941, but others arrived. There were 3 children from West Ham London, and 6 children from Doncaster School in Bristol admitted in June 1941, but these had returned home by January 1942. There were 7 evacuated children in May 1943 including 1 evacuee from Portsmouth, but at one point in this year there were just 2 evacuees at the school. In July 1944 children from Kent and Surrey arrived and in October 1944 there were 14 evacuated children from Kent, London, Surrey and Croydon.

By June 25th 1945 all evacuees had left. There is mention of one family with 2 children leaving the school in 1940 to go to Canada.

Late in 1942, the Drill Inspectress visited the school! After this, there was emphasis on Physical Training lessons, and in July 1946 equipment was bought for P.T.

School Meal provision was a requirement of the 1944 Education Act. School dinners could cause problems and once in 1949 did not arrive until after the start of afternoon school! Washing up was done in combination with caretaking duties, but did not always get done! Teaching staff changed several times post war, some travelling to school by unreliable buses.

The 1944 Education Act was a further milestone and again pressure about building conditions and maintenance arose. In 1947 a Yeovil Education officer visited Marston Magna School. Early in 1948 the schoolyard and site were visited again. A new Headmistress arrived and was told that small constructional repairs would be carried out. During 1948 the Architect visited on several occasions to examine the structure and decoration of the building. HMI also visited the school at the end of the year when school managers, the decorator and architect were in discussion. At the end of that school year the architect visited to see the structure and internal decoration of the school. In November the Managers of the school met with Education Committee members.

Conditions at the beginning of 1949 were described as chaotic. The caretaker was ill and workmen were present alongside the children when electricity was installed, the building was redecorated and washbasins were fitted.

In July 1949 correspondence from the Education Committee was sent to the vicar. It was a letter remonstrating that the only improvements made to the school since the architect's visit a year before were the redecoration of the school paid for by the Education Authority and the installation of electricity. An assurance had been given on behalf of the Managers that the work to remedy defects would commence by April 30th 1948. This work had not commenced and now an ultimatum of improvements being completed by the 3rd September 1949 was made. The Education Authority would cease to maintain the school without the necessary improvements being carried out.

The Revd. Bartlett responded. His letter notes the task of dealing with the matter had become almost a full time job, that he would call a meeting of the Managers but that he had had a very serious illness and now one of the members of the Sir John St. Barbe Trust (which was helping with the repairs) had met with a very serious accident. He asked for due consideration in the light of these difficulties.

In May 1950, oil stoves were delivered to the school, when the architect was again in attendance. A new stove was bought and fitted in November 1950, when there was also flooding, followed by snow in December. The school remained cold that month, as fires were not often lit. The Rector opened the school on Dec 15th 1950 when the Headmistress was delayed by snow. On Dec 19th Revd. Bartlett conducted the school carol service, but sadly he died just a week later, on Boxing Day 1950.

The summer of 1951 saw the closure of the school. One pupil transferred to Ansford Secondary Modern School but the rest of the children were transferred to Queen Camel School. Arrangements for school transport were made at the time of closure. The Parish Magazine of September 1980 announced there was to be a meeting regarding School Transport:

A meeting will be held in Marston Magna Village Hall on 8th September to discuss possible means of transporting our local children privately to Queen Camel School consequent upon the removal of the County Council's subsidised transport scheme.

In the 1990s transport to school was still available but the County again mooted the idea that transport be removed. It was suggested in discussion that children in Marston Magna living under the statutory 2 miles from the village school should walk to school. It was argued that the road was considered too dangerous and school transport from Marston Magna to Queen Camel has continued beyond 2000.

After the closure, the school building was then back into the care of the charity. The Sir John St. Barbe Foundation spent its limited funds on the maintenance of the "Listed" buildings. The schoolhouse continued to be let at a peppercorn rent, but in the mid-1980s the letting of the Old School building meant that there was a small annual surplus. The original Sir John St. Barbe Trust had been set up in 1736 in memory of Sir John to educate poor boys in the parishes of: Ashington, Marston Magna and the tithing of Draycott in the parish of Limington. With the Trust fund's small increase, the Trustees decided to revive the educational purpose of the fund. Sir John's interest in music prompted the introduction of bursaries to children from the specified villages to help fund their musical studies.

Many children from the parishes have benefited from the bursaries to help their musical practice and studies. Lieutenant Colonel Russell R. B. Anderson of Limington House, who in his own words stated that he was "an umpteenth great-nephew of Sir John St. Barbe" and as trustee took a keen interest in the children's studies, worked hard to keep the charity going, together with the other trustees who have given their time to sustain the charity.

The School, and the schoolhouse were sold as a private home in 2003. This meant that the Trustees were able to consider more awards after 2006. In 2012 14 bursaries for 13 students were provided via 5 different music teachers. The charity founded in memory of Sir John St. Barbe in 1736 is still fulfilling its objective of educating children in the parishes in which he held land.

FAMILIES

The Chainey Family

The Chainey family arrived in Marston Magna in 1932. Maurice and his wife Beatrice had run various Public Houses including the Crown in Yeovil, which stood on the site where Tesco now stands and also the White Post at Rimpton. They rented a cottage in Camel Street, which was built around 1840. Beatrice was quite a character, as Brenda Darch remembers. During the war, when the trains were delayed due to bombing further up the line, they would be kept amused by Cyril Chainey's mother, who had a large repertoire of jokes and stories. Maurice played the piano so they probably ran a fun place to visit and to enjoy a drink or two.

Life for the five children, all boys, was not always easy however, as the father was an alcoholic and the cottage was very small. The eldest enjoyed a variety of names, which are worth explaining. His birth certificate was in the name of Arthur George, but his mother and her side of the family called him Hurford, because of all the children he was most like her husband Maurice Hurford. When Arthur George first courted his future wife he gave the fictitious name of Ron, in case he wanted to abandon the friendship. He didn't, and it stuck! Ron, as we will call him, joined the army at a very young age and travelled extensively throughout the Empire during these youthful years. At some time he had an operation, which resulted in him being classified as 'not fit for active service' so, when war was declared, he spent those years as a Sergeant in a training capacity. He married early in the war and raised a family of two children living in Sherborne, where he eventually took employment as a postman.

Reg was the second eldest and despite the fact that Ron had left home to join the Army, the little two-bedroom cottage was too small for the growing family. It was decided to find alternative accommodation for Reg as he was deemed old enough to deal with it and of course it would be one less mouth to feed. He was found a place in the Yeovil Workhouse when he was around the age of 9 or 10. The Workhouse was built in 1837 on the north side of Preston Road. (It was converted and opened in 1967 as Summerlands Hospital). It was a very grim institution when Reg arrived.

The 1901 census showed over 100 inmates described as paupers, 26 of whom were over the age of 70. Infirmities were described as 2 imbeciles, a lunatic under observation, epilepsy, tuberculosis, palsy, deaf and dumb, blind and syphilis. It also provided overnight accommodation for itinerant tramps. A Franciscan monk described conditions in the Yeovil Workhouse for these homeless men in an article published in the Western Gazette in 1928. The accommodation was in cells; there was no heating; they were given insufficient bedding and slept on the floor; they were given dry bread and inedible cheese to eat; the washing facilities were almost non existent and they were tasked in the morning to do cross-cut saw work in freezing conditions. There were 31 children under 14 years of age.

Reg arrived some twenty years later and probably stayed there until its closure in 1928. He must have been aware of the adult inhabitants and no doubt the whole experience made a deep impression on him. He moved then to a children's home near Frome, which he did not care for. The children had to scrub the floors and the religious pictures and quotes seemed to have little relevance to his life. As soon as he was of working age, in those days 14, he returned to Marston Magna.

When war came Reg tried to join up, but he was in a reserved occupation as a driver and it was quite some time before he was accepted into the RAF. His first deployment was operating Barrage Balloons in London and he also spent time in South Africa, North Africa and Italy. At the end of the war, in his late 30s, he married the twin sister of his brother Ron's wife and they bought the little cottage in Camel Street from Mr Hockey. Granny Chainey (Beatrice) lived with them for a while before moving to one of the Almshouses. Reg never forgave his father for the treatment he had received, and always condemned him for drinking and wasting the family income. It gave him the determination that no child of his would suffer as he had done.

Reg was a founder member of The British Legion branch when it was formed in 1955.

The Act of Remembrance reported in the April 1979 Parish Magazine made special reference to Mr. Reg Chainey who had died suddenly the previous day. His wife remained in the house until her death in 2001.

Reg's son, Ron Chainey, spent his childhood in No.3. He remembers that when he was quite young, the occupants of No 2 were an elderly lady called Mrs Talbot and her companion called "Nurse". Young Ron found Nurse rather frightening as she always sported a huge ginger wig and wore a great deal of make-up. She would also bash the walls to keep the evil spirits away. On one occasion Reg fumigated the top of their house because they had a plague of flies. Nurse decided that the dead flies were a very bad sign.

Milk, bread and eggs were delivered to the house regularly. Every Tuesday Mr Baker would arrive in a green Morris Minor van to receive the weekly grocery order. His brother would then deliver on Thursday from a bigger van.

Ron did well at school, became a gifted linguist and won a university education, as did his two children. He still owns the little family home in Camel Street.

Cyril was the third born son and also joined the RAF. He saw war service in India and Burma amongst others, but on returning at the end of hostilities, he settled down in the village, marrying Kath Hobbs-Webber in 1947. Kath was born in 1922. Her mother was the parlour maid at the Manor House, while her father worked as carpenter at the big house in Chilton Cantelo, before it became a school.

Cyril was a bricklayer and ended his working life doing site maintenance at the Winery. He would also open up the Old Village Hall every Friday for the village youth.

Kath attended the village school and remembers sitting the 11+ exam, but found when she turned the paper over she could answer very few of the questions. The senior school was at Queen Camel and she travelled there by horse and cart, until she was deemed old enough to ride a bike.

When war was declared Kath was 17 years old and on a visit to Bristol she signed up for the WAF. She started off her 5-year stint working on the Barrage Balloons that were manufactured in Bristol and following an accident, which prevented her from continuing that work, she transferred to the transport section and became a driver for the remainder of her service.

Cyril and Kath Chainey on their wedding day at St.Mary's Church in 1947.

When Kath was planning her wedding, her mother and sister gave her enough clothing coupons to purchase her very smart wedding outfit of dark and pale blue check suit with matching accessories. She could have purchased a white wedding dress but decided the suit was more sensible. There were not enough coupons for both outfits.

Having tried without success to start a family, they were told that it was not possible, so Cyril and Kath took the brave decision to adopt, firstly a little boy and two years later a little girl, both received at 10 days old. They were greatly surprised three years later however, when a baby girl was born to them, conceived naturally. To the credit of Kath and Cyril, the eldest child reported as a mature adult that they had never been treated any differently.

Kath and Cyril's eldest child, Michael, remained in the village. He is remembered for collecting a substantial sum while still a youth, by going on a sponsored walk from Dorchester Football Ground to the Red Lion Skittle Alley in support of the 1979 Poppy Appeal. The total raised that year was a record £660.

Michael was apprenticed to Westlands at the age of sixteen and spent all his working life with this company. He travelled to many foreign countries in his role as an aircraft fitter. He married Helen Pearce at St. Mary's Church, Marston Magna, in July 1989, and raised a family living in a cottage in Little Marston Road, where he had once lived as a child. Helen served the village on more than one occasion as Clerk to the Parish Council.

James was the fourth son of Maurice and Beatrice. As a lad James (Jim) was in the A.T.C., which was in its infancy at the commencement of WW2. It was first set up in 1939 to give part time training to young men in various aviation related skills. He also did agricultural work for Freddie and George Noyce between 1939 and 1941, milking cows in many fields around Marston. He would always turn to count the Barrage Balloons over Yeovil and the number was always 24. He joined the RAF and was mainly concerned in operating heavy plant, used in constructing landing strips, for example. On VE day in 1945 he found himself at Base 58 Melsbroek, which occupied the same site as Brussels Airport, assisting in the repatriation of British POWs. Coincidentally Jack Batson, a fellow Marstonian, was one of the released prisoners. Jack was unable to communicate with Jim, but was pleased to inform Jim's mother of his whereabouts, and to tell her that he was safe; since all she knew was that he was part of the British Liberation Army.

Jim never married and was always a very correct and polite man. He continued in the RAF for much of his working life, relocating to the Cambridge area. He was instrumental in researching and publicising the famous RAF memorabilia bar at the rear of The Eagle Inn, Cambridge.

Maurice, the youngest boy, also served in the RAF and moved to Cambridge, but apart from Jim did not keep contact with the rest of the family.

The Chainey family can therefore claim four generations living in the village during the 20th century.

The Noyce Family

The Noyce family were at the heart of Marston Magna village life at the turn of the 20th century. Joseph Noyce and his wife Martha arrived in the village in 1894. He was 27 and his wife a year older. They took on the licence of The Marston Inn, offering a transport service as well as hospitality. Martha had learnt the pub trade from her parents George and Sophia Lane who ran the "True Lovers Knot Inn" at Tarrant Keynston for many years. Joseph had been employed as a gamekeeper for the Earl of Pembroke at Grovely Wood Wiltshire.

At the Marston Inn Joseph cared for the horses and had a brake for hire for trips to the station or into Sherborne or Yeovil. Sadly, he died in 1912 while still only in his forties. After his death, Martha continued as the licensee - well, she had little choice with 12 small mouths to feed and no man! However, she did go on to marry for a second time and ran the pub for 45 years, in all probability retiring in her early seventies. She was outlived by her second husband, Jack Giles, who lived in one of the Almshouses in old age and subsequently at Home Lea.

The large family of seven girls and five boys fathered by Joseph will have kept the couple remarkably busy. Mrs Noyce was apparently never happier than when she had something to worry about and with twelve children she had plenty of practice. The only times when she was really unhappy was when she had nothing to worry about as she thought the family was keeping something from her!

Mrs Martha Noyce with her 12 children.

The Noyce boys would often get into mischief and were always on the alert for a practical joke. On one occasion they took a cattle dealer's horse and cart from outside the Inn into the field opposite, unharnessed the horse and took it back into the road, pulled the shafts of the cart through the field gate and then re-harnessed the horse, which left the horse on one side of the gate and cart on the other. Later on, the owner is reported as having stood in the road scratching his head at this spectacle, not really being in a condition to reason it out at that point in time!

The eldest son Fred married Ginny Hayward and farmed at both Garston Farm and Park Farm, but also found time to follow his interest in training horses. Fred served with the Dorset Yeomanry in the First World War and did his bit to satisfy the great demand for horses. Many would arrive by rail and be led into the fields behind the Cider Factory where Fred would get to work on them. He was also very proud that one of his horses called Peepadawn was entered in the Grand National. The name lives on above his stable door, which has now been converted to a dwelling at Garston Farm.

Fred's son George remained in the village doing agricultural work until his retirement. Fred's grandson and great grandson also chose to stay, resulting in four generations of this family working in Marston Magna within the 20th century.

Fred's brother Jim was a butcher, who undertook slaughter work when asked. He eventually moved on to farm work. He served in World War 1 with the Royal Horse Artillery, which was responsible for light mobile guns that provided firepower in support of the cavalry. He was probably a late teenager when he was posted to France. His expertise with horses stood him in good stead, and also, in view of his slaughter experience, he was detailed to collect bodies from the battlefield. After the war at the age of 29 he left the Marston Inn to marry Alice from Milborne Port, only to move to another part of the village. He worked in agriculture for his brother Fred for many years and then went labouring for the building trade, often for Dennis Darch.

Jim and Alice celebrated their Golden Wedding in 1977, having lived at 8 Townsend for 45 years. Mr Noyce said, *"Our friends and neighbours are like a family to us. We have never had a cross word with them in our lives."*

Two years later, in December 1979, Henry Trim reported the recent death of his uncle Jim Noyce, who at the age of eighty-one was the oldest 'Marstonian' in the village. It seemed to mark the end of an era. With the exception of his army service in World War I with the Royal Horse Artillery, Jim had rarely spent a day outside his beloved village. Many residents recall being conveyed to Queen Camel School by means of his horse and buggy. The donkey cart or "Camel Cart", as it was called by the children, would collect, chiefly girls, for the school run. It stopped at Marston School corner and Ralph Bartlett and James Chainey, without bikes, would run behind and jump up on its back axle. Jimmy would get very cross and wave his whip.

Of the remaining three brothers, Jack went to work for the Earl of Pembroke on the Wilton Estate for a year to learn game keeping, and while there he was taught how to use a gun. He spent the remainder of his life in and around Marston, spending many years as a driver for Marston Cider Factory doing deliveries. His son Geoff lived in Mudford and served as a postman for over thirty years.

Billy died of pneumonia at the tender age of 12 and is buried in St Mary's churchyard. The remaining boy, Gilbert, also did not make old bones.

Of the daughters, we know that Hilda remained in the village, living next door to Garston Farm with her builder husband Walter Thomas.

Another daughter, Jessie, married George Libbey and spent two different periods in Australia. They also were employed in farming and the Pub trade.

Dora Noyce married an Australian soldier called Jack Divall, who survived WWI after being wounded in Gallipoli and then again when serving in Belgium and France. His recovery and recuperation took place in Bath Hospital, where he probably met his future wife. Everyone knew this couple as Dora and Jack but they were christened Margaret and Sidney - how did that happen? Their son Fred, living in Sydney, prospered and established a plastics business, but subsequently reverted to his agricultural roots by moving out, buying a farm and raising Hereford cattle. Fred's children have also prospered in the New World. Susan has been back to the UK tracing her roots and made contact with the Marston arm of her family. Her brother, Richard Divall, is a highly respected conductor and musicologist who, on the invitation of Dame Joan Hammond, became the Music Director of the Victoria State Opera in Melbourne for much of the final quarter of the 20th century.

The Marden Family

At the turn of the century in 1900, E.D.Marden was already well established in Marston Magna, having progressed from being a tenant farmer at Home Farm Rimpton on the Genge-Andrews Estate. His brother Walter was also a farmer at Middle Farm Rimpton and the two brothers married two sisters. E.D.M. made good profits on the production of cream and butter and was able to diversify into Cider, with a Factory on the same site as the Creamery. He was a big employer with employees spread across his various business enterprises and also in the home. His groom, Grant, progressed to chauffeur with the advent of the motorcar. E.D.Marden was a very keen motorist and initially owned the only car in the village. He went on to own a fine collection.

There is a delightful tale of a motorcar excursion undertaken by Mr and Mrs Marden together with the family nurse into Yeovil to visit Denners. Mrs Marden and nurse were happily viewing the wares on offer, when Grant suddenly appeared and uttered the words "Come on! Come on! Tidn't I, tis he!"

E.D.M. (as he was commonly known) was in his fifties in the early years of the twentieth century. He and his wife Jennie had already established a mature family of six sons and a daughter. John Peppin, the vicar's son, remembers that the only houses in the village whose inhabitants were considered 'gentry' were The Manor House and The Court. Everyone else was considered working class, although the exception was the Mardens. They inhabited a sort of middle stratum between gentry and labourers, but were categorised as 'commerce' in that class-ridden society. He also remembers "Old Marden was a Churchwarden who often failed to put in an appearance, sometimes for weeks together."

Of the boys, Bert worked in the creamery and married Madge. They had three boys Phillip (Bill), Ted and Peter.

Doug and Gray managed the Cider Factory. Doug served in World War 1 in the West Somerset Yeomanry and was commissioned lieutenant. He served part of his time in Egypt. Doug was a keen cricketer and headed the village cricket team, which was active in the 1920s. He married Maisie in 1930 and took on the responsibility of her two children by a previous marriage. He fathered no children of his own, but helped Maisie to rear Jim and Averil successfully.

Doug retired from the Cider Factory in 1947, when Clifford Hockey bought out the business, and passed away in 1954, aged 70.

Sadly, Gray, who lived at Brookside opposite Wickham Farm, became depressed as a result of a failed marriage to Catherine and shot himself. There were no offspring.

Stanley worked for Marconi. He married Lola from Blackpool, who was a showgirl. Stanley and Lola visited the Marden home quite regularly and Lola was considered a rather 'fast' woman. Photographs from the period show off her extrovert personality to the full. He was fascinated with radio and had a huge aerial installed on the roof of Marston House.

Stanley and Lola eventually bought a house in Yeovil, and he had just landed a good job at Westlands when he died suddenly of a heart attack in 1938. Lola lived on in the house off West Coker Road until her death aged 90+.

Stanley Marden with his "radio" at Marston House in 1923.

Arthur Cecil, known as Cecil, was the Village Scoutmaster and served as Second Lieutenant in the Royal Garrison Artillery. He died of his wounds towards the end of the First World War in 1917. His grieving parents installed stained glass windows in St Mary's Church in his memory.

Monty undertook training for the priesthood and emigrated to Australia, where he contracted a disease and died a bachelor at the young age of thirty-three. His parents dedicated one of the new church bells to his memory, when the peal was increased from four to six.

The only daughter Hilda married John Petter, an architect. He formed a partnership with Percy Warren and is probably best known for the row of Nissen shaped houses known as Petren Houses set back from the A303 near Queen Camel. Hilda and John had two children.

The family tie with the Creamery continued into the next generation with Bill Marden (son of Bert) taking employment with Aplin and Barrett Ltd, which was eventually taken over by United Dairies. He then worked for the Milk Marketing Board, but resigned when he tired of commuting to Thames Ditton. His final position was with the Ilchester Cheese Company.

In their retirement Bill and his wife Muriel, a clergyman's daughter, played an active role in church and village life. He was Churchwarden for 5 years. There is a plaque in the church remembering that money raised at his funeral funded the gate to the gallery.

The Pitman Family

Paul Pitman was a farmer who lived at Vine Farm House in the centre of Marston Magna. He had a son named Sam who was born in 1890. Sam was sent away to Bristol as a lad to learn the butchering trade and returned to work with his father before his marriage to Lily Stretch. Lily was nine years older than her husband and it is thought that she had come down from her home in Cheshire to take up employment in service somewhere in the area.

Sam and Lily immediately started a family and had four children in quick succession. Their first child was born in 1913 when Lily was 32 years old. His name was Kenneth and he remained single, working with his father on the farm. He died in his sleep around the age of 42, which must have been quite a shock for one of his sisters who discovered him. Josie was the next, born a year later, and she too stayed at home with her father keeping house and helping out on the farm. Leslie was the middle child born in 1915 and probably quite an extrovert who enjoyed his visits to The Marston Inn. He married and moved out of the village to run a smallholding and a scrap metal business in Dorset. Dulcie came next, born in 1916. She remained in the village and was very close to her sister, but enjoyed a clerical career in insurance and later at the Yeatman Hospital. The fifth child, born after a gap of a couple of years, was Dennis, born in 1919 when his mother was 38. He was called for service in World War 2 and tragically died whilst travelling home on leave in 1945. A cow ran in front of his motor bike and caused the fatal accident. He was only 26 years old.

In 1923 when their eldest child was 10, Sam sold Vine Farm to Mr Ashworth Hope of Marston Court and bought Park Farm where Lily let rooms to augment the family income. It is believed they did not know that the intention was to demolish their old home in order to improve the outlook from Marston Court. It must have been a sad day for them. At Park Farm, Sam pursued his dairy and arable farming, but he also enjoyed a good trade with the pigs that he bred. Since he was also a master butcher, he was able to sell direct as well as supplying the local butchers. His granddaughter Suzanne remembers accompanying him on his deliveries. In addition he was a skilled cider maker and was noted for it over a wide area. Some Sunday mornings he probably entertained as many in his cellar as the village pubs put together!

Sam Pitman

Upon Sam Pitman's death in 1963, Dulcie and Josie remained at Park Farm and let out the land for grass keep. They were both very active in the village especially with events in support of the church and Josie helped with the Meals On Wheels service. When Josie died in 1982, Dulcie found it impossible to stay at Park Farm, so it was sold, together with the two cottages at the end of the farm drive that face the road into Sherborne. She moved to 5 Court Gardens, which stood on land that had previously been owned by the family.

Dulcie Pitman drove for Meals on Wheels in the village, and was apparently quite intrepid when it came to driving through floodwater. Eileen Newell remembers accompanying her!

Dulcie arranged for the remaining land known as Moat Field or Court Garden to be sold to the local authority with covenants that it would never be built on. She passed away in her 93rd year. There is a plaque in St Mary's church in memory of the sisters.

Personalities

Sallie Brown

Sallie Brown lived in Marston Magna for 35 years. She arrived here with her family in 1953, when her husband, Gilbert, was appointed manager of Martins Bank in Yeovil. They had three children, Claude, Liza and Cally.

Known as Sallie, Lalla, and Mrs. Brown, she was an excellent organiser. Sallie became a Churchwarden, an active member of the Women's Institute, organiser of the Fête, the Harvest Supper, and also the local Conservative party.

Her great love was St. Mary's Church, and for many years she and Henry Trim worked together as Churchwardens. Sallie organised the rotas for church cleaning, flowers and the washing of altar linen. She ran the Embroidery Group, and was responsible for organising the work resulting in the beautiful kneelers, which are used and admired in the church to this day.

Sallie's contribution to the Women's Institute included the production of their plays. She worked hard, and, according to Peter Clarke's tribute at her funeral:

> *...always obtained the best from her performers ......the results were such fun and a joy to watch.*

At election times, Sallie's home became the Conservative Party headquarters, and during the years in between she took on such tasks as organising functions and chairing meetings.

Sadly, Sallie's husband Gilbert died suddenly one Christmas Day, so she was a widow for eighteen years, continuing to live in the village for the rest of her life. The beautiful pewter cover for the font is a memorial to Gilbert, inscribed with his name and dates.

Her adored family gave her great comfort, and she was very proud of her grandchildren.

In Peter Clarke's tribute to Sallie, given on November 14th 1988 at her funeral in St Mary's Church and subsequently published in the Parish Magazine, he spoke of all these achievements, and of her lively, warm and caring personality:

Sallie was consistently.... doing what she felt needed to be done in her quiet and unassuming way...meticulous in her thought for others...always making sure everything was properly done.

To spend time in Sallie's company was tremendous fun, with that wit and irrepressible laugh, reducing us sometimes to tears.

Sallie Brown was very much missed in Marston Magna. The gallery screen in the church is a memorial to Sallie. Her name is inscribed in the woodwork of the screen, visible from the Lady Chapel.

Peter Clarke

Peter Clarke and his wife Ann came to Marston Magna in 1971 and settled in Kyle, which lies close by the church. They had a daughter Sarah who attended Queen Camel School where she flourished and gained her 11+ exam. There were no Grammar Schools in the vicinity and so she was given a place at Bruton School for Girls, fully paid for by the Local Education Authority, even including the transport.

Peter Clarke

Hubert De Jersey Hunt was the vicar and the Clarkes quickly found themselves a part of church life and the village community. Ann Clarke started a Sunday School which she organised in their own home.

During the 1970s the Anglican Church encouraged men to study for the ministry while they continued in their regular employment. Peter was Deputy Clerk to the local Magistrates, which took him over a wide area but he was based in Yeovil. He studied for the ministry for 2 years in his spare time and was ordained Deacon in 1976, appointed curate in his own parish and became a priest in 1977. He was the first non- stipendiary priest in the diocese covering the parishes of Marston Magna, Rimpton and Corton Denham.

Peter says that Marston Magna was the most perfect village community that he has ever lived in. During his 17 years residing and working here he is proud of the following achievements:

He served as Clerk and subsequently as Chairman of the Parish Council.

He was instrumental in organising the 6.30am - 2pm refreshment stop in the Village Hall for three or four years when the road was officially designated a "Holiday Route". The profit from this initiative purchased the playground equipment in the field next to the hall. The field was donated to the village by Farmer Wadman.

In the severe winters of 1976 and 1977 there were 18 foot high drifts making the roads impassable to vehicles. Peter walked or fought his way through to Queen Camel and obtained vital medication for villagers in need. He subsequently became responsible for a case of drugs for a few years, which was kept in the cupboard under his stairs, in anticipation of future inclement weather.

Along with the rest of the villagers, he took an enthusiastic part in the Queen's Silver Jubilee Celebration recreation of the popular TV Show "It's a Knockout". (See chapter on Social Life).

In 1976 Peter introduced the Marston Magna Monthly Magazine, possibly his most enduring legacy to the village, which he produced, edited and printed. The Magazine is still going strong!

Peter left the village in 1988 to take up the position of Rector at Tintinhull. This was close enough for him to remain constantly in touch with friends and parishioners in Marston. In the Parish magazine he wrote:

As Ann, Sarah and I prepare to leave, we do so with full hearts, for 17½ years in one place is a mighty long time, and for 12 of those years I have had the immense privilege of being your parish priest....and haven't we had the most wonderfully happy and gorgeous times here.

Henry Trim wrote this tribute:

This month saw the official announcement of the pending departure of The Revd. Peter Clarke, Ann and Sarah from Marston, as he has entered the Church as a full time minister and been appointed as Rector to the Benefice of Tintinhull, Thorne Coffin, Chilthorne Domer and Yeovil Marsh. Some members of the congregation did not realise that as a member of the Non Stipendiary Ministry, Peter will not be replaced, as in the case of a Rector or Vicar. Perhaps that is as well, as it would be well nigh impossible to find anyone with Peter's calibre! We must all be thankful for the bonus of his 17 years in Marston and close ranks to continue to keep our beautiful Parish Church of St. Mary's in the same healthy state as it is now.

Eventually, Peter and Ann retreated to West Camel in a delightful spot overlooking the church, to enjoy a well-earned retirement.

David Crabb

David Crabb

Samuel David Crabb was born in 1953 when his parents, Samuel Edward and Molly Leonora Crabb, were living at Broughton's Farm, Ilminster, which was farmed by David's grandfather Samuel Jeffrey Crabb. Within the family Samuel David was called David to avoid confusion with his father Samuel Edward, who was known as Sam. Two further children were born, Richard and Caroline, before the family moved in 1963 to Marston Magna, when they purchased Wickham Farm. David's father had successfully built up a herd of Friesian dairy cows, landrace pigs, poultry and turkeys. It took 2-3 days to get all the animal stock, farm equipment, household furniture and personal possessions moved to Wickham Farm and the boys were introduced to their new school at Queen Camel.

David won a place at Yeovil Grammar School, where he was fortunate to be sent on a twinning exchange in St Aubin sur Mer in Normandy. This eventually resulted in David attending school at Douvres la Deliverande for a short period and as the only English pupil it was learn French or sink!

David's early career was with Lloyds Bank. Whilst at his first branch in Wincanton he asked for and secured a loan to buy an MGB sports car. It was unusual in that the repayment terms depended upon David selling a heifer in two years time, which was a first for a member of Lloyds Bank staff! His career progressed, working variously in training, securities, as an inspector and finally manager at Lloyd's branch Berkeley Square, London.

Together with his second wife and two young daughters, the family had progressed out of London to Bath but in 1988 he called an end to the daily commute and resigned his position.

Alongside this impressive banking career he had a second "calling" with the Territorial Amy, having joined B Company of the 6th Battalion Light Infantry based in Yeovil in 1974. The Light Infantry had a 'home defence' role in the event of call up. He won the 'most promising recruit' award at the passing out ceremony. In 1976 he was asked if he could attend

Sandhurst for officer training but the Bank refused leave, which would have involved quite a considerable period of time. At the T.A. summer camp that year David was surprised to be named the fittest soldier in the regiment by the PT instructors. This was possibly because he would fly over assault courses, being used to climbing up ropes and swinging on them in the barn at Wickham Farm. He could also do huge numbers of press-ups and sit-ups! The following year he transferred from The Light Infantry to The Royal Army Ordnance Corp, based at Heston. Life in this unit was very different as it was aligned to NATO defence and in the event of call up, David would have been sent to Germany with the unit.

A life long asthma sufferer, David crashed his car in the course of an attack in 1989 at Lambrook between Queen Camel and Marston Magna. Luckily, the vehicle behind was carrying a Nursing Sister from Yeovil hospital. She cut the seat belt and kept him alive until an ambulance arrived. He was in a coma for a week but recovered well.

Having moved to the Insurance world, David also utilised his fluent French to undertake translation work for people wishing to buy holiday homes or move to France. With this experience under his belt, he progressed to work in Edinburgh managing luxury winter ski chalets.

Tragedy struck his family in the early days of January 1999. They were preparing to drive home from Scotland having celebrated Hogmanay, when his daughter Rowena collapsed and later died at Edinburgh Royal Infirmary. At the age of 15 she had died of heart arrhythmia, Sudden Death Syndrome, which kills 12 young people every week in this country. Rowena's picture has been used by CRY (Cardiac Risk in the Young) to push for better heart screening of young people. A heart arrhythmia can be detected by having an ECG, and tablets can stop a fatal attack.

David first became interested in politics when his brother Richard had a problem with American Express, where the amount had been altered up by 300%. Paddy Ashdown MP sorted it out for him and David was very impressed by his whole attitude. From 1997 David served as a Parish Councillor and a Somerset County Councillor. He also served on the Avon & Somerset Police Authority and was involved in the Glastonbury Festival policing. Despite all this, he remained interested and involved in life back in his home village of Marston Magna and in June 1994, together with his mother Molly, he took on the editorship and printing of the Parish Magazine. As we write in 2015, this amounts to 20 years of unbroken service, and the villagers appreciate their dedication.

Jim Nowell

Jim Nowell

Jim is the stepson of Doug Marden. He was born in Coventry on 31st March 1926, the second child of a Bank Manager and his wife Maisie. Jim was 6 months old when his father died in his 40s of pneumonia and septicaemia. Maisie, aged 21, was left with a baby and a toddler daughter. She went on holiday to Bournemouth with her friend Daisy and met Doug Marden who was holidaying at the same hotel. Four years later, in 1930, they were married and Maisie arrived in Marston to take up residence at Braggcroft, next door to Marston House where Mr E.D. Marden lived with Jennie his wife. Maisie was widowed for a second time in 1954, but remained in the village for the rest of her life, passing away in 1996 at the grand age of 91.

The two children, Jim and Averil, did not attend the village school but instead were educated in the early years by governesses. Miss Cox schooled them for a while and then they shared a teacher called Mrs Fraser with Jean Baillie of Rimpton. Their stepfather was quite a disciplinarian, although fair, and life became difficult for him as he suffered with depression from time to time. At the age of eight, Jim was packed off as a boarder to Prep. school at King's School Bruton, and Averil attended Sunny Hill Bruton. The Prep. school immediately presented Jim with a Latin textbook, which he not unnaturally found very intimidating, but by the time he had progressed to the senior school he was well adjusted to the life. The teaching staff had been reduced to old men during the course of the war, and Jim was co-opted to help with teaching in the Prep. School before commencing his training with the Air Force.

His mother and stepfather took part in the housing of evacuees, hosting 2 children from Hastings in the first wave and then later, when city bombing had stepped up, Agnes, a Catholic teenage girl arrived.

Jim was not suitable to train as a pilot due to poor eyesight and was offered the role of Radar Operator, which he happily accepted. He spent a year at the Radar Station on the Isle of Lewis and during the demobilization period he lived at Ringstead, travelling every day to Portland, where he was on guard duty at the Radar Station sited in a disused quarry. He would get regular calls from the local constabulary warning of prison break outs and took the precaution of keeping a pistol close by, although he had no ammunition for it.

After demob he underwent several years of agricultural training before settling down eventually to farm Easton Farm, which the family had retained when the Factory site was sold. In the fullness of time his farm employee Graham Norman became a partner and his son Richard followed in his footsteps.

Jim was a Parish Councillor for approximately 30 years and in those days the Parish Chairman was also automatically Chair of the Village Hall. He served on the Rural District Council from 1967-1973. He continued to serve as an Independent when the rural councils were reformed to Yeovil District Council, eventually losing his seat in 1987.

During those years of Public Service he stood firmly against street lighting, he co-operated in the Civil Defence Plan, even undertaking training courses on how to blow whistles and use Geiger counters, and more importantly how to deal with all the refugees that would be streaming out from urban areas. He was a team leader in the notorious "It's a Knockout" event and was the Club Leader of Sparkford Young Farmers for approximately 30 years.

The Camelot (Yeovil) Group of the Institute of Advanced Motorists formed in 1980 and Jim became Chairman in 1990, having passed the Advanced Driving qualification in 1986. He went on to serve for 25 years in that capacity until its amalgamation with another group in 2015.

Les Sayers - a portrait by Tony Birks-Hay

Les Sayers

The contribution made by Mr Les Sayers to the village during his lifetime was immense. He was born in 1919, living in one of the little cottages that fronted Rimpton Road next to the Mill entrance. These have long since been demolished. He left the village for his early farming jobs and returned in 1956 with a wife and a four-year-old daughter in tow.

Les was a true countryman and loved the village to which he had returned and also the countryside which surrounds it. He was an active churchgoer and in the fullness of time he was elected to the Parish Council. There is a plaque on the church wall at the entry to the graveyard commemorating the work that he gladly undertook in 1987/88, renovating the wall.

He was a motorbike enthusiast and displayed his bike and sidecar for all to enjoy at the Village Fete in 1979.

For many villagers his most precious contribution was recording the local footpaths for the pleasure of generations to come. The following extracts from the Parish Council Reports demonstrate the progress with this initiative:

August 1987. A major project of providing stiles and bridges to enable the footpaths of the parish to be used was put in hand by the former Parish Council and the work is now being carried out through a Man Power Services Commission Scheme with the Parish Council providing all the materials. Les Sayers is the liaison man for this work. It was subsequently reported that all footpaths abutting into a road had had marker posts installed. There would now be the task of putting further marker posts at various stages where the footpaths meandered through the parish.

By November 1987 forty stiles and eleven footbridges had been erected, paths had been drained and cleared, hardcore laid on two paths and signs erected.

In January 1988 Councillor Sayers handed over an anonymous donation of £25 to be used towards the cost of producing a footpath booklet for Marston Magna. In March of that year the Parish Council Chairman advised that preliminary discussions had taken place regarding the booklet on the footpaths. Mr. Sayers had already written out detailed descriptions with maps for nine walks around the village.

A fitting tribute to the esteem that Les inspired is the portrait painted by Tony Birk-Hayes, which his daughter Ann says is an excellent likeness, right down to his 'sleepy' eye. He died in 1997, shortly after the birth of his great-grandson.

Henry Trim

Henry or 'Our Henry', as he was known from his column in the Marston Magna Parish Magazine, was well loved and respected throughout the village and beyond. He was born in Mudford in 1916 during World War I. His father died two years later in France just before the end of the war, leaving his mother to bring up Henry on her own.

Henry Trim

They moved to Burnham-on-Sea where they kept a small sweet shop. Henry went to school in Burnham at first, and then he won a scholarship to Dr. Morgan's School in Bridgwater. Later on he went to Yeovil to work at Taylors, progressing to their accounts side, and lodged with his aunt in Queen Camel.

He was keen on sport, playing cricket for Queen Camel and football for Sparkford. One day he went home with Ralph Bartlett to hear a cup final match on the wireless, and met Ralph's sister Grace. He was 19 at the time and Grace was 14. Three years later, in 1939, they were married at St. Mary's church in Marston Magna and were a devoted couple for sixty years, bringing up three children, Ann, who sadly died at the age of 20, and Maureen and David. Later on the grandchildren came along and also gave them great joy!

In 1939 Henry was in the Territorial Army and, as he explained in the Parish magazine many years later, he "suffered the rigours of a T.A. camp at Corfe Castle in July" where they were up to their knees in mud. They subsequently "cast aside their rusty mess tins and mud-stained puttees" only to find themselves called up for war service a few weeks later. He joined 'A' Company, 4th Battalion The Dorset Regiment T.A. and five other lads from the village joined up too. Henry was slightly wounded in the second wave of the D-Day invasion but recovered and was transferred to the Pay Corps.

After the war he was a leading light in the Marstonaires, a variety group made up of young villagers who put on lively concerts during the 1940s and 50s. He also 'trod the boards' later on in the 1970s, when all the village organisations provided a turn at concerts which seemed to include most of the villagers, either taking part or in the audience.

Henry was a village stalwart. As in his working life he was an accountant, this led to him being Treasurer to several organisations in the village including the Church, the Village Hall, the Royal British Legion and the Whist Club where, as recorded in the November 1976 edition of the Parish magazine, it was estimated that "Resident M.C. Henry Trim" had officiated at over 1500 whist drives in Marston! He was also Churchwarden for over 40 years. He hosted many other events, including the village celebration for the Queen's Silver Jubilee in 1977 where he kept score in the "It's a Knock Out" competition. He was a caller at Bingo, and a very popular Auctioneer at the Harvest Suppers, where he managed to persuade many people to pay extraordinary prices for half a dozen eggs or a handful of vegetables. He was also once brave enough to umpire a ladies hockey match between Marston and Queen Camel!

Grace was also involved in many village events. She was a flower arranger, W.I. member, Mothers' Union and a staunch member of the Royal British Legion. As Revd. Peter Clarke said in his address at Grace's funeral, Henry and Grace lived for each other and "made a wonderful double act in the village, even earning the title of Mayor and Mayoress".

In 1976 when the Parish Magazine was first produced by the Revd. Peter Clarke, Henry was asked to contribute his regular column, which was always thoughtful, fun, informative and very popular. In the summer of 1979, there was a very important day when Henry and Grace went to a Palace Garden Party. He described in his column how they "entered the Palace through the main gates, crossed the inner courtyard, up the grand steps to a great hall with very fine oil paintings and rather rude statues!" (See Chapter on Social Life).

Henry's sense of humour and fun were well known. When confined to hospital for some weeks after an accident in 1981, his magazine column contained his plans for an escape tunnel! While assuring readers that he was being wonderfully looked after there, he deplored the 'reducing' diet he was put on, saying that there was "no pastry, no potatoes- not a Desirée in sight!"

He was a great character in the village, kind, thoughtful and willing to give help to anyone who asked. He was a friend to all and was sadly missed when he died in 1999.

Walter Raymond

In Yeovil Library there is a plaque to Walter Raymond (1852-1931):

"*His love and understanding of Somerset and her country-folk live in his books.*"

Walter Raymond worked in the Yeovil gloving industry before pursuing a writing career. Some of his early life was spent in our village. He lived at Marston Magna schoolhouse with his aunt and his grandmother, following the death of his mother from typhoid.

"Underneath The Spreading Chestnut Tree" A Volume of Rural Lore and Anecdote by Walter Raymond was published in 1928. The chapter entitled "Early Reminiscence" is based on his childhood years and indicates that his early love of the countryside stems from those childhood years spent in Marston Magna in the 1850s.

Evelyn V. Clark's tribute to him states:

> *If the love of the countryside can be transmitted, it is certain that Raymond's passion for his native county was inherited from men and women whose very existence depended upon the soil, and whose interests were centred upon work connected with the farm and rural homesteads.*

This connection to the land seems to be the very essence of the village of Marston Magna at the beginning of the 20th century.

A Century of Childhood

A childhood in Marston Magna 1905-1922

(Taken from the memoirs of John Peppin)

I was born in my parent's second flat in Clifton and I think my arrival must have provided an incentive to my father to find better paid work than Precentor at the Cathedral. No doubt he consulted his Bishop and in due time was offered the living at Marston Magna, a modest living, worth about £275 per annum.

My parents came to see the parish and the house sometime in the winter of 1904/05 and my mother was appalled at the prospect. This was hardly surprising. The roads were not tar macadamised and were rutty and muddy. She spent a long time brushing the mud off her skirt. There was no street lighting. The church was undistinguished, though my father was quick to point out that it had examples of every period of English building from Saxon to Victorian incorporated in it. The worst horror was the Rectory, a long rambling house (said originally to have been a tithe barn, but I doubt it) facing east and west with only two small windows looking out on the south side. My own belief is that the south end was added at a later date to the rest of the house, which may

* *Photo: John Peppin as a boy*

well have been late Tudor. The older part was in a deplorable condition. The floors were riddled with dry rot. On one occasion when there was a choir supper and the dining room table had been extended to its full length and laden with viands, the floor gave way where one table leg stood. The northern most ground floor room was considered too risky for normal use and was used for prams and bicycles. The kitchen had an ancient black stove which was supposed to heat the bath water above as well as cook meals. It did neither with efficiency. There was a large crack across the back of the oven from which most of the heat from the coal fire escaped. Water came from a well in the garden and had to be pumped up daily.

Cook's Timetable

	Monday	Tuesday	Wednesday	Thursday	Friday	Saturday
7.	Kitchen & Dining Room sweep through Hall &c.					
8.30	Your Breakfast					
9.10	Dining Room Breakfast					
9.30	Help make beds.					
9.45	Clear breakfast & wash up.					
10.30	Help with washing	Study	Hall & anything that wants doing.	Own room Attic stairs alternately with larder & back premises	Mistress's Bedroom	Hall, Pantry Kitchen Stairs
1.30	Dinner					
3.30	Be dressed & ready to answer the door					
5	Dining room tea & wash up					
6.30	Missie's bread & milk					
		Night out	Clean tins etc.		Clean Kitchen utensils if any	
8.30	Supper					

Cook's timetable drawn up by Mrs. Peppin

It is necessary to point out that a stipend of £275, a steadily increasing family, two maids, gardener and boot-boy precluded the purchase of expensive replacements or improvements. My father was in debt to his bankers from as early as I can remember such things, and only moved into credit in the last year of his life after he had inherited the bulk of his elder brother's estate about seven years after he had left Marston Magna.

So far, I have tried to look at the Rectory from my parents' point of view. From the children's point of view it was an earthly paradise. We had no worries about the floor, or the draughts, or the household problems. We just enjoyed the space, the garden, the trees and the birds. The house itself was tremendous fun. There was a long attic running from the north end to where the later building started. It was approached by a rickety staircase leading from the maids' bedrooms. When you got there you were greeted by a mixture of smells made up from decaying leather trunks and decaying fruit - mostly apples. The floors creaked and one end was considered unsafe. We were warned off, in case we fell through to the first floor. One of the delights of this eerie place was the water-tank, refilled daily from the well. There was a long brass chain attached to this tank, which activated a plug. The chain went through a hole in the floor, which at that point was the ceiling of our one and only indoor loo. It ended at a convenient height in the loo and its great merit over modern flushing systems was that one could use exactly the right amount of water for flushing purposes - neither less nor more. This was a valuable asset, when all water had to be pumped up by hand. However, it also created a hazard and a temptation to the young. One had only to sneak up to the attic when the "throne" was known to be occupied, pull the tank end of the chain to loose a flood of water onto the seat of the victim.

A feature of the garden has disappeared. A curious multisided single floor building containing three small rooms. One was a two-seater loo for the use of the maids, another was a single seater for the gardener and the third (and largest) was a potting shed and tool house for the latter. The closets had no amenities and were periodically emptied by the village factotum at the dead of night. It never occurred to me that there was anything peculiar in the different arrangements for the maids and ourselves. There was no mains drainage for the house. A cesspit was situated at the rear of the house outside the dining room window. Here the grass was soggy and mostly moss but if it ever smelt, I did not notice it.

My mother had to swallow her dislike of the look of this ramshackle homestead and my parents moved to Marston in about March 1905 at which time I was eight months old. My first clear memory (I must have been two or three) is of an accident while having a seesaw with Tom, which nearly resulted in my becoming a eunuch. I remember the look of horror on my parents' faces when they saw what had happened. To get a doctor, they had to send a telegram to Yeovil and I remember the discussion that went on as to how to word it. I think they settled for 'between the legs'. It must have been quite a problem as the telegram had to go through the local postmistress, who was as gossipy as the rest of the village. After a few hours, the doctor came, sewed me up and all was well.

We had a large house and a large garden. Outside our back gate there were several disgraceful hovels, in one of which lived a boy named George Greatwood. I used to play with George, who had nothing. My parents found out and contact with him was forbidden. In our class-ridden society, there was scarcely any other child in the village with whom we were allowed to associate. The Court was inhabited by a Mr Gould, a bachelor and his sister. They were rich but colourless. He had one complaint against society, which he used to repeat in a monotone: "I'm an Eton man and a Cambridge man, but nobody cares for me". No children there, of course. In our early days, the Manor, across the Green, had not been restored and was occupied by the gardener to the Court. There were children there (one of whom ended up a Bishop), but could hardly be classed as 'gentry' and I do not recollect ever going there to play. Apart from these two houses, all others were thought to be working class - labourers is perhaps a better word - though there was 'Marston House' where lived the Mardens. Actually, the Mardens, in a sort of middle stratum between gentry and labourers, were very important members of the village populace. The old boy, E.D.Marden had started the cider factory and was a big employer, but they were of course in commerce and anyway, their considerable family was all grown up.

With whom could the rectory children associate? Although there was a back entry into the village school from our garden, we were never allowed to use it. What about neighbouring parishes? Rimpton had a bachelor vicar known as 'Longshanks Taylor'. He was so tall; he had a bicycle with two crossbars. He was also known for his inability to control his wind. Oddly enough he had a pony similarly afflicted. He once took us for a short ride in his pony-trap and his pony farted at every step, all the way from Marston to Rimpton. We were reduced to hysterics. He, being devoid of humour, pretended not to notice.

Queen Camel had a Rector and two daughters, a good deal older than we were.

There remained Mr French at West Camel. His kids were roughly of our age and we met occasionally for parties and later for tennis, but there was no regular friendship between the two families.

Having disposed of the so-called 'gentry' of the neighbourhood, I turn with pleasure to the ordinary folk, with whom I always felt much more in sympathy. Apart from the maids, who were usually local girls earning their keep at £1 per month, I suppose my first contact was the gardener whom we inherited from the previous rector. Mr. Miller always seemed to me to be at least eighty. He used to hobble through our gate, smoking a broken clay pipe about one inch from his nose. If the weather were damp, the pipe would be upside down. He had a grizzly grey beard and white hair and he took a depressed view of life in general.

The following conversation was quite common: "Good morning, Mr. Miller. Is it going to rain?" Mr.Miller: "Yar". "Are you sure?" Mr.Miller: "my veats do tell I". I think he secretly hoped it would rain, for indeed, he was already past heavy work.

Later, he gave up and was succeeded by Mr. Foote, who was one of the best characters in the village. I could never quite make out how he managed to make a living. His life seemed to be made up of odd jobs. Basically, he delivered coal from the truckloads that arrived at the station to clients in the villages around. For this work he had a cart and a horse called 'Colonel', a sturdy brown beast of enormous patience and strength. But Mr Foote was also the sexton, bell-ringer, gravedigger, bass singer in the choir and general factotum. It was he who would come with the cart and Colonel, stealthily, by night and empty the maids' earth closets and occasionally our cesspit. His moments of greatest triumph occurred when the village brook overflowed its banks and flooded the road and also (we children hoped) the rectory garden. The depth of water in the road was sometimes deceptive and the few motorists who came that way would think it worthwhile to take a chance. Before they had gone ten yards the car would stop in two feet of water and the motorist would be hopelessly stranded. Delight in the Rectory garden! Where is Mr Foote? Well, he might be delivering coal in Sandford Orcas, working in someone's garden, improbably digging a grave or just sitting at home. Anyway, exciting news like a stranded car always spread through the village in no time and usually Mr Foote could be tracked down fairly quickly. Out would come 'Colonel', cart less, but with all necessary harness attached and led by Mr Foote carrying a length of stout rope. They would come sploshing through the water to cheers from the rectory garden and haul the vehicle to dry land around the corner towards Queen Camel.

My brother Phil arrived, unannounced in May 1907, when I was nearing 3 years old. I have no recollection of his coming. I think my mother, who had always wanted girls, must have been a little disappointed at having a third son, it was bad enough when I turned out to be a boy. I do remember, rather vaguely, the arrival in 1910 or 1911 of yet another boy. I was sent away to stay with the aunts and granny at Glastonbury - no reason being given for my departure. Then suddenly one day, an aunt announced that I had another brother. He was called George after the new king and according to my mother he was the most beautiful boy of the lot. Unfortunately he had some sort of tummy trouble and by the time I arrived home from Glastonbury he was dead and buried. He was put in a tiny grave just adjoining the North Porch and no stone was erected. I never knew why. There used to be a thing against burying anyone on the sunless north side of a churchyard, which I think was reserved for the unbaptised. I have wondered, though I do not know, whether George died before my father had had a chance to baptise him.

Undaunted, my parents tried again and in 1912 my mother was again pregnant. Our doctor lived at Yeovil, 5 miles away and the extent of mother's pre-natal care was that my father measured her tummy monthly and sent the results by post to the doctor. Consequently when, on 30th December, Mary was safely delivered, the midwife announced, "There's another one". Twenty minutes later Geraldine arrived and you may guess there was some hasty work to be done.

Geraldine was put into a bottom drawer, which someone remarked looked very like a coffin. Both infants weighed somewhat under 4 lbs and for some time their futures were uncertain and my mother was also ill for several weeks.

There were wars going on in the Balkans when I first went to school. I followed brother Tom to King's School Bruton in about 1912 at the age of eight. Until then I had been taught in a rather desultory manner by my parents. My father taught us to read and write. It was an advantage to follow an elder brother at this very minor public school.

King's School Bruton had for headmaster a rather formidable personality named D.E.Norton and his sister used to do quite a lot of teaching. Sometimes she took us for walks and we used to walk behind her giggling at the way her bottom wiggled. There was a French master named Galadaveze and it must have been about 1912 when he came prancing into our class in a state of high excitement. He had just heard that a young Frenchman named Carpentier had knocked out a British champion named Bombardier Billy Wells in the first round of a heavyweight fight.

(The following story does not appear in John Peppin's memoir but was recounted to his children)

Tom (John's older brother) absolutely hated blancmange and one day it was served up at school lunch. At the end of the meal the other boys filed out leaving Tom sitting in front of his uneaten pudding with a senior boy who was supposed to make sure that it was consumed. Once everyone had gone this boy lifted up a loose floorboard revealing 'The Glory Hole' and into this went the blancmange!

There used to be an annual outing to Alfred's Tower - a prominent landmark on the Somerset/Wiltshire border, not far from Stourhead, which at that time was not open to the public. We used to go in a horse-drawn carriage called a 'brake', in which the passengers sat facing sideways.

From the time of the birth of the twins, my father gave up his Sunday night whisky and bought a barrel of beer, which in those days cost about one penny a glass. No doubt it was about then (1913) that he began to think how he proposed to educate his five offspring. Feeding them, in early days, was no great problem, since much of our food came from our large garden. Tom presumably tried for Christ's Hospital at about that time and in 1915 I found myself there as well. (John Peppin had a miserable time at this school and was always longing to return to his beloved Marston Magna home. His daughter recalls her father explaining that he was forced to wear his school uniform in the school holidays, as there was no money for other clothes. The uniform of the 'Bluecoat School' was a modified version of the 16th century uniform; a long navy coat with brass buttons, knee breeches and yellow stockings. The Marston village boys would chant, "You've dipped your legs in the mustard pot"). There were small fees to be met for these clergy assisted places and they were undertaken by an uncle.

We usually went for family holidays to Weymouth. I think we always went into cheap rooms overlooking the harbour. We brought all our vegetables from the garden in a hamper and gave them to our landlady who cooked for us. Later on when there were two small twin girls to come with us, my father, Tom and I cycled the 30 miles or so, while my mother travelled by train with the girls and the luggage.

I left Christ's Hospital and came home near my 17th birthday in 1921. With Dad having so many financial commitments involving the other children it was up to me to find employment as soon as possible. I paid for not working at school and leaving early. No one ever suggested that if I worked I might get to a University and then life would open up before me. Eventually I learnt that I had been accepted as a junior clerk in The National Provincial and Union Bank of England Ltd.

I spent the end of the summer of 1921 (glorious sunshine) and the autumn and Christmas of that year at home in Marston giving my young sisters some lessons. I enjoyed it and looking back I think I might have been a schoolmaster. I left to take up my duties at the Rugby branch of the bank on January 2nd 1922.

Early in their lives my sisters began to show exceptional musical abilities. It became evident from 3-4 onwards that both of them had perfect pitch. This was first demonstrated when one of them kicked the metal potty under their bed and immediately announced what note it was. A check at the piano confirmed the accuracy.

There was insufficient money to send them to a fee paying school and of course it was impossible to send them to the village school so they were taught at home with a shared tutor. Their musical talent was progressed firstly by their mother and then by their Uncle Arthur who taught music at Clifton School. They were very famous within the village and would give concerts playing together on one piano or two. They left the village at the age of 11 and moved with their parents to Henstridge and gave their first recital in Sherborne Abbey at about the age of 13. They left for London at the very young age of 15 to further their musical careers.

They never went to Music college but studied privately with Mabel Lander who also taught the young princesses Elizabeth and Margaret. They went on in the 1960s to teach for many years at the Guildhall School of Music and Drama in London where they were made Honorary Fellows despite their lack of a formal diploma. They appeared at The Proms and also performed on the BBC Radio 2 "Friday Night is Music Night".

(On 25th April 1987 a service of Thanksgiving and interment of ashes was held at St Mary's Church of Gerard Sydenham John Peppin, son of former Rector. His ashes are buried in Marston churchyard and commemorated by a small stone).

Down the Lane

A childhood memory from Mrs. M.I. Davis at the turn of the century.

We had been back at school for four or five weeks. There wasn't much time for play outside after we had tea. I remember asking my Mother the meaning of the word "equinox" and she told me it meant "equal day and night" and explained exactly what it was and how it happened. I still think of her when March and September come round, but although the time of sunrise and sunset are different now we have this new-fangled Summer Time the days and night are still twelve hours each. However, the darkening evenings drew our thoughts forward to Christmas – always a beckoning light although a long way off.

The lane, except for late and overlooked apples in Mr. Salmon's orchard, was losing some of its interest and was slowly becoming damp and overgrown, and full of slight disappointments when we saw the many birds' nests we had not found earlier in the Spring. There were a few flowers in shady places – buttercups or robin-hoods - but all we could find to take home (for we never returned empty-handed) was a bundle of sticks to help light the kitchen range in the morning. Put on the top overnight they would be dry by the time they were needed next day.

So we were obliged to play in the yard, among the stacks of tiles, bricks, slates and drainpipes of all sizes for an hour or so, till it became too dark to bowl hoops or spin tops or play marbles. There were no lights but we were perfectly safe for there was no traffic in the yard after half past five.

By the end of the month there was no play out-of-doors and the movement up and down the lane might be an odd cart or so going to fetch a pig or a heifer, or Mr. Higdon in his high two-wheeled trap collecting a truss of hay from his field at the end of our garden. His old once-black coat was a sort of murky myrtle green, and his hard wide-brimmed hat matched it. It was said that he bought the Western Gazette every week and used it for a tablecloth for the following seven days. We never spoke to him nor he to us.

Being the eldest I was the last to go to bed and any spare time I had was spent in knitting or sewing – long black stockings, white woollen vests and cream flannel petticoats, these last being done in herring-bone stitch with perhaps a little feather stitching on the hem for decoration.

We made most of our Christmas gifts during these evenings. We had no regular "pocket money" and depended for ready cash on uncles and aunts so we ransacked the ragbag and the bead-box from under the stairs to find suitable material to make needle-books, pin cushions, bookmarkers or hair bands to give our friends and relations...these were always accepted gratefully. Does any little girl now know how to do french knitting on a cotton reel I wonder? It will make a nice mat to prevent marking a polished table.

NOW AND THEN

Extracts from the Memories of

L.H.SAYERS 1925-1938

My name is Leslie Sayers and I was born in Marston Magna in 1919 and had one brother and two sisters. My brother, mother and father are buried in Marston Churchyard.

Until I was eight I lived in the middle of three old tumbledown cottages that stood by the stream in front of the Mill. They have been demolished now but there are still signs if you look carefully. The living conditions were not good. The water tap was outside and also the toilets, which boasted a long bench seat with different sizes. Cooking was done on an old black range with the oven on the side with a hook up the chimney for a kettle and for smoking bacon. There were two bedrooms and we had a paraffin lamp and candle to go to bed. When we had floods in winter, water would spread from Station Bridge to Park Bridge and we would watch the water come up two treads of the staircase. We moved everything upstairs. In front of the house was a drinking place for cows and horses, as you must remember that when cows went to market a drover drove them on the roads.

The things I really miss are walks across the fields. Now there is not even a rabbit, mouse or mole and the birds do not sing so much as there are so few. The wild flowers are going fast, also hedges, lanes and footpaths that were so nice.

As a young boy I would often sit upon the church wall listening to the bells of St Mary's ringing out over Marston - that was well over half a century ago. Today I still sit there (thanks to God) but how times have changed! In 1925 I was just six years old and I remember if you go up Station Road (now known as Rimpton Road) to the top of the Railway Bridge, turn right and then carry on down to Netherton House, this was a coal merchants. The coal used to be delivered by horse and cart. Then continue on down Netherton Lane to the bridge over the stream. It is an old bridge we call Cradle Bridge. Follow the imprint of the lane, which will bring you out over the railway on the Sherborne Road to the bottom of Park Bridge.

One of our nice walks was straight to the top of Garston Lane and keep straight on. Here there was a nice stile, where many pretty girls were stopped. Across the kissing gate and out onto the Sherborne Road, which takes you to Adber where we would get our hair cut, and shoes repaired at the same time. Footpaths were a must in those days. Men would walk miles to work and these were all the short cuts.

Studleys Farm House in Rimpton Road had a lovely old thatched barn, which is gone now. The barn comprised a cart shed, a stall for cows, and a large store for hay, cake, swede, mangolds and pigsty. This is where I first started work before and after school aged 9 and not forgetting Saturdays. It is where I learned to milk my first cow. The farmer's daughter was about my own age and was a pretty little girl with ringlets. We would have some fun when I finished work. On Saturday I would have to clean the knives and forks, clean out the fowls and that little girl would lock me in, if I forgot to put the key in my pocket. Milking in the summer was in the fields. We would load the milk float up with churns, buckets and stools. The farmer nearly always took his gun for a rabbit or a pheasant. It was hard milking before school and after. It meant I had to go to Thorney Lane at half past six in the morning.

Camel Street was not very wide then as from the footpath to Little Marston (now beside the Telephone Exchange) and up as far as Woollen Lane there were no houses and the last house in the village was Lambrook Cottage. The road ran right past the front door and you can see how wide it was by the width of the bridge outside the house.

At the stream by St. Mary's Church the steam engine would stop and fill with water and also the carter would stop to give the horses a drink and their nosebag dinner of oats and hay. On Sunday I was a choirboy in church. It was a large choir including tenors and basses. Friday night was choir practice, Sunday morning the service and Sunday School in the afternoon then the evening service. One Sunday I played truant. I went out and cut a stick in the hedge and cut my hand. I went home and Mum said "Why are you not at church?" and would not tie it up until church came out. I did not play truant again. At Christmas time Percy Rainey and others would go around playing the hand bells and the choir would go around the village as well. In those days we would share the money collected. As choirboys we would also have to pump the organ (no electricity). The sexton would toll the bell if anyone died in the village. The grass was cut by scythe and all the paths were gravelled. The church was very pretty in winter with its hanging oil lamps and the big candles at the altar and the coconut matting up through the centre of the church.

Many of the old buildings in the village, particularly farmhouses, were built of Camel Hill stone extracted from quarries south of Somerton. I spent a lot of my early days at a local dairy farm and slaughterhouse. My Mum did some housework there and I played with the farmer's son. We would get up to a lot of mischief. We would watch the cows being killed with the poleaxe. We would watch from the loft looking down through cracks in the floorboards.

Another farm made cider and as boys we would help ourselves. The men had a cow's horn, which they drank from and when they hid it we would take the big bung out of the barrel, and put a straw down. We would drink too much and get drunk - very naughty boys.

The moat field always held plenty of water and we made some lovely slides on the ice in winter. The big pond on one corner is now filled in. Along Garston Lane is Marston Court, a big employer in the village, servants, gardeners, grooms and a chauffeur. A little further along is the engine house that drove the electricity for Marston Court and two cottages, one for the head gardener and one for the head groom.

There was a field called Homelea on the left as you enter Little Marston Road and in the summer there would be a big marquee to teach the gospel and I still remember singing "I am H.A.P.P.Y." Mr and Mrs Penn and Mr & Mrs Bartlett lived there later on. On the right hand side past two farm cottages and the farmhouse of Mr & Mrs Ralph was a field given over to allotments for the village and most villagers grew their own vegetables. The right hand corner of this field was a sheep dip.

As you walk from Garage Corner, the first house on the right is the Post Office and smallholding and on the left an orchard. On the right are almshouses founded by charity for poor (usually elderly) people run by the village. There are three houses facing the road and their gardens were in front with a pump in the middle and a lovely old ham stone trough.

What a sight the blacksmith shop was - so dark, with horseshoes hanging on the wall, a wheel or two brought in by the carpenter to have the iron bonds put on the wheels, a horse waiting to have his new shoes on. I can see Mr. Newberry now pumping the big bellows to blow the fire up and the smell was really nice when the red hot shoe was put on the horse's foot just to burn it to shape, and the ring of the hammer on the anvil, to shape the shoe. Heading towards Yeovil from the forge the next on the left was a horse's only access to the stables of Marston Court and then the main drive.

My Mum did some housework for the Marston Inn. It is a real old country pub with farmers going in with guns over shoulders maybe a couple of rabbits and a pheasant and of course a dog. There was a pond and there were always ducks in the road and chickens running around the yard. A horse drawn caravan always stood in the yard and Mr Bugby had a carpenter's shop in the outbuildings.

Every year we would have a large fair in the field opposite the Marston Inn, all driven by steam. In the same field is the footpath to Portway Farm.

The children had to make their own games when I was young. We would spin tops, which we hit with a piece of string on a stick and we would flick with cigarette cards, which the landlord of the pub would put back for us. In the right season we would do bird nesting. When I was ten we had real guns, single-barrel shotguns and we would shoot rabbits, pheasants, partridge, pigeons and wild duck. Once when I was out with my gun after some wild duck up by the stream I shot some tame ducks by mistake. I took them home but I could not fool Mum. We would catch moles for their skins, which would be nailed on a board to dry. We would save rabbit skins to sell, not forgetting the fox, as gins and snares were used to catch wild animals. We would take moorhens eggs for eating. To get their eggs we would have a long stick and tie a large tablespoon on the end. The next thing to do was to see if the eggs were all right - if you put them in water and they sank you could eat them. If they floated we would put them back as we would always leave one or two in the nest and she would come back and lay some more. The moorhen in season would make a nice dish and you would find plenty, as there was a pond in every field.

We would also do bird baiting for blackbird pie. You get two long sticks about 6 feet long and put a 6ft x 2ft net on them. You need four boys and a candle lantern with three sides blacked out. Get a nice dark night and a good thick hedge. Two boys hold the net, one on each pole, one boy with the lantern on a stick to hold shining on the net, and the fourth boy on the other side of the hedge. He hits the hedge and the birds make for the light and fly into the net. We would also shoot rooks in season and ferret for rabbits to make pies or stews and we would fish for eels, stone roach and stickleback in the millpond.

There have been enormous changes in village life from 1919 to 1985 and I think my life as a boy was so much nicer than a boy today.

Life in Marston

Memories from Nigel Penn 1948-1960

I was born at home in Marston Magna in 1942, right in the middle of the war. My mother was from Switzerland. She had come to England to work in service for a wealthy family, and shortly afterwards she met my father who worked as a gardener at that time. They were married in St John's Church, Yeovil (where I was also married) in 1936 and lived initially in Rimpton at 5 Daisyfield.

My father was away in the army when I was born. In those days, the first child was born at the nearest nursing home, but as I was the younger of two, I was born at home. The District Nurse looked after my mother. I am told that my brother Tony, who is four years older than me, on hearing from another child in the village that their mother was expecting a baby, told him to "make sure you get one from the Nurse at South Cadbury, they are good ones".

The district nurse used to visit regularly, and came on an upright bicycle with a basket on the front. I particularly remember that she delivered concentrated orange juice, which we thought was wonderful. My earliest recollections are from after the war, when food was rationed. We had a ration book with weekly coupons in it that we had to produce in order to be able to buy restricted items of food and drink (which were most things). Although it sounds very harsh, we never went short of food, and we enjoyed everything.

There was a sweet shop in the village at that time. It was in one of the small cottages along Church Walk and was run by Mrs Willshire. We used to go there every week and buy our ration of sweets (normally a very small bag of fruit drops or something similar). The shop could be reached either from Church Walk at the back or via a small footbridge over the stream (or the brook as we called it). Mrs Willshire's husband often used to sit outside the shop (which was also their house) chewing tobacco, and he would spit a steam of tobacco juice onto the garden.

Our house was number 1 Townsend, the first of the Council houses along the Little Marston Road. Our father worked as a Chauffeur/Gardener for Mr Gerald Urwick who lived at Ashe House. He was a local businessman who had a glove factory in Yeovil. My parents managed then to get a council house in Marston, which was easier for my dad to get to work. Mr Urwick was a kind man and my dad enjoyed working for him. They became good friends, albeit always respecting their different situations in life. My dad particularly enjoyed going on shooting trips when he would form part of the team of beaters for the "guns". Afterwards there were always a few drinks together. Later, my brother Tony was allowed to join in as a beater, but I was deemed too young. I remember being quite disappointed.

At one stage Gerald Urwick bought a new car (I think it was a Rolls convertible) and he took us as a special treat to the point-to-point races at Babcary. I was very taken with the car, and commented to my Parents "Mr Urwick must have come up on the pools".

Quite a few "characters" lived in the Council Houses. The local coal merchant Charlie Rainey was one. He had his depot just over the Railway Bridge from the station, and had a couple of old trucks to haul the coal around. Apparently, during the war, he used to listen to the broadcast of Lord Haw Haw, and was the prophet of doom about the outcome of the war. Consequently, he was known (behind his back) as "Hitler".

As dad was a gardener by training, and food was always needed, almost our entire garden was given over to growing vegetables. We also kept a few chickens.

Later we also had an allotment at the back of the council houses and both Tony and I helped to dig it. I still have the spade I used. In those days, everyone had a large vegetable garden, and there was a certain amount of competition between families to produce the best crops. It was always done on a very friendly basis, and everyone gave each other some of the surplus crops when they all became ripe at the same time.

We also stored as much produce as possible, bearing in mind that at that time we did not have a fridge or freezer, only a cold larder. Runner beans were kept in salt in an earthenware jar, and eggs were preserved in isinglass, as very few were available during the winter months.

I remember in particular Tom Dole (Winnie Dole's husband) whose garden was always immaculate. Our neighbour opposite, Tom March, was an old Boer War veteran and he used to wear an old Boer War hat when gardening. It annoyed my father that Tom would dig his garden with a pitchfork (rather than double digging etc. with a proper spade, as one should) yet managed to produce magnificent crops. I think the main reason was that he had a regular supply of chicken manure.

Next to our house was an apple orchard (the nearest tree was a russet) and it belonged to a small farm in what is now Laurel Cottage. We used to buy our milk there every day. The milk was cooled but not pasteurised, but it didn't do us any harm. I collected it in a small milk can. The farm also had a small shop and I was often sent there to buy tobacco for my dad.

Life in Marston was wonderful for young children. There were very few cars on the road, so we were able to wander about the village quite freely. There were quite a few children of our age group, and we played together a lot. There was no formal sports ground, so we did our sport where we could. The most popular venues were Court Garden, and the field next to Wickham farm (which was flatter). For football matches, the goal posts were a couple of coats thrown down on the ground, and impromptu teams of about 5 or 6 a side were made up.

From time to time, a football match took place between Marston and West Camel. I remember that the West Camel captain was Graham Wreford, the baker's son. One particular match was played in the field opposite our house. I was too young to play, but I was a keen spectator. I had a whistle at the time and I remember blowing it during the match. All the players stopped, and asked who had blown the whistle. I had to own up and was told off!

For cricket, it was a little more complicated. Ron Batson was about the only one of our group who owned a cricket set, so we needed him around to have a proper game. I recall that from time to time there was some discussion as to whether Ron was out or not (usually an LBW decision) and some times he would threaten to go home and take his cricket set with him. He was usually given the benefit of the doubt.

As there was no team in Marston at that time, some people went to play cricket for Queen Camel. Tony played regularly with Bill White (a fast left arm bowler) and Henry Trim (an aggressive left-hand batsman). Tony was a good all rounder and played regularly. I played a few games but was too young at the time to get into the team.

We did have old bicycles, which in those days were as much a necessity to get around as a leisure object. Just beyond the Station on the site of the old ammunition dump (where the agricultural machinery depot is now), there was an old water reservoir formed like a concrete funnel set into the ground. It had water in the bottom, and sloping sides of about 45 degrees. Tony and some of the other boys used to ride around it, calling it the "wall of death". I think that one or two did fall in, and I was too scared to do it.

In summer, when there were long light evenings, we sometimes played "fox and hounds". We would delineate the boundaries of the village for the purposes of the game, and one person (the fox) was given a head start to go and hide somewhere in the village. The others then went off to find him. It may seem unlikely, but the fox was usually caught, and in doing so, we must have run for miles. We loved it.

During the 1940s and early 1950s the village school was still running. There was one teacher (initially Mrs Standing) and the school room was split into two by folding doors, with the infants in one side and the juniors in the other, all taught by the one teacher. Mrs Standing later retired and was replaced by Mrs Woodier who came from Yeovil on her bicycle.

The school was very cold in winter, and was only heated by a cast iron coke heater. One of the older children was charged with keeping this filled during the day. Our desks were equipped with a ceramic inkwell that slotted into a hole in the desk. One of the pupils was appointed as "ink monitor" and would have to mix up a jug of ink powder and water, which was then used to top up the inkwells every day. We also had school dinners delivered. The meals were pre-cooked and delivered in containers like milk churns. All the food was grey and it was difficult to know what we were eating. I remember once being offered what I thought was mashed potato and I asked for "plenty please" only to discover, when I sat down, that it was in fact mashed swede which I detested. I was made to stay in during the whole playtime to stir this food around the plate (I just couldn't eat it). I was more careful in my choices thereafter!

We only went to Yeovil on odd occasions. There was even a village barber in those days. Herbie Chant, who lived in one of the cottages at West End Farm and worked on the farm, offered a barbering service on Sunday mornings. This took place in a shed at the rear of his cottage, and you sat on a wooden chair while he cut your hair. There were no electric clippers of course, and I would regularly come back from there with one or two nicks in the back of my neck. One big advantage was, however, that you could catch up on all the village gossip.

There were several working farms in the village at this time. The most notable was Wickham Farm owned by Stanley Dare and his wife Frances. He had a herd of Friesian cows, which were moved twice a day for milking up and down the road from the farm to the field opposite our house. Mr Dare had one of the first Land Rovers, and used to drive around with his pet Fox Terrier. The dog had one paw missing where it had been cut off by the corn cutter (binder) and was called Nelson.

The Dares were also lay preachers at the Methodist chapel in Camel Street. At that time there was no Sunday School at the village Church, so we went to the Methodist Sunday School. Mrs Dare played the harmonium, and Mr Dare preached.

Once a year, the Dares organised, and paid for, a trip to Weymouth for all the Sunday School pupils and their parents. I remember that we were given two shillings spending money. This was one of the highlights of the year. On the way back from Weymouth, the coach would usually stop at a pub so that the parents could have a drink. We children had to stay in the coach as we were not allowed in the pub, but we did get some lemonade and crisps. I don't think the Dares knew about this, as they did not travel with us, and they were strictly teetotal.

In the early days, Mr Dare farmed using horses. He had two magnificent shire horses called Ruby and Violet. Only in the late 1940s did he acquire a David Brown tractor. He also used a wooden four-wheeled cart for many years. In summer, the wooden wheels would shrink so that the iron "tyres" could slip off. To combat this the wheels were put into the brook along the Little Marston Road to "plim". The wood swelled against the metal rim and so worked fine.

Frank Ralph then ran West End Farm. This was at that time a rented farm, and obviously had fewer funds available than some of the other farms. Frank Ralph used to sow seeds in the field opposite the farm using a "fiddle". This was a device somewhat like a banjo that contained seed, and as the farmer walked up and down the field, and pushed a lever across the banjo, seed was dispersed.

Frank Ralph retired and went to live in the house along the railway line down from the station, and the farm was taken over by Dick Sansom. He also kept chickens, and we used to buy our eggs there. There were often soft-shelled eggs available, and these were cheaper. The chickens were free range and we often had double yolks in the eggs.

Harvesting was always an exciting time for us in the village. As boys, we regularly attended the corn cutting in order to catch rabbits. The corn was cut in those days using a "binder" which was drawn behind a horse or tractor, cut the corn and bound it into sheaves. The sheaves were then stood upright in groups of about six to from a stook and left to dry. Some days later the farmer would collect the stooks, and make a rick to store the corn. Eventually the corn needed to be threshed, and this was another occasion when we went along with our dog to catch some of the numerous rats that came out of the rick as it was being loaded onto the threshing machine. It was only later towards 1950 that the first combine harvesters and baling machines began to appear in the village.

There were many cider orchards in the village at that time, and cider making was an important business in the area. Sam Pitman at Park Farm was the principal maker of cider in the village, but there were a few others who made it on a smaller scale. Several people had cider orchards and sold the apples to the local producers.

We also had one or two shops in the village. Mrs Thorne who lived in the small farm now known as Laurel Cottage ran the main general store and post office. There was a smaller general store on Camel Street opposite the Methodist Chapel run by Miss Cox. This shop did not last for many years. The local butcher was Bob Rideout and he had a small slaughterhouse right behind the Old School House.

Mr Smith who lived at Wisteria cottage (his daughter later married Clifford Hockey) owned the field at the rear of the village hall. When I was young there were still a number of Nissen huts around the perimeter of the field as well as the old village hall and the cookhouse installations at the back. Other buildings on the field had been removed, but the concrete foundations remained. I recall that these had been broken up, and sometimes my brother and I would work for the farmer by picking up stones and pieces of concrete to clear the ground. We were paid a few pence for each bucket full that we collected.

Some of the grocery shops in Yeovil would provide a service to villages such as Marston. At one stage, Mr Knight from Queen Camel supplied the groceries. He would sit with our mother and go through a long list of shopping requirements that were then delivered in a large cardboard box at a later date. Later the World's Stores from Yeovil had a mobile grocery van that came and parked up so that people could collect their groceries. This was still mainly staples and tinned goods etc. as most people grew their own vegetables or bought them in the village.

Mr Wreford, the baker from West Camel delivered bread on a regular basis. There was also a baker from Sherborne who delivered to a few people, but he always seemed to come in the evening at the end of his round.

In the late 1940s and early 1950s we were quite interested in football, and we sometimes went to Yeovil to watch the team play. One of the villagers, Reg Hawkins, who lived in Church Lane, ran a garage at Ilchester. He owned a mini bus, and a group of us would go together in the minibus and contribute to the cost. Sometimes the bus was full, and as the youngest of the group, I would have to sit on the engine at the front. Reg Hawkins was one of the few people at that time to own a television, and he used to invite us to his house to watch the Cup Final.

Fancy Dress competition at a Fête in the 1950s

One event in the village, which was always a highlight of the year, was the village fête. In the days when few people owned a car, there was no television etc. the fête was very much more important than is these days, and people went to some trouble to support the various events involved. As a small child, I was generally involved in the fancy dress, and my mother made various costumes for this. Ursula Samways was the leading light in the fête committee. I recall that she was also very much involved in the revues run by the Marstonaires.

I remember once when the fête was held at the house of Mrs Marden on the Rimpton road, and there was a dog show. The show was judged by Mrs Dally, the wife of Colonel Dally who lived at Marston house. It must have been a cold summer day, as she was wearing a long fur coat (although she wore open sandals with no stockings). The dogs were put in a circle and she walked around inspecting each one. As she was carefully looking at one particularly fine pedigree specimen, another dog walked behind her and cocked its leg against her fur coat. We children watching were in fits of laughter.

Another highlight for the adults at the fête was the skittles competition for which the top prize was a pig. Skittles was a popular pastime and every pub boasted a team. I remember when a new skittle alley was built at the rear of the Red Lion. It must have been in the mid to late 1950s.

On Sunday afternoons in the summer, Wakes Coaches from Sparkford would run "Mystery Tours". The coach would pick us up from the garage at Marston early on Sunday afternoon, and we would travel to visit somewhere interesting in the local area. It usually lasted for a couple of hours and was always an exciting outing for us.

At other times late on Sunday afternoons, we would simply sit on the wall in front of the garage and count all the cars returning from Weymouth (we assumed). It was about the only time there was any real traffic in Marston.

One of the highlights of the winter was bonfire night. For weeks, in advance we children would gather all sorts of old rubbish to make a huge bonfire in Court Gardens. We usually had a good number of people who came along, and most of us had a few fireworks, which we could buy, from the village shop. In those days, there was no formal organisation of such events, and it was simply a group of village boys and girls who did it.

One special occasion was the Coronation in 1953. A television (black and white of course, and not very big) was set up in the village hall. We small children were allowed to sit at the front, so we had a good view, but I remember that the hall was packed.

As we grew older, we needed to get some pocket money. I took over from Tony, an evening paper round, delivering the Bristol Evening Post. Although I didn't earn very much, I was very pleased to have some money at least. It was quite difficult at times, especially in winter and sometimes I would have to cycle through the floods. Garston Lane was notorious for flooding. On Saturday evening there was a late evening sports paper called the "Green 'Un" which was printed on green paper. It carried all the racing results, football scores and early reports, and I had to deliver it at about 8 o'clock in the evening. Fortunately, there were only a few people who wanted it delivered, but I usually took about 10 copies to the Red Lion to be sold there.

Tony's job then was as Butcher's boy for Bob Rideout at the village butchers. He would ride around on Saturday morning on the old butcher's bike with a big carrier on the front, delivering meat. He would then have to help cleaning up the butcher's shop and scrub the chopping tables. All very hard work.

My evening job became a problem when I was at secondary school, as I then had homework to do as well, so I gave it up and Colin Dole took it on. Instead, I would sometimes work weekends, helping with the farm work at West End Farm. The hardest was cleaning out the cowshed, especially in winter when it was very cold. In summer, I used to help with haymaking and this was good fun as I was allowed to drive the Ferguson tractor from time to time. I still remember, however, that I was disappointed at how little money I earned for what I considered quite hard work. Dick Sansom, the farmer, always assured me that it was "the standard agricultural wage for someone of my age"!

Looking back on it now, I suppose life was tough, but they were very happy days, and Marston was a great place to grow up.

The Life and Times of the Moore Brothers in Marston Magna
1945 – 1955
Through the Eyes of a Schoolboy – Tony Penn

The Moore brothers were not the subject of constant surveillance by the boys of the village, but on the occasions when the boys got together to 'chew the fat' as it were, as well as discussing football, birds nesting, rabbiting and the village girls, any slightly different family would also come up for discussion. Initially, the brothers were judged to be bachelors, who all lived together in the grey stone house opposite the village school along Camel Street on one side and opposite the churchyard along Station Road on the other side.

The village boys thought the Moore brothers 'different' because their household had no women or children, leaving the lads always being 'slightly suspicious' of them. The other thing the boys thought odd was the fact that the Camel Street entrance to the Moore's household was via a pair of very large barn doors that incorporated a small door for pedestrian entry. The oddity was that no one had ever seen the large doors open, but everyone wanted to know what was kept behind them.

The problems of young people in judging the age of older people are that they can never get it correct or even near. In the case of the Moore brothers the situation was no exception, but opinion among the village boys was that Erne Moore was the eldest and that the other three were quite a bit younger. However, rather than judge their ages it was decided to categorise the brothers by their roles within the family. Erne was regarded as the boss because he spent most of his time going around the village talking to everyone he met, but not actually doing a lot of work. He was however treated with a certain amount of reverence by the boys because it was rumoured that he always carried a bag of gold sovereigns in his pocket and they all hoped he would give them one but of course he never did!!

Ed was classified as a farmer because he spent most of his time at the family smallholding towards the bottom of Garston Lane. Ed was also classified a 'pain in the backside' because he spent so much time in the farm buildings that the boys could not gain access to check for birds nests! Fred's duties were twofold; he was responsible for the housework and cooking but in the afternoons, the only time he was regularly seen out of the house, he went to the smallholding to help Ed with the milking. Fred was also known as 'Toilet Soap' a name the lads always thought was appropriate because of his household duties. The name Toilet Soap was rumoured to have been given to Fred because of his poor pronunciation, he apparently could not pronounce the letter 'S' and so Toilet Soap became 'Toilet Toap'! Little was seen of Frank Moore because he spent much of his time away from the village, it was rumoured, in Yeovil. At that time most of the village lads regarded Yeovil as a very large town with more shops than Sherborne, and a place where the people were smartly dressed and the girls were prettier than the girls in the village.

One day a caravan appeared in the farmyard down Garston Lane and very soon after Frank took up residence in the caravan. The village rumourmongers had a field day analysing the reason for this event, and they came up with any number of explanations. The most highly rated story was that Frank had had a relationship with one of Yeovil's 'ladies of the night', had fallen out with her and was consequently thrown out of her house. It should be noted that most of the village lads had quite advanced knowledge of the relationships between men and women gained from observing US servicemen and local women and girls!! The lads had also come across the stand-in Vicar 'Willie Warmington' in some compromising situations! In point of fact the village lads missed very little of the 'goings on' of the times.

The mystery of the Moore's barn doors was finally solved. Following many checks by the boys to see if the small pedestrian door had been left unlocked, they finally hit the jackpot and waited excitedly for Fred to leave the house to go milking. When it was judged that Fred had gone a good distance a file of boys piled into the barn. There they discovered an extensive collection of old and rusty farm implements and for the rest of the afternoon they explored the building and played on the machinery before leaving the barn and closing the door.

With the mystery of the barn sorted out the boys thought it might be fun to subject Fred to a session of 'knock down ginger'. Knock down ginger was a well-known prank of the time but the lads had devised a novel variation for the unsuspecting Fred. Half a dozen village lads had gathered on the bridge leading to 'Bridge Cottages' opposite the Moore's household and it was decided that with the aid of a 'reel of cotton' they would gently knock Fred's front door. Fred had returned from his milking duties so the boys knew that he was at home alone. The lads decided via the 'stone paper and scissors' game that the last man standing should attach the cotton to the doorknocker. The winner duly crossed the road and crouched below the wall entering through the gate and attaching the cotton to the knocker before retreating and carefully unreeling the cotton. With the cotton attached to the Moore's doorknocker at one end and the reel with the remaining cotton in the hands of the lads on the bridge, action began! Initially the cotton had to be pulled very gently to test its strength. Once the cotton capability was adjudged OK, in unison the lads gazed into the stream with one eye on the Moore's door whilst the door was being knocked. Immediately the door showed signs of opening the cotton was slackened off to avoid breakage and discovery. Fred opened the door looked left and right swore loudly and closed the door. This series of actions was repeated several times with all the lads collapsing in peels of laughter whilst continuing to monitor the front door. At that point, with the door being gently knocked, Fred appeared in the upstairs window trying to see who was knocking his door. Because the door had a porch above it Fred was rapidly moving from left to right with his nose against the windowpane to see who was there. He could see no one but again opened the door cursing loudly then rushing back to the upstairs window getting even more wound up. Eventually he rushed downstairs and out of the front door shouting loudly 'I know who is doing this you little b******* and when I catch you look out'. Fred made the mistake of starting his rant immediately he came out of the front door and this provided the opportunity for the lads to scatter in all directions out through the churchyard and across Court Gardens. Fred made it up to the churchyard path to the stile before returning to the house and slamming the door! For safety reasons the lads did not meet on the bridge for several weeks.

Like many farmers of the time the Moore's had a cider orchard along the Yeovil Road with a wide variety of cider apples, and when the apples were beginning to fall off the trees the village lads would visit the orchard to enjoy the best and sweetest apples in the crop. The Moore's orchard had a superb tree of 'Morgan Sweet' apples, large yellow juicy apples that were a favourite at the time. On a visit to the orchard a group of about ten lads descended on the tree, some lads climbed up the tree while others shook the branches to encourage the apples to fall. It looked like a plague of locusts. Suddenly, the lookout lad spotted Ed Moore climbing over the road gate and sounded the 'alert'! The lads up the tree either jumped or scrambled down and everyone raced to the far hedge away from the road. They all went through the hedge and turned left in the direction of Sherborne Road, quickly observing the movement of Ed Moore.

He was seen to go back over the gate, and jumped onto his bicycle with the obvious intention of getting around to the Sherborne Road to intercept the lads as they came through the field. One of the more 'canny' lads read the situation perfectly and immediately called for a one hundred and eighty degree course change. Once the lads understood the reason for the change they immediately responded, crossing Thorney Lane, then Yeovil Road before circling back to the village via Little Marston Road where they rapidly dispersed - with their pockets full of apples.

One day in the early 1950s one of the lads reported that he had spotted an unknown 'youngish' women walking in the village. He described her as being very smartly dressed with bright lipstick and blondish hair piled up on top of her head. Over the following days every member of the village lads' gang had seen the young woman and they all agreed that she was 'different' and a bit special. It turned out that the young women was the daughter of Frank Moore and she had come to Marston to stay with her Dad in the caravan.

As a result of this discovery the lads reclassified the Moore brothers as three and a half bachelors!

Memories of Marston in the 1970s

From Philippa Mitchell (née Pemberton)

In 1971 our family moved in to what was previously just a field. A row of a few new houses was built on a bank above the brook and ours was the middle one. We children used all the left over building materials to make our own dens and met our neighbours, riding in a dumper truck and paddling in the river. Marston Magna turned out to be a quiet village with lovely fields all around and lots and lots of children, or so it seemed to me.

Philippa in the 1970s.

We caught the old Wakes bus to Queen Camel each school day to Countess Gytha Primary with Mrs. Mabb escorting us. My teacher was old Mrs. Kirk and although she took us on many walks, she rarely let us out to play. We had tests every day and she was not too impressed if we didn't do well.

Out of school, we roamed the fields as our playgrounds. Some hedges made hidden dens with extra branches woven in. The barn beyond the Rimpton turning had infinite possibilities for den making. We used the rectangular bales of straw to stack and build. There was a really old car we used to sit in, pretending to drive and if the farmer turned up we hid! We all used to get around on our bikes all the time but with no helmets in those days. We could be out for hours in the summer and as there were no mobile phones, we just stayed out as long as we liked and probably went home when hungry, or to our friend's houses. In the winter the water in moat field froze over and we 'skated' around it or cracked the ice if it was not thick enough to hold our weight.

I remember bell ringing at the church. It was fairly easy to learn to do but if you didn't remember to let go of the velvety blue, red and white part of the rope at the right moment you would be swiftly lifted off your feet and upwards to the ceiling, where you could bang your head if you were not quick enough to let go and fall to the floor! I remember learning the number sequence of the bells written on the boards in order to 'ring the changes' - the tunes - which I remember being quite tricky, but it sounded great when it all worked out well.

When we reached the end of primary school, we took the 11 plus exam and then we were bussed off in different directions to new schools. This broke up a few village friendships but we made more friends further afield. There were also the Guides at Rimpton, the discos at the Sparkford Inn and a bus to Yeovil on Saturdays to spend our pocket money.

Dean Noyce
1983-1995

My name is Dean Noyce and I have lived in Marston Magna since I was born in 1977. The Noyce family have lived at Garston Farm for many generations and I personally have lived there for 38 years and owned it since 2012.

Dean Noyce

I remember my childhood quite clearly, the weekly video van where I would rent a movie for £1, the Deacons bakery van (I looked forward to that) I remember the smell of those cakes to this day! I would also spend hours in the front garden watching the purple lorries travelling up and down the road to the winery just yards from my house. The winery is now Perrys recycling.

I remember buying penny sweets from the local village post office, whilst on route to the butchers to get chops for tea. I also remember going to the local pub with my granddad. I used to have coke and crisps whilst my granddad George downed numerous ciders.

In the school holidays I would leave the house first thing in the morning to meet my friends. We played in the park, made dens, and played with blow up dinghies in the moat field, which I do now with my own three sons. There were never any worries for safety as everyone knew each other and would always look out for each other.

There was a youth club in the Red Lion pub, which was very popular. We'd play snooker, darts, billiards, football and we had a lovely tuck shop. I got my first job there sticking up the skittles, and to this day I remember a wall at the rear of the skittle alley, made entirely from old glass bottles.

Christmas time in Marston Magna was always a jam-packed fun filled time. We had lots of activities in the local pub such as football matches, tug of war over the river, children's parties, "It's a knockout" skittle competitions and even a village bed race! There would be several hospital beds decorated in different themes, and these would be frantically pushed around the village with children on board. All the kids would be dressed in fancy dress and a good time was had by all.

Yes, I have lots of wonderful memories of my childhood in Marston Magna, and hopefully my own children will be writing their happy memoirs in the future, as I am today.

St. Mary's Church from Rimpton Road

Methodist Church

The Old Village Hall

The Red Lion

Snow at Cooper's Farm 1978

Floods in Rimpton Road in the 1990s

The Manor House

St. Mary's Church from the Moat

Extreme Weather

As the name of the village refers to a marsh, it is not surprising that flooding occurs. This had consequences for many villagers over the years, and particularly regarding attendance at the village school in the first half of the century:

From the School Log Books 1904-1951

A school log book entry for February 1904 notes there were continuous rain and floods, which affected attendance. On November 29th 1908 3 children were absent and flooding was near homes. In December of the same year heavy rains caused the roads to be flooded in some parts. This was also the case on January 28th 1910. Flooding again was noted on December 6th 1912. The beginning of 1913 saw floods again with children from outlying districts unable to come to school.

On January 24th 1913 the roads were almost impassable. Early March in 1914 affected attendance and a heavy snowstorm on March 20th meant attendance figures at the school were down. In the following year on February 17th 1915 14 children were sent home from school in the afternoon "as the water was rising considerably" and the roads were becoming impassable.

In November 1915 there was a week of heavy rain and floods. The following November saw floods again and the school closed for Christmas when there was flooding in December 1916.

1917 was a particularly hard winter right through until the beginning of April. The ground was so hard that potatoes could not be lifted from the ground.

At the cottage at the entrance to Park Farm, which was below the level of the road, the snow was so deep that the door could not be opened to help at the birth of a child. A ladder had to be obtained to gain access to an upper storey window to assist the mother.

There was a severe snowstorm on March 17th 1917. 1918 may have seen easier weather but 1919 saw flooding on January 10th whilst March brought flooding on March 20th followed by a snowstorm on March 31st. The year ended with floods on December 5th.

In January 1922 there was a cold, wet start to the year. The children from Thorney Lane were absent from school being hindered by weather right through until early April. A former pupil of the school reported that children from Thorney Lane were often away from school because of poor weather conditions. In 1923 Thorney Lane was under water in January. Snow often seems to have occurred in March and on March 3rd 1924 11 children were absent from school due to snowfall. There was heavy rain on May 8th 1925. Towards the end of the decade there was a heavy snowstorm on February 15th 1929. Attendance was not counted for afternoon school that day, as only 18 pupils were present out of 41 children on roll.

During the 1930s the school log records little of weather events except for June 7th 1935 when there was very inclement weather with only 12 out of 26 scholars at school.

Weather comment was infrequent during the years of World War 2 but the spring term of 1940 saw poor attendance for the whole term as a result of very severe weather and sickness in the infant class.

The school was closed due to poor weather on January 30th 1947. Early February saw bad weather and floods. On March 6th of the same year the school was closed for half a day as there was no bus service and the headmistress had to travel by train, which was very late due to bad weather conditions. The school closed for 3 days in March on account of bad weather. There was further disruption towards the end of 1950, when on November 21st school began 15 minutes late as the bus could not negotiate the floods and snow caused the late opening of school on December 4th.

The school was very cold on December 4th, 5th and 6th 1950 with the school thermometer registering less than 2 degrees Celsius in the morning and at best 10 degrees Celsius in the afternoon. On December 15th the Rector opened the school when the headmistress's bus was late due to heavy snow and she did not arrive until 9.30a.m. Records of such weather conditions came to an end with the closure of the school in 1951.

The winter of 1947 was certainly one of the longest, hardest winters in living memory. The winter of 1962-1963, often referred to as "The Big Freeze, was particularly harsh too. The temperatures were exceedingly low, with January 1963 reported to be the coldest month of the twentieth century. The blizzards and easterly winds left huge snow drifts, and there was a fatal incident on White Post Hill that year, when sadly two people were asphyxiated when trapped in their car.

It was not until March that the thaw began to set in.

Most of the surviving records date from the onset of the Parish Magazine, which gave villagers an opportunity to record their memories of severe winters in Marston Magna:

Floods: 1979

The tribulations of weather in 1979: January gave us an icy cold beginning, recording -13C on January 2nd somewhere in the British Isles. February was also cold with frosts, and then March was not merely cold but wet as well, nearly as wet as in 1977. All contributed to making it a long delayed spring when we were able to count the losses of our gardens to the severity of the winter. Hebes, escallonias, pittosporums and other half hardy shrubs were either killed outright or severely damaged, while in kitchen gardens the brassica family suffered ferociously.

April was still cool and May showed some improvement until the last third, with wet and showery weather giving an unpleasant Bank Holiday, and finally unleashing upon us on May 30th the wettest day of the century in this area at 2.03 ins.

The area of really heavy rainfall was restricted to West Dorset/East Somerset but the flooding and its consequences had nationwide publicity.

The Spring (March/May) rainfall topped 10 ins instead of the usual 6 ins. June was a great relief, while July was predominantly dry and warm, but certainly without threat of water shortage.

Peter Clarke wrote then:

The worst flooding within living memory occurred at the end of May. Coming as it did with frightening rapidity some parishioners suffered considerable damage to their property and possessions. Who will ever forget the sight of the Village Green almost totally submerged by water or the houses so badly flooded to at least 2 feet deep with possessions floating around each room.

Further memories on this flood from Peter Clarke:

*The village had been very badly flooded and was impassable, and a coach full of people had ground to a halt outside the village hall. Word soon got round and in one of my capacities (*perhaps several, curate, parish council clerk, Chairman, member*) I got involved.*

It was obvious the coach could go no further that night, so I suggested they should use the village hall for as long as they wanted. Beds, blankets, food were required and in time all villagers turned up bearing their gifts. It was a terrific community effort and the passengers were terribly appreciative, and later the coach proprietors gave a generous donation as a token of their gratitude.

Fame came too, as local TV reported the incident that night, extolling the virtues of the village and the use of the "village shed" as they quaintly described it. After being fed the passengers settled down to a night's sleep. At that time the old hall could be divided in half by curtains, and my abiding memory was quite late that evening popping my head round the curtains where the females were bedded down, and seeing a dear lady lying on a camp bed, blanket up to her neck and still wearing her hat! The purpose of my visit was to ensure all was well and they were all comfortable. The next morning the community continued to rally round and I think we probably provided some sort of breakfast before they were sent on their way. A wonderful memory of the Marston Village community coming together to help others.

Ricky Gibbs, owner of Gibbs Yard, remembers the winters of these years in the late 1970s:

I think it was possibly in January 1979. It was snowing heavily with a very strong east wind that was drifting the snow. A large snow clearing train was operating on the Weymouth-Castle Cary line. The train was made up of two engines back to back, with snow plough units on both ends. I understand that having cleared the line in the afternoon to allow the passenger trains to operate; it waited a while with the intention of getting the line cleared for the following morning. The cutting on the north side of the railway bridge on the Rimpton road had filled with drifting snow almost level with the fields on either side. When the snow-clearing unit came down the line it ploughed into the deep snow and eventually came to a standstill some 100 yards from the bridge. When it attempted to reverse out the packed snow held it in place and despite its best efforts was unable to move. The following day they attempted to move the train without success. Eventually a new crew was brought to the train by a helicopter. I think it spent another night stuck and was eventually freed the next day. It backed out some distance and then came forward again. This time the snow plough blasted away the snow in a most impressive manner, and the train sailed under the bridge towards Yeovil. I am sure there are others who will remember this, as a lot of people walked out from Marston to watch.

A couple of years before this, there had been another severe snowstorm with an easterly wind that had cut off Rimpton and Marston for sometime. I remember the road out of Rimpton towards Villa Farm was filled with snow level with the top of the hedges. I have some 8mm film of one of our tractors clearing snow on the Camel Road out of Marston! In places the drifted snow was well over 6ft deep.

I remember after the second incident, we spent a lot of time sealing up our workshop building to stop the snow getting in under the eaves. Strangely, in some 35 years since, there have never been any remotely comparable snowstorms, and our efforts to seal up the building have never been put to the test.

A Hard Winter: 1978
A Memory of Snow - 18th to 22nd February 1978

The snow was not deep, but the wind force was strong. The snow was blown off the fields and filled in the roads between the hedges. Villagers had to make their way on foot. One youngster even had to be brought home by sledge over the hedge height snow. Cars and tankers were parked in the roads approaching the village for several days. The church service could not be held due to the drifts.

This turned out to be quite a social time, particularly in Rimpton Road, with invitations to coffee or something stronger! Everyone seemed to be out to have a look at the train stuck on the line just north of the bridge. A train plough approached from the north to come to the "rescue" but this also became snowed in.

Mrs. Shapley, who lived by the bridge, was making bowls of porridge to keep the driver and crew fed and warm. Milk was available from the farm door – bring your own jug! Wrefords, the bakery arranged with the Royal Navy at Yeovilton to fly in a helicopter with a delivery of bread.

Of course, when the snow melted, we had floods.

Blizzard

Mary Martin remembered:

When we were living in Rimpton, we awoke one Sunday morning to find the village engulfed in snow. Lanes out of the village had become blocked to about 10-12 feet. This was because the snow on the fields had been blown into the lanes by a blizzard.

Everyone was out walking around the village chatting. One villager was at the start of the blocked lane with a shovel saying, "Someone has got to make a start!" The lane was blocked all the way to Marston Magna.

Some villagers went to dig snow out of a barn to help the farmer, whose sheep were lambing. Three of us with bean canes, to probe the snow, walked across the fields to Miss Bugler who lived on her own in an isolated cottage. It was thought that she had run out of bottled gas, having no electricity! The police subsequently took supplies to her on a motorized sleigh. Bread was dropped by helicopter from Yeovilton. There was a well -worn path across the fields, which led to the Red Lion (in Marston Magna). The thaw came at the end of the week.

In March 1978 the vicar, the Revd. de Jersey Hunt wrote:

While the ferocity of the blizzard and the consequent snowdrifts experienced during February disrupted normal life for everybody, two benefits were forthcoming. One was a spirit of neighbourliness shown on all sides and the other was the blissful quiet. We have become accustomed to rushing about on our own affairs and it was no bad thing to have to slow down for a few days. We have also become accustomed to an awful level of traffic and aircraft noise and not to have that was a blessed relief.

Peter Clarke, at this time curate of the parish, wrote this fascinating account of the March 1978 weather problems in the Village Magazine:

Whoever could have dreamt that we should actually witness a Royal Navy helicopter from Yeovilton, landing on the Glebe field to deliver our bread? Whoever could have dared to imagine that 10-15 foot snow drifts would cut all road communication from our village for four days?

On Sunday morning, we all awoke to a silent, white, deep world. Strangely silent, with only a biting hurricane force wind drifting the snow into indescribable patterns. The task of digging ourselves out was predominant. For the first time in many, many years a church service could not be held owing to the drifts outside. However, after the initial shock and clearing up, it seemed as though we were all intent on enjoying ourselves. Thanks ought to be extended to so many people; to those who made the lives of their neighbours so much easier by their kindly help; to all the farmers for supplying us with milk; to Mrs. Wreford for having the admirable foresight to arrange with the Royal Navy for our bread to be delivered; to those who kept our phones and electricity supply going and to those valiant diggers and shovellers who eventually did the necessary work in order to open up once again the wide open world.

Henry Trim's column also gave a lively account:

The fall of snow experienced in February was certainly much heavier than that of 1963, when at least I was able to get to work in Yeovil each day, although it was only single line traffic. One lesson learned in 1963 was of practical use this time. Our section of the council estate was built in 1921 and there is no felting to one side of the roof and snow can get through into the attic. In 1963 the weight of snow collapsed a ceiling at No. 3. At that time there was no means of getting into the attic, but trapdoors were cut following those snows and these proved of immense help now. 19 sacks of snow were taken out of No.1!

It was very heartwarming to see the way neighbours and friends were helping with path and attic clearing.

Molly Crabb of Wickham Farm also remembers the winter of 1978. She adds that the helicopter landed in the glebe field next to Wickham Farm, from where the bread was taken to Mr. Rideout's shop.

Molly and her husband Sam gave their milk away to villagers, who made milk puddings with the excess! The milk tankers were unable to collect their milk due to the roads being blocked with deep snow, which had blown off the fields. A caterpillar track vehicle was sent from Yeovilton to organize the collection of medical supplies for the village inhabitants.

With no sign of a thaw, Sam Crabb and Mr. Pat Upwood decided to go and fetch a plastic bulk tank for the milk from Mole Valley Farmers in Yeovil. As the roads were impassable, they decided to walk along the railway line. However, on their return journey, as they were struggling along the track with the plastic bulk tank, they heard a noise, which they assumed to be an aeroplane. A few seconds later, they realized that it was in fact a train, so they had to jump off the line with their tank just before the train thundered past! Sam told his wife that they had had a very narrow escape.

A Hot Summer

Molly Crabb remembers the very hot summer of 1976 on Wickham Farm:

All the trees on the farm were already dead or dying. Many had been killed by Dutch Elm disease. They had no leaves, and it was summer.

The ground was very parched because of the long drought, which had lasted for several months. The grass and field pasture was turning to dust.

When the dairy cows had been milked and turned out to pasture, they were a very sad picture as they walked onto their field. They seemed to disappear in a huge cloud of dust, and could find little or nothing to eat. Sam came indoors very upset and crying because his cows were suffering.

THE WARS

The Boer War

The first mention of war in the village comes from Mrs M. Davis in the Parish Magazine. She writes:

In May 1900 our eighty-five year old grandfather from Castle Cary was staying with us. He made us each a whistle from the willow tree growing in the lane; Mother made us each a flag of red turkey twill tacked on a stick and waving our flags and blowing our whistles we went down the lane, through the narrow part, over Cradle Bridge and along the rest of the lane as far as the gates where the level crossing leads over the railway. I was seven and we were celebrating the Relief of Mafeking in the Boer War.

World War 1

Henry Trim records the following in the Parish Magazine dated November 1979:

This month marks the 61st anniversary of the end of World War One and it is interesting to look back in the Parish records and see the names of men in the village who were already serving in that terrible conflict in December 1914.

Commander C.G. Chichester R.N. serving in H.M.S. Hornet
Stoker 1st Class William Herridge H.M.S. Bulwark (drowned off Sheerness 1915)

Serving in the Regular Army:
Driver Arthur March 22nd RFA
Driver William March 118th RFA
Driver W.A. Linthorne 235th RFA (killed in action 1917)
Private Samuel March 5th Dorset Regt. (killed in action 1915)

With the Territorial Army were:
Ted Bow - N.Somerset Yeomanry and
W.D.Marden, P.G.Higgins, W.Mant, E.Knight and J.Thorn - W.Somerset Yeomanry

With the Kitchener's Army units were:
Private W.Higgins 10th Devon Reg (missing 1917)
Private Samuel J.Linthorne Somerset Light Infantry (killed in action 1917).

Others listed but with no further details included:
Thos.March, E.Mant, W.Orchard, E.March, G.Walters, J.Gillard, H.Biddiscombe, E.G.Florence, J.Short, Goodyear, B.Rose and G.March

John Bush who was the brother of Mrs M.Davis adds the following additional information:

John Bush thinks he was the youngest of the village to join up at fifteen and a half in 1916. His first ship December 1917- May 1920 was the 'Barham'.

Commander Chichester was later appointed to HMS Forward (the Birmingham home to Reservists) returning to the Manor for a while around 1930.

Cecil Marden died of his wounds in France (he was the village scoutmaster).

Ray Davis was with Allenby at the Relief of Jerusalem.

Basil Grant (son of the Marden's chauffeur) saw service at Archangel (North Russia).

William Drake of Thorney Lane joined the Navy as a stoker.

Cecil Marden

Keith Hockey was in the Flying Corps at the end of hostilities.

Cromwell Bugby came over with the Australians.

Ern March was an Anzac man and wore the Aussies Hat.

Bert Webber (the village postman) served with the Artillery on the breakwater at Portland.

Jack Mant (eldest Mant boy) stayed in the village as head of the family caring for his widowed mother and sang in the choir for many years.

We also know that the following lost their lives as they are recorded on the War Memorial inside St. Marys Church:

Tom Rowland Thorn R.A.M.C. Died of fever in India September 2nd 1916
Private Bertie Foot 1st Royal Berks Regt. Killed in action August 23rd 1918
Private William John Bowden Innis Fusiliers. Killed in action October 20th 1918
Private George William Brine 6th Wilts Regt. Died prisoner in Germany Dec 25th 1918

The following names appear on the 1918 Electoral Roll marked with NM referring to Naval or Military Voter:

William Alfred Arnold
Francis Albert Cannon - Mill Cottages
John Coote - Manor House
William Thomas Rowe
Leonard William Bishop - Rimpton Street
Ernest John Bush - Hawkes Cottage
Eli Highmore - Rimpton Street

Henry Trim's father served in France during WW1 and he tells the following strange tale.

My mother was cooking on November 5th 1918 when her wedding ring, which normally fitted quite securely, rolled off under the grate. On Armistice Day, November 11th 1918 - a few days later - she received the news that my father had died in France on November 5th.

Before WWI the Magna Cider Company started jelly and pulp making from apples. Sour or jam apples were graded, put into large boilers until they were reduced to almost a liquid. A machine then extracted cores and pips. This product was then stored in sterilised containers until it was used for jam making. More than 100 tons of this was made, but the output was restricted due to the unavailability of requisite machinery. This was unfortunate, because there was a bumper harvest that year, whilst the following year was a poor crop when more could have been produced. The apple pulp could be combined with plum pulp.

Before the war, apple pomace, a by-product from cider production, had to be used immediately otherwise it would rot. During war time the company started to dry apple pomace, to develop cake food for cattle. This was done on a small scale but in 1917, in conjunction with the Food Production Department, the product was much increased. The apple pomace was put through a rotary dryer to extract excess moisture; the product could then be stored and used in the winter as a concentrated food when there was not enough grass keep.

Apple jelly was made by using fresh juice from sweet apples. No added sugar was necessary. The juice was put through an evaporator where it was reduced to a fine, clear jelly. The jelly was potted, then cooled and labelled ready for sale.

These processes increased the food supply for both animal and human consumption.

During WWI the Revd. Peppin was one of those workers helping in this enterprise. John Peppin writes that his father, who was 47 when the war started, felt he ought to be doing something additional to his job to help the allied cause. Having been told by his Bishop that he was too old to volunteer for active service, he tried putting in a few hours at the cider factory. This was a task he was certainly unfit for, and which he gave up after a short while:

My older brother Tom and I were pressurised into helping with the corn harvest, which, for us, involved tying bundles of corn into stooks - an undertaking which, at age 10 and lacking any experience of such activity, I soon gave up.

He went on to say:

Hatred of the Huns in 1914 knew no bounds. First they marched through Belgium, with which country they had a treaty of non-aggression. This took the Western Powers by surprise. After that, our propaganda soon joined the realms of fantasy. Huns were slicing up babies, raping women, and committing every crime in the book. Ordinary ignorant Englishmen were driven almost to frenzy by the awful Huns. That Christmas my father went in to Yeovil to buy his two elder sons a really remarkable present - so remarkable that it had to be shared. He came back with a large box containing a steam engine, complete with an elaborate coach, and a large circle of rails. On THE DAY, the box was opened in an aura of excitement. Then the discovery - on the bottom of the box was stamped the fatal words "Made in Germany". My father was livid. After all, this present had cost him 5/- (25p) and here he was, apparently helping the Huns! Should he take it back to the shop? Presumably realising, in a calmer moment, that the Huns would already have been paid for this engine, probably as far back as the summer, and that therefore they would not gain from his unfortunate purchase, it was decided to forget all about it and just enjoy the Huns' ability to produce so much toy for five shillings!

The village responded well to appeals for men and money. Following Lord Derby's scheme Mr Charles Ketley of Millbrook House acted as recruiting officer for Marston Magna, Rimpton and Chilton Cantelo. Married and single men gave their names but farmers and farmer's sons listed themselves as cowmen or carters who were amongst the "Starred" (essential) occupations.

Men aged between 18 and 40 were told that under the Derby Scheme of 1915 they could continue to enlist voluntarily or attest with an obligation to come forward if called up later on. Men who attested and were accepted under this scheme were divided into two groups: Group A and Group B. They were also classified in their groups as to whether they were married or single. Group B agreed to immediate service. Group A deferred their service. Those who were wished to defer were paid for the day they attested but then returned home until they were called up. They were given an armband with a red crown as a sign that they had enlisted, been rejected, discharged or were in starred occupations. The next day they were put on the Army Reserve B. This was a scheme that was somewhere between voluntary enlistment and conscription. The Group scheme recruits did not have a say into which regiment they were recruited. Recruits could appeal against their call up and were referred to a tribunal. The scheme was not considered to be successful as not enough men enlisted and conscription followed in March 1916.

The villagers supported the scheme for contributing eggs for wounded soldiers. Five members of the Boy Scout Patrol including the Patrol Leader Davis assisted by Scouts B.Grant, C.Florance, A.Lucas and L.Linthorne collected the eggs. Mrs E.D. Marden took these to the Yeovil Depot each week.

A Land Girl was killed in an accident in the village around the time of the First World War. At the time of the accident she was lodging in one of the Bridge Cottages. Her name was Lily Davey from Tiverton in Devon. She was twenty-two years of age.

Lily Davey was working for Farmer Jackson of Little Marston Farm when the accident occurred along the road between Little Marston turning and West End Farm. She was driving a four-wheel wagon drawn by a fairly spirited horse - not a heavy carthorse - who somehow crossed its front legs and fell. Miss Davey was sitting on the front board of the wagon with her legs on a shaft and she was thrown into the road where the wheels passed over her. She died in Yeovil Hospital and was laid to rest on 14th June 1919 in an unmarked grave, under the wall of St. Mary's Church.

Mrs M. Davis aptly sums up the outcome for those that survived the War:

> *On November the 11th an Armistice was signed between Great Britain and Germany and the Great War was over, at least as far as fighting was concerned, and London went mad. In Marston my Mother among others went to St. Mary's for an impromptu Thanksgiving; in London the streets were soon filled with cheering singing mobs.*
>
> *So the fighting stopped and the war of words began. A Peace Treaty was signed and the long task of re-settling returning soldiers began; this was not easy. One disturbing factor was that women had been free to earn good money for themselves - often for the first time - many had lost their husbands, some had invalids to care for, others had now no chance of marriage. The Victorian idea of men working, with wives and mothers in the home, had gone forever.*

World War 2

Almost as soon as the war started soldiers started arriving in the village - the first were Royal Engineers and Pioneer Corps. The Royal Engineers were responsible for laying the track into the railhead (where Gibbs yard now is) and the Pioneers laid out the yard itself.

Armaments were transported to the South West using the rail network. Two caterpillar tractors were used to flatten ground at Gibbs Yard and a fan of sidings was laid northwards from the goods yard and brought into use on 16th December 1940, to serve as an ammunition storage area.

The Royal Engineers were under canvas when they first came but over a period of a few months the Pioneers put down the bases and roofs of the Nissen huts (the remains of some can still be seen from the field at the back of the Village Hall). They also had huts around the station and the Cider Factory (the last one of them was demolished in the late 1980s). As these were built the soldiers moved out from under canvas and into them.

After a while the Engineers moved out and these were replaced by Ordnance Corps and Service Corps who also brought lorries with them. A lot of the Pioneers were Scotsmen and if you lived near the Camp you were awoken by the Bagpipes early in the morning - not a pleasant sound if they were not played properly!

Once the Ordnance Corps got settled in, the trains of ammunition started arriving at the station. This was unloaded and put under metal roofs, covered in canvas which was green to blend in with the fields and hedges, and placed alongside the roads all around the area. The British Soldiers were housed in the hall field. They built an extension on the old Hall and also the stage. E.N.S.A. concerts were held in the Hall, and films were also shown.

During this time, the soldiers in the camp could often be seen going round to houses in the village asking people if they could put up their wives for a couple of weeks, so that they could have a rest from the bombing in the large towns where they lived. Many of them came and stayed and remained friends for many years after the war.

Brenda Darch tells us:

One couple used to visit my mother every year on their way to or from Cornwall. One of these soldiers was a Sergeant whose wife used to stay with my parents and he was nearly always on the door of the Hall when the concerts and pictures were held. I could always get a few friends and myself in the Hall on the nights he was on Duty.

The British Army also requisitioned the Creamery, but they moved out on the arrival of US troops in the spring of 1943. In fact, in the run up to D-Day, all the English soldiers moved out and in came 500 black Americans and about 30 American Officers and N.C.O.s, plus a fleet of lorries. For months they were unloading trains and taking ammunition to fields along the roadside for miles around. It was rumoured that there was ammunition for a 20 mile radius.

The American G.I.s arrived in southwest England to prepare for the D-Day landings in June 1944.

A further railhead was constructed in late 1943/1944 at Sparkford by US Army Engineers to serve the Marston Magna ammunition depots. The depots stored US ammunition but remained under British control. The Marston Magna depots had been using Sparkford GWR Station goods yard since 1940 for in and out loading of ammunition.

Fortunately, Brenda Darch recorded many memories of the Americans in Marston Magna:

The American Senior Officers were mostly living in The Manor House but the Corporals and Sgts (all white) were billeted out in private houses. My parents had seven different ones billeted on them at different times - one of whom wrote to my parents until their death and continued (to the family) long after. In 1979 we went to visit with him and his wife in Indiana. The first Saturday he went to Yeovil to see what a small English town was like, - he had got off the boat at Bristol and came straight to Marston - and when he got home my Mum asked him what he thought of it to which he replied "Ma'am I've never seen so many buggies in all my life" In those days there always seemed to be a lot of people who took their babies out in prams on Saturday afternoons in Yeovil.

The US Army operated a segregation policy at that time and black soldiers were largely employed on labouring duties in separate units rather than integrated with white soldiers on combat duties.

In the immediate area, troops were based at Sherborne and the remains of their buildings can still be seen in fields just beyond the immediate grounds of the castle. There was a reported tragedy when US soldiers were practising laying land mines outside Sherborne Castle. One soldier threw a mine to another, which resulted in an explosion, killing several men. Coldharbour Hospital Sherborne was commandeered as an American hospital.

There was a camp at Rimpton at the top of Back Lane, on the right hand side, in what is now called Camp Field. White soldiers would go to The White Post for a drink but if black soldiers were already there, they would be turned out. Segregation was flouted however by the local residents much to the amazement of the American white soldiers. Marstonians were happy to enjoy any perks such as Camel cigarettes and sweets that were offered. Most of the local population had not seen black men before.

The Marston Magna camp was in the field at the side and rear of the Village hall. The Nissen huts can still be seen and are now used as farm buildings. The old Village Hall, which stood beside the road, was used as the Mess and when it was pulled down various mementoes were found, including a packet of Camel cigarettes. The Officers were billeted around the village and the Manor House was in constant use.

Brenda Darch continues:

The first thing they did was to cover up the Village Green with large chippings, so that it could be used as a Car Park. The Fire Watchers hut was still down by the stream but I don't know whether or not it was used after they took residence. The Officers were billeted in The Manor and had their quarters upstairs as part of the bottom half was used as a telephone exchange. The other part was used as an Office where the Senior Officer had his Meetings etc.

The attic was used as a Radio Station for the American Forces Network over a large area of the West Country. Sgt. Roy Snyder and Sgt. Frank Halley ran this. This Radio Station continued to operate long after D-Day when all the other Americans had gone from the village. From then on most of the children in the village from II to 16 (if missing) could be found up in the attic listening to the music. B.B.C. programmes in those days did not have things like "Top of the Pops" and more modern music could be heard in the attic. There was always at least half a dozen there when not at school. These two men used to get their food delivered from Sherborne after the rest of the soldiers had moved on, but when they were using the cookhouses in the field at the back of the old Hall they got it from there.

Things that couldn't be got here because of rationing were often sent to them like tin peaches, and pineapples also ice cream. If it were something they didn't like, they would put it back so that one of us could have it - there was certainly a mad rush if they had ice cream, as we hadn't seen any since the early part of the war. Ray Snyder had been training to be a missionary before being drafted into the Army and said that when the war was over he would continue his training.

Just around the corner from The Manor House is Stokes Cottage, which was owned before the war by a Miss Hall, who moved away. This cottage was also taken over by the American Army as a dispensary. Bill Samways and his family were the first occupants after the war and I remember him saying that he took a large tin of nails out of the walls before he could start decorating. He could only assume that they must have had notes and orders nailed on to the walls upstairs and down.

Dances took place at Marston Court with Wrens travelling in from Yeovilton. The troops were an attraction, so many women living outside Marston Magna visited the village, walking from Queen Camel and other nearby villages, or catching the train from Yeovil.

Many years after the war, Jim Chainey recalled service with the Marston National Fire Service in the Parish Magazine of February 1995. This was the single fire service created in Great Britain in 1941 during World War 2. After 1947 fire services reverted to local authority control. Active members were Ralph Bartlett, George Noyce, Aubrey Wadman, Bill Smith and George Frampton Jnr. Clifford Hockey was in charge:

They started with a push cart from the Rectory but were later promoted to a trailer pump and did water training in the stream at Portway. One call out was to an ammunition fire towards Chilton and another to a farm fire at Mudford Sock. On both occasions Yeovil Fire Brigade arrived first!

The High Explosive bombs and other dangerous items were kept in Thorney Lane. Before the war it was impossible to walk through from one end to the other, but the Americans put down a concrete road beyond the house. They were then able to go in one way and out the other. If villagers wanted to go into Thorney Lane they would find it closely guarded by the Americans. A special pass was required, which had to be renewed by the C.O. at the Manor House. Members of the public were blocked from visiting the area.

One soldier was given special permission to be married in St. Mary's Church. However, family and friends were not allowed to attend. The villagers made up for that disappointment by offering a three-night stay at the stationmaster's house, and a wonderful party at the Village Hall.

The Americans improved the higher road from Middlemarsh to Dorchester, to make it easier to transport heavy equipment and munitions to the departure ports.

There were holding camps all along the south coast as the troops massed ready for the invasion. One such camp was in the village of Broadmayne between Dorchester and Weymouth. The camp accommodation areas were carefully chosen, as military planners were aware of the danger of camps being visible from the air. Hedges, farm buildings and woodland were all good camouflage. The journey to Weymouth carrying troops and all the munitions and equipment involved a fairly narrow country lane out of the village and up to the top of the Ridgeway. It had two very sharp bends that tanks and large vehicles would struggle to negotiate, so the bends were straightened and remain in this new shape to the present day.

It must have been very eerie back in Marston Magna when all the soldiers and all the vehicles departed. Suddenly it was quiet, because they disappeared in the blink of an eye.

Brenda Darch tells us:

A lot of young men of the village went away in the forces including Ron and Ralph Bartlett; The Chainey brothers - Reg, Hurford, Maurice, Cyril and Jim who were all in the RAF; Henry Trim; Arthur Penn; Bill Hunt; George Frampton; Les Sayers; Greville March; Ted Cannon; J.Batson; Tom Doel; Doug and Ray Miller; Stanley Highmore; John Webber; Percy Rainey; Dennis Pitman; Stan Sharp; Harry Tremlett and there must have been a few more which I can't remember.

The Memorial to the Fallen inside St Mary's Church lists the World War 2 fallen as:

L/Cpl. Percy N.G. Rainey 6th Bn.Grenadier Guards. Killed in action at El Alamein March 17th 1943 age 29. Buried in a war grave Tunisia.

Percy Rainey was a very keen bell ringer and had rung in most Somerset towers. His brother Ern said that Percy was able to ring in Durban Cathedral on his way to the Middle East.

Pte Dennis W.Pitman N.C.C. Killed in an accident May 21st 1945, lies in a Commonwealth War Grave. Non-Combatant Corps in Marston Magna churchyard.

Herbert Eldon Hope died as a result of war service 2nd February 1946. His parents, Mr. and Mrs. Ashworth Hope, commissioned carvings of The Stations of the Cross in his memory. These can be seen in St.Mary's Church.

Henry Trim was a member of the Territorial Army in 1939 and having survived the rigours of a Territorial camp at Corfe Castle in July 1939, he was very soon called up for War Service with 'A' Company, 4th Battalion The Dorset Regiment T.A.

Many years later, Henry wrote in the Parish Magazine of June 1989:

As a private in the Territorial Army at the commencement of WW2 I drew the princely sum of 14 shillings per week. Well, I didn't actually draw all of it as 7 shillings had to be put towards the Wife's allowance and 2 shillings retained for "leave" and "barrack room damages", so that one saluted smartly for 5 shillings. Stationed at Weymouth in the early weeks of the War, it cost 5s 3d for a return rail ticket to Marston on a day pass. Try and balance that out Chancellor of the Exchequer!

Henry married Grace in St Mary's Church at the beginning of the War. He caused some minor upset to the postal services by despatching a telegram to his unit immediately after the ceremony saying: "Sergeant, what do I do now?"

Other young men who went from the village were Doug Northover (who was a gardener at Marston Court), Bill Harding, and Bert Dorrington. Before war had been declared the T.A.s were stationed at The Drill Hall, Sherborne.

Agneta Hickley wrote a record of the first eighty years of the Marston Magna Women's Institute. In the booklet, she writes about life in wartime for many of the women in the village:

In 1936 there were sixty-seven members and in 1938 Rimpton joined Marston Magna with a vote of twenty for and twelve against.

As the threat of war became more a question of when than if, various charities appealed for help and this was given whenever possible. The Personal Service League received knitted blankets with gratitude. This was followed by the Overseas League for tobacco for the troops. Knitting wool was supplied and socks, helmets, mittens, gloves and scarves were made for the Somerset Comforts Fund. After a bring and buy sale, parcels of biscuits and cigarettes were sent to each member of the forces from the two villages.

With the arrival of so many evacuees from London the Reverend C.V. Borelli gave a talk on the life and conditions of these Londoners, hoping it might help to create a better understanding of the differences between town and country.

Miss Gregg from Rimpton ran the National Savings Campaign and after just two weeks she had raised seventeen pounds, seven shillings. This increased to well over a thousand pounds by the end of the war.

In September 1939 the meeting was cancelled due to the outbreak of war. This was the only occasion when no meeting took place, but in October 1940 it was delayed for a week because of an air raid. By September 1940 the Army had commandeered the Hall and the meetings took place in the skittle alley of the Marston Inn.

In true British style the children's party with Pongo the Clown, the WI Birthday Party and the New Year Party all went ahead as usual, but refreshments became more difficult and meat paste sandwiches were on the menu. For the birthday cake all members gave Mrs Sharpe one ounce of sugar, fat and fruit and she made the cake.

As the war progressed a scheme was set up for members to qualify for the Ministry of Food allowance of sugar for jam, provided the jam could be sold in the local shops. Thirteen hundredweight, one hundred and one pounds of sugar was supplied and the jam was made in Mrs. Dare's kitchen, but this was disbanded after one year because of the shortage of fruit. In the meantime Mrs Ashworth Hope allowed waste paper and cardboard to be stored at the Court for collection by the salvage team.

There was some trouble in 1941 when the Army commandeered the skittle alley, but the WI could meet in the Hall provided the meetings were held in the afternoon.

During the whole war the WI contributed to an endless call on their services and fund raising. It was sometimes difficult to find a venue, although several events were held at the Court, including outdoor whist drives, socials, concerts and three-penny parcels. The money raised would be sent to such appeals as:

Russia Week
Aid for the Merchant Navy
Occupational parcels for Prisoners of War
Wings for Victory Week

Warship Week
Medical Aid for Russia
St. Dunstan's
Salute the Soldier week.

The need was endless. In addition to these countrywide appeals, five shillings was sent to every serving man and woman for Christmas and this was increased to ten shillings in 1944. The Foresters Hall was vacated by the Army in 1944 and was available for meetings once more, but the cost had risen to one pound, eight shillings and sixpence which was considered to be too expensive and meetings were held in the school for three shillings a night. There was some difficulty when the Hall was re-opened because there were no chairs and no heating and the Foresters could not supply either. Eventually chairs were hired from the Church for two shillings and sixpence and whist drives and meetings returned to their old haunt.

This record shows that the Marston Magna Women's Institute played its part patriotically as the war years drew to a close.

Evacuees

Brenda Darch wrote:

Our quiet little school was suddenly expected to hold a lot more pupils as Evacuees came to the village from London. The village children had the big room and the evacuees had the small one. They had all come from Camberwell and as far as I know were all Roman Catholics. I know the village children couldn't understand why these children could do the things that they did and then confess to Father Berelli and all would be forgiven. Some of them must have come from some very poor homes as one lady in the village had awful trouble with the boy that she had. He was absolutely filthy when he arrived so she gave him a bath, showed him where his bedroom was and his bed. She called him to have a meal, after he had unpacked his things, and sent him to bed about an hour after. When she went to bed he was sleeping under the bed so she woke him up. She told him to get into bed but he wouldn't - he said he had never slept in a bed before - always underneath!

Some of these children stayed in the village until the end of the war but a lot of them were taken back to London by their parents. Over the war years we also had Evacuees from Essex & Kent who were sent as their towns were being bombed so badly.

Les Dewey

Les was evacuated from Southampton along with his brother and sister at the outbreak of war. They spent several months with Revd. and Mrs Bull at Tincleton Rectory in Dorset, before being collected. However, towards the end of 1940 Southampton was subjected to large-scale air raids resulting in extensive damage. There were particularly intensive attacks in November and early December, which subsequently became known as "Southampton's Blitz". Les remembers walking into the city centre with his sister and finding the whole of London Road flattened, save one building. His own home was rendered uninhabitable with not a door, window or ceiling left.

A second wave of evacuation took place and Les found himself amongst a throng of children and mothers on the platform of Southampton Station. As instructed, he wore his identification label and carried his gas mask, together with a small bag containing extra clothing. The train took him to Wincanton. From there, a coach carried the children to various nearby villages. Six of them were dropped at Galhampton, which lies between Castle Cary and Sparkford. Les was billeted with Sam Harper at the home of Oliver Hares and his spinster sister at Foxcombe Farm. Sam Harper and two of the other children ran away within days and Les never heard of them again.

Les attended school in North Cadbury and passed the 11+. His education was still the responsibility of Southampton Education Department where his parents resided, so he was awarded a place at Bournemouth Grammar, which now shared its buildings with Southampton's Taunton School. He spent 3 years there, residing in lodgings nearby, but in the school holidays he always returned to the home of Oliver Hare in Somerset.

Les finished school at 14 years, so in 1943 he returned to work at Foxcombe Farm. Oliver worked his farm in partnership with a skilful business farmer named William H. Longman. Farmer Longman would snap up farms that became available to rent or buy and offer a partnership to hard working farm hands, giving them a first leg up the ladder. He specialised in dairy cows and pig fattening. He also had a big farmhouse cheddar cheese operation as well. Any partnership deals featured the requirement to supply milk for the cheese making.

In September 1945 Les and Oliver came to Lambrook Farm on the outskirts of Marston Magna and before long took up residence at the one of the purpose built cottages opposite the farm entrance. Oliver's sister kept house and Les was kept busy doing general farm work and milking. Les' father would come from time to time to visit his son and on one occasion they visited Farmer Longman, who privately assured Mr Dewey the elder that he would help Les into a partnership when the time was right.

Les was given his chance in 1955 when he and his wife moved into a farm at Wincanton with just 12 cows.

By the time Les reached retirement he owned three farms outright and was just as successful as his early benefactor. His experience as a wartime evacuee from Southampton was the start of a successful career on Somerset farms.

Joan and Betty Mercer

Joan and Betty were approximately nine and seven years old when they came to visit Aunty Gert for a holiday in Marston Magna in the year 1939. Little did they think that it would be six years before they returned home to Stockwell. Their father served in the London Police Force and he and his wife decided to leave the girls in the care of Mrs Mercer's sister. Granny and Granddad were also close by at Bradford Abbas. Gert was married to Tommy Aplin who ran the garage business and the girls settled down to village life very quickly with an older cousin Marion keeping an eye on them.

Joan and Betty attended the village school where Mrs Jones was the headmistress. Both girls went on to pass the 11+exam and were awarded places at Charles Edward Brooke School, Lambeth Education Authority. Evacuees receiving education remained the responsibility of their home authority and arrangements were made with a school in Yeovil. The girls got lifts from villagers into Yeovil every day and at the end of the war took their rightful place at the school in Camberwell Green. While in Marston Magna, they attended church regularly, and since the boys that sang in the choir at that time used to 'mess around', before long Joan and Betty were asked to lend their voices. They were also both confirmed in St. Mary's Church.

Joan reports that she remembers American soldiers everywhere in the village with the white officers at The Manor. Uncle Tommy had most of his petrol pumps requisitioned by the Americans and she also remembers that he got casual jobs for them with neighbouring farmer Mr Wadham, picking potatoes and pulling vegetables.

Both girls retained very fond memories of their years in Marston Magna. When the time came, they did not want to return to London.

Charles Lodge

Charles Lodge was one of twelve children who were evacuated to Marston Magna and Rimpton from war-torn London during 1939. His family's house had suffered bomb damage, and his parents were pleased for him and his stepsisters to come to the comparative peace and safety of Somerset. He came with others from St Alban's School, Camberwell.

Charles was nine years old, and went to live at Marston Court with Mr. and Mrs. Ashworth Hope. He and two other boys lived in the servants' quarters, and he recalls that they "couldn't have been better looked after."

The boys went to Marston Magna School for six months, but the school became very crowded, so they were moved to the school in Rimpton. Mrs. Ashworth Hope insisted that they should return home for lunch, so they walked back over the fields every day.

They had a wonderful 2-3 years in the countryside, playing in what is now known as the Moat Field (Court Garden), and every morning Mrs. Ashworth Hope would come in at breakfast time to see that the boys were all right. They did not go into the main house very often, but Mr. Ashworth Hope played the organ in the Music Room and they were able to go in and listen.

One of the village farmers taught the boys how to milk cows, so then they were allowed to help him with the milking on the farm. The farmer also took them ferreting. At Marston Court, there were stables full of horses, and a paddock. At that time the Court had three entrances. Charles remembers how the Head Groom, Mr. Crawford, and the Gardener lived in cottages down Garston Lane.

Charles remembers attending the wedding of the Ashworth Hopes' daughter at St Mary's Church. His own step-sisters stayed with Mrs. Bryant, but her son was killed serving in the RAF, so the girls were moved to Mrs Woof's cottage, which was then near one of the village shops.

When it was time to return to his parents in London, Charles did not want to leave Marston Magna and the Somerset countryside.

Years later, he and his wife came to visit the village, but it was during the foot and mouth epidemic and they were unable to walk over his favourite fields. However, they have been back since, and in March 2015 Charles wrote in the visitors' book in St Mary's Church: *"Fond Memories."*

National Service: 1950s

Tony Penn writes:

Tony Penn in National Service uniform

As far as I am aware there were three of us who did National Service between 1955 and 1960: myself (Tony Penn), Ron Batson and Albert White.

Ron Batson did his service in the RAF. He went to Exeter for his Medical and his selection interview. Ron joined the RAF at Cardington on the 8th May 1956. He did his basic training there and a further training course in 'time and motion studies'. Throughout the remainder of his NS career he practised time and motion studies in various aspects of aircraft maintenance. He was known as a 'work study recorder'. Ron said that his period of NS turned out to be the most enlightening period of his life at the time! He was demobbed on the 9th May 1958.

For myself, I did my NS in the army, in fact the REME (Royal Electrical and Mechanical Engineers). I also went to Exeter for my interview and medical examination in July 1957. I was then called up on 24th October 1957 and I was posted to 1 Training Battalion REME at Blandford where I did my basic training. I was then posted to 7 Training Battalion REME at Barton Stacey where I did a course on workshop planning and progress. The course became irrelevant because I was then posted to 8 Training Battalion REME at Taunton, mainly to play football for the battalion team. In those days anyone who was a relatively accomplished sportsman could always find a comfortable 'slot' on their NS! I became orderly room corporal and in the process I met the Commanding Officer's secretary who two years after my demob in October 1959 became my wife. Quite clearly NS had a huge impact on my life. In addition to meeting my future wife I took every course and educational opportunity available and attended night school at the local technical college in Taunton, providing me with the background I needed for higher education.

A further interesting coincidence relating to the history of Marston Magna occurred during my NS. Whilst on cookhouse duties at 7 Training Battalion REME I was tasked with issuing the bread and butter rations. I served a corporal who I recognised. His name was Percy Miller and he was the son of Mr Miller who had a professional photographic business in the old army buildings on the site of the cider factory in Marston. The business was started during the war and carried on after the war, but finished when the Millers moved to Brighton in about 1951. Percy had been at school with us prior to his move. One of the specialist workers in the business was an Austrian lady named Fraulein Strauhuber who later became Mrs Miller, the original Mrs Miller having passed away. Fraulein Strauhuber was a lodger in our house at Marston.

Further conflict that occurred in the latter half of the century always involved serving military personnel only and with limited involvement of any village inhabitants. All military conflict makes distressing reading and alongside the long term skirmishes in Ireland, there have been several other very serious engagements which our government has supported. The following accounts have been written by people who lived elsewhere in the country at the time of the action, but they chose Marston Magna subsequently as their home and we appreciate their willingness to tell their stories:

The Falklands War: 1982

Second Lieutenant Tom Martin, Royal Artillery:

In 1982 I was a young Gunner officer serving in The Royal Artillery, based in Aldershot, when on the 2nd April 1982, Argentinean forces invaded the Falklands Islands. My Falklands War began on the 16th April when I received a telephone call with the code word 'Pegasus' recalling me back to barracks. We were recalled due to the fact that the Leading Parachute Battalion Group was added to the Task Force and my section, 29 Battery, was an integral part of that group. Earlier that morning I was to propose to my girlfriend Lieutenant Jill Harrison.

The following days were incredibly busy, not only getting both the equipment and ourselves ready to sail, but also to find a ring! I sailed on the North Sea Ferry - Norland from Portsmouth on the 26th April (D-25) to begin our 8000-mile voyage south. The days and weeks ahead were filled with endless lessons, drills and PT, punctuated by the briefest of stopovers at Ascension on the 7th May (D-14). This gave way to final planning and preparations and ultimately our orders for the re-invasion. The balmy tropical weather soon succumbed to the full might of the South Atlantic; giving us an insight to the weather we were about to face. Our specific plan detailed how we were to fly our 98 all rank unit and 6 Light Guns ashore. My part was to lead the first of 2 Sea King helicopters and a 30-man party, with orders to secure our designated gun position, and then hold it until the remainder of the Battery flew ashore. At the end of the afternoon of the 20th May (D-1), the entire Battalion Group was assembled for 2 Para's Commanding Officer – Lt Col'H' Jones' final address, which was followed by a brief church service. The mood was most sober. 'H' Jones' address steeled all hands to the task ahead, while the Padre prepared everyone, not only to the reality of what we were about to do, but allowed individuals to contemplate and make peace with their maker. At the end, there was no overt show of bravado, as everyone was focused on what they had to do and we all filed out in relative silence.

When I first packed my kit, rations, machine gun and ammunition, as well as my technical gunnery bag, I could neither physically fit it all in, nor pick it up! After halving some of the extra ammunition I was able to do so and was ready to go. I was detailed to go in at first light on the 21st May (D Day). The mood was sombre and nobody spoke as we made our way out, each filled with the feeling of 'right - this is it'. As dawn broke to a fair day, I could make out our new surroundings and thought, much as others, of its striking similarity to Scotland's Hebrides.

We landed and set up the position centred round the abandoned farmstead called Head of the Bay House, at the southern part of San Carlos Water. The house and all of the buildings conformed to the non-tactical highly visible paint scheme of white walls and red roofs! Our position was to see ammunition flown in at a rate never before encountered. The 105 mm Light Gun could fire a 35 lb high explosive shell 17,200m. Little did we realise that the amount of ammunition we had on the position was only a taste of what was to come in the weeks ahead. Towards the end, we were resupplied with 2000 rounds, of some 64.5 tonnes for the final push towards Stanley.

My role was that of a Command Post Officer (CPO), where I led a small team of technical assistants and radio operators. When a call for fire support was received, my task was to convert that request into firing data and collectively coordinate each gun to fire on my order. We used an archaic combination of protractor/plotter boards, slide rules and books of firing tables to 'compute' the solution - a world away from our early Land Rover mounted computer. It was 'old school', simple but effective. The following day saw us, as a Battery, fire the first Artillery rounds of the War. This was the first time that the Royal Artillery had fired in its conventional role in action, since Malaya in1960, although Gunners did fire in a limited capacity in 1967, during the crisis in Aden. The reality was that 29 Battery were the first to fire their guns and I was in the hot seat. As a Command Post we had survived our first baptism of fire.

During my time at Head of the Bay House I was to witness events not seen in modern times, from the multiple air attacks on the anchorage, the explosion of HMS Antelope and its ultimate sinking, numerous aircraft being shot down, along with our own offensive efforts. The news hacks tagged San Carlos Water 'Bomb Alley'. I have no idea what the Argentinean pilots called it, but I can only assume it was some form of hell on earth. What wasn't in question was their incredible bravery, which was clear from the way we saw them press home their attacks.

On Thursday 3rd June (D+13), we flew forward to Bluff Cove, some 22 km from Stanley, in preparation for the next phase of events, which also brought us into range of the Argentinean forward positions. Due to the nature of the terrain, we were actually the furthest forwards of our own troops. Being closer meant our firing increased with a steady influx of helicopters bringing in more and more ammunition. It was here at Bluff Cove on the 8th June (D+18) that I sensed an incoming air attack. I gave out the warning and we opened fire but it didn't deflect the Argentineans from bombing Galahad and the ensuing tragedy. We moved forward on Thursday 10th June (D+20) to our final position, some 6 km closer to Stanley, which put us just in range of its outer reaches. It was here for the next three days that we came under harassing enemy artillery fire. We were incredibly lucky, as our position was unsighted, with rounds exploding closely all around and overhead, but mercifully not amongst us. Eventually that harassing 155mm gun was silenced and we remained there until the end of hostilities, firing at an ever-increasing rate.

The islands themselves have a stark intrinsic beauty and the weather is generally unforgiving. The relatively low lying peaty 'camp', as the Islanders referred to it, was either barren rock, or covered in waterlogged tussock grass. The weather was best described as brutal. The sun did shine and the wind did drop, but it was never warm. It was quite feasible to experience all four seasons in a day. For the majority of the time, the incessantly strong winds, lashing rain, wet and at best damp clothing, along with the wind chill made it hard. Thankfully the Arctic clothing and rations were up to the task. However, rationing resupply was intermittent. For example, we went ashore with 3 days rations and it wasn't until the end of day 5 that we were resupplied. Taking matters into our own hands, a sheep was butchered and the farmstead's fallow vegetable patch gave up some potatoes and carrots. The subsequent stew was cooked in an old dustbin over a peat fire, which was cleaned to meet any health and hygiene standard. The biggest issue was the chronic shortage of the solid fuel blocks, akin to firelighters, required to cook our rations. On some days it was necessary to make a conscious decision to either eat or drink something hot. The only irritation was the lack of variety of the rations. There were 8 menu options, and I was to eat an overwhelming percentage of the 'mutton granules' menu, which is a dehydrated mince and gravy. As a result, I had an aversion to lamb and mutton for some 10 years afterwards.

Notwithstanding that, morale amongst the Gunners remained high and I was to witness northern humour at its best! We were generally in an information vacuum, but mail did get through, and I even received two cards actually on my 23rd birthday! We did manage to tune our HF radio into the World Service, and towards the end of the War, the Football World Cup began. In between missions I was able to pass out the scores, which raised more of a cheer than the tactical updates! Hostilities finally ended on Monday 14 June (D +24), with the Argentineans in full flight, retreating back into Stanley. At 1520, all Artillery was ordered to stop and by 1525, we were told that the Para's were marching through Stanley and morale couldn't have been higher.

On Thursday 17 June (Day 28) we repositioned back into the settlement at Bluff Cove, where we were to remain until our repatriation back to the UK, enjoying the company of the islanders there. I had a chance to briefly visit Stanley and it was in a truly sorry state, which was matched by the Argentinean Prisoners who, to a man, cut a dejected sight.

On Tuesday 29 June (Day 40), I was ordered to take a party of 27 onto the Landing Ship Sir Geraint, expecting a long voyage home, but thankfully we were overtaken by events and flights were arranged at Ascension for the final leg. We arrived at Ascension on Saturday 10 July (Day 51) and flew out a few hours later, arriving back at RAF Brize Norton at 0810 on Sunday, to our families and a small official welcoming party.

I did not do anything worthy of note, save trying to do my job to the best of my ability. What I can claim, is that when a call for fire came, when I was on duty in the Command Post, the Battery were first in the race to respond in the overwhelming majority of fire missions, and that all rounds landed where requested.

Lieutenant Jill Harrison, Women's Royal Army Corps:

Meanwhile, back in England and having seen Tom go off, I was to find that my services as an Officer were required in an unexpected way. I was pressed into service as a Visiting Officer for the South West, which I kept as a secret from Tom until his return.

Visiting Officers were the first point of contact that families had when it came to being informed of either the death, or serious injury of an immediate family member. All servicemen were required to notify whom their 'Next of Kin' was on a specific record card, in the event of their families having to be told if anything untoward had happened to them. When required to deliver such a notification, I would be taken by my driver to the family's address, and dressed in full Service Dress would make that fateful 'knock on the door'. The sight of an Army Staff Car pulling up outside one's house and an officer in full dress uniform getting out could only mean one thing, and families knew that they were about to receive devastating news. I would pass on the facts as known and offer the services of a Padre, before leaving the family to come to terms with their news.

I was required to make one such visit to a family of a Private Smith from 2 Para, just after the Battle of Goose Green, but thankfully it was just to notify them that their son had been wounded. As was often the case in these early days, the system kicked in and acted with scant information of the facts, believing that getting the information out was more important than the detail. In this instance, I was sent out with just a surname and an address to deliver the message. When I arrived at the door, the family knew that they were about to be told bad news. I began with formalities, by first confirming the identities of the family and that of their son. When I asked - 'are you the parents of Private 'Smith' they paused for a second and then replied - 'yes ... but which one ... we've two sons down there?' You can only imagine my horror at their response and I didn't know the answer. After a frantic phone call I was able to clarify which of their sons was involved. The family was just relieved to hear the positive news that their son was alive and didn't dwell on the failure of the Army's Welfare System, in how the news came about.

The news that Tom was finally coming back filtered through on Saturday 10th July. I arranged with Tom's parents to meet them at RAF Brize Norton early the next day, where we formed part of the homecoming crowd.

Following their engagement in 1982, Tom and Jill were married at Aldershot's Garrison Church on 18th June 1983. The following year Tom embarked on a flying career in the Army, gaining his pilot's wings in 1985. Service life eventually brought them to Somerset where he spent his last four years in the Army on exchange with the Royal Marines and Royal Navy at RNAS Yeovilton. They moved into Marston Magna in September 1993, along with their three children, as the first occupiers of The Oaks in Yeovil Road. As with other children in the village, Victoria, Charlotte and Andrew went to Countess Gytha Primary School before continuing their education at Ansford Secondary School in Castle Cary. The association with Countess Gytha went further than just the children's education, as Jill was a School Governor for 15 years, the last 6 of which as Chair of Governors. Jill was also active in the village sitting as a Parish Councillor for 4 years and for 10 years she set up and ran a Youth Group for over 10's.

Gulf War 1 and Croatia

Wing Commander Mark Willis

Mark Willis and his family came to Marston Magna in 1998 and bought a house in Little Marston Road from where he served out his time in the RAF until his retirement in 2003. His final tour of duty, on promotion to Wing Commander, was at MOD Abbey Wood where he was the Chinook Programme Manager, responsible for the purchase and introduction to service of new Chinook helicopters.

Mark Willis writes:

From my original home in the Black Country, I joined the Royal Electrical & Mechanical Engineers (REME) as an Aircraft Engineering Apprentice on 10 September 1969 – the very day that the troubles began in Northern Ireland. I met and married my wife Kate during this time in the army. She was serving as a Teleprinter Operator at RAF Upavon. I served in various locations including three tours in Aldergrove, Northern Ireland, where we flew photographic reconnaissance missions in an attempt to detect improvised explosive device sites.

Whilst at RAF Akrotiri in Cyprus, I saw that the 'grass was greener' in a light blue uniform so I applied and was accepted for a commission in the Royal Air Force; I returned for Officer Training to RAF College Cranwell in August 1986.

A prizewinner during my commissioning course and after Engineer Officer Training, my first appointment was at RAF Binbrook – the only hill in Lincolnshire – as Officer Commanding Engineering Wing Headquarters Flight. Several postings later I was posted to RAF Guetersloh as the Junior Engineer on 18 Squadron working on the Chinook Mk 2/2A helicopter or "the banana helicopter" as our German hosts called it. Two years into the appointment Iraq decided to invade Kuwait and Gulf War 1 began.

For the RAF helicopter force the early months of the war belonged to the Tornado. They deployed very early in the conflict and established operations on Saudi airfields. The helicopter force undertook a number of false starts and my Senior Engineer, Squadron Leader (now Air Vice Marshall) Julian Young and I became adept at putting together deployment plans. Having spent Christmas at home, the Chinook Squadron Middle East deployed from Hannover Airport to Al Jubayl by Kuwait Airways Boeing 747 on 28 December. Home in Al Jubayl was a motel-style foreign workers' hostel – relatively comfortable and the food was good if a bit repetitive. The helicopters arrived by ship a day after we did and we then spent 3 days continuously re-building and test flying them prior to them being parked on a specially laid dispersal adjacent to the docks.

The next 5 days or so saw the Chinook Detachment preparing to deploy into the desert. Money appeared to be no object. Our supply officer, armed with his

Amex Gold Card purchased photocopiers, 4x4 vehicles, paper plates and plastic knives and forks to avoid stomach problems, and 2 x 100 KVA generators which we mounted on a 40 foot articulated trailer. In order to be able to power the flying site, he also purchased 2 miles of armoured electrical cable.

In the second week of January, I led the advance party into the desert to an area called Logs Base Alpha. We had two days to set up the flying site prior to the rest of the Squadron and the helicopters joining us. We were located adjacent to a US Chinook Squadron and, at first, I could not believe how happy they were to see us – all would become clear in time. The US guys helped us build a barrier of sand around our site using a fleet of bulldozers. Payment for the favour was two boxes of Compo Rations to each driver. For some inexplicable reason, the Americans tired of their Meals Ready to Eat and looked forward to the change of eating something different, and Compo fitted the bill.

Scavenging parties were sent out to various areas and we soon had a set of shower blocks and the infamous diesel toilets. It is surprising how one gets used to doing your daily Number 2 sat next to a colleague and hearing the plink plonk as it drops into a couple of gallons of diesel below you. Sites were easy to spot as the daily poo burning took place to get rid of the human waste.

The rest of the Squadron soon joined us, we prepared to 'step up' (the term for the advance party moving to our next location) and we all stood in line to get a cocktail of inoculations. Surprisingly, only one or two guys experienced side effects. Having checked out the step up equipment, I then took the advance party forward to Logs Base Echo, which was on the Saudi/Iraq border on 12 January. A large sand barrier marked the border and we were within about 500 metres of the barrier.

Back at Logs Base Alpha the US Chinook Squadron was having a few problems with the sand getting into the Rotor Head seals. The US supply chain was tortuous so we were able to lend them some new seals until their spare equipment arrived. This example of coalition cooperation was repeated a number of times but the Americans were saddened when the Squadron left for Logs Base Echo, leaving them and their unofficial source of supplies behind.

The Squadron joined us at Logs Base Echo on January 16. The Air war had started the night before and those of us in the forward area found ourselves digging trenches for safety. It's amazing how quickly you dig even though it's your allies doing the bombing.

Once the Squadron deployed to Logs Base Echo the daily routine became almost predictable. The engineers were supporting flying operations; we were coping with aircraft unserviceabilities and working a day and night shift pattern. The routine was interspersed by the occasional warning of a chemical attack, which usually came to nothing and was caused by vehicle exhaust affecting the sensing equipment. Despite the inconvenience, we were highly amused by one of the airman, SAC Sweet (Isney), who held the record for getting into his protective clothing.

The ground war was short and sharp (24 February to 28 February). There are a number of books which tell the story better than I but it was the clear up after the Iraqi surrender that struck me most. Our helicopters worked 16 hours a day to collect and transport Iraqi prisoners to the various holding areas. We had never seen such pitiful human beings in our lives as the Iraqis. After the transportation operation we had to decontaminate the inside of the helicopters and the aircrew had to obtain new flying clothing because their original clothing had become infested with human fleas. A couple of the engineers and I flew out to view the road North from Basra, called the Highway of Death. I was somewhat affected by the sight and smell of the destroyed vehicles and their occupants – some 10,000 casualties in all.

Later in my career I was appointed Senior Engineer Officer on 1510 Flt – back to operational Chinooks, this time in Split. Many books have already been written about the conflict in the Former Republic of Yugoslavia so I will not attempt to explain the conflict. Suffice to say that I have never in my service career encountered a more violent race of people. The sight of a seven-year-old child attacking another child with a piece of wood populated with 4-inch nails is not a pleasant one. The look of bewilderment on the face of the attacker when he is relieved of the wood to prevent further bloodshed left me perplexed.

Mark is now pursuing a career in Defence Consultancy.

SERVICES

The Buses

Reg Wake, an eighteen year old lad, started his bus company in 1930 with just one second hand vehicle. By 1937 the fleet size had grown to four vehicles. From 1940 the business operated from Hancock's garage at Sparkford, now the site of the McDonald's Restaurant beside the A303.

The making of the business was perhaps the extensive wartime contracts to carry workmen to and from Yeovilton, Henstridge, Charlton Hawthorne, Corsham and other airfields and camps in the area. At its peak in the summer of 1943 over twenty vehicles were needed for this work alone.

After the war the business thrived, catering for the demands from schools and private hire as well as running bus routes. Our Henry's Column in the Parish Magazine notes that in 1956 there were 21 buses each way serving Marston Magna. He had the times of the service noted in his diary for that year.

National Buses served the village at one time alongside services run by Wakes.

Reg Wake died aged 78 in 1990, and the business continued to be operated by his sons Dennis and Michael, until their desire to retire led them to sell out to South West Coaches, a privately owned bus company, in the year 2001.

Electricity

By the end of the 19th century some companies and individuals installed electricity into their factories and homes using their own generators. Public supplies were initially set up by private companies or local authorities. By the beginning of the 20th century it was becoming apparent that electric lighting was as good as gas lighting.

During World War I the government established the Electric Power Supply Committee. Following the Electric Supply Act of 1925 the Central Electricity Board was formed. At first domestic supply was limited and used mainly by wealthy people. The introduction of electricity pylons into the countryside met with opposition. Street lighting was one of the early uses of electricity and first discussed for use in Marston Magna as early as 1911. In 1930 some local authorities brought in assisted wiring schemes to encourage people to connect their homes to the supply. Rural areas were often not connected until much later in the century and then the connection to individual homes was a gradual process.

Papers relating to St Mary's Church, Marston Magna refer to the Silver Jubilee Memorial Fund for electric lighting. There was correspondence with Wessex Electricity Company during 1935-6.

Electricity at Marston Magna School was not installed until January 1949.

Marston Magna has had difficulties with electrical supplies and during the 1980s and early 1990s the supply was subject to disruption with frequent power cuts. Sometimes only parts of the village were affected. Fortunately, an employee of Southern Electric living in the village during the 1990s, was exasperated by the disruption and work was carried out to renew faulty lines. Since renewal work took place in the mid 1990s, the supply has been much more reliable.

The Railway

Mrs. M. Davis wrote in her wonderful publication 'Marston Magna at the turn of the Century'

> *If you stand on the railway bridge and look north, down on your right you will see an overgrown patch of ground on which, before the railway came, a row of three cottages stood. Each had a neat garden in front open to the south, leading to the road going east to Rimpton and west to the village. A lane went south to Park Farm, with footpaths going to Rimpton and Mudford and further afield.*
>
> *But, with the coming of the railway a bridge had to be built over the east-west road, so that tons of soil and stone were brought, taking away part of the little front gardens and blocking the view to the south. A steep stony path thereafter led down to those little homes.*

She speculates that the coming of the railway through Marston must have been a great event causing much discussion and protest as men came with theodolites and chains measuring the fields, bridging the streams, cutting corners off fields and roads and taking slices from cottage gardens. One has only to stand on Park Bridge and look north to see exactly how the fields were divided and the old footpaths carried across the 'iron road' on level crossings. It is possible that men came from other parts to do the skilled work of constructing the permanent way, but there was a great deal of digging out and filling in that could be done by local men. The three bridges - Sutton Road, Rimpton Road and Park may well have employed local masons and bricklayers.

Revd. Peppin, who was vicar from 1905-1924, had a fairly reliable watch and he used to go to the station (often to collect his daily paper which arrived in the guard's van of the first train from London) and get London Time from the Guard, who had a chronometer which had been set right that morning in Paddington Station.

Mrs Davis also says that in those early 20th century days few people took a daily paper, many had the Western Gazette. Any startling news would be sure to come via the guard on the train straight from London.

John Peppin, the vicar's son, would take the train daily when he was a schoolboy at Bruton School. The first hazard to negotiate was a flock of hissing geese in the station road. He loved the train and remembers:

All the luggage racks had a legend 'These racks are provided for light articles only', which I once saw altered to 'These backs are provided for eight tickles only'. Sometimes the coaches were provided with electric lights; sometimes they had gas fittings and had a lovely smell of gas, but gave very poor light. The engines were a constant source of delight. There was one called 'Ilfracombe' and this was always a favourite of ours.

The 8.40am train from Marston Magna conveniently deposited us at Bruton just before 9am. There were two intermediate stations - Sparkford and Castle Cary, known to all the children as 'Castle Canary'. On one or two occasions the engine driver and the guard allowed us up to the driver's cab (a flagrant breach of railway law, but we came to no harm).

I remember arriving at Marston Station on our way home one evening; I thought I would try to emulate the guard, who, boarding or leaving the train, never waited for it to stop. I had not noticed that the guard, when performing these feats, always faced in the direction in which the train was moving. I just stepped out sideways and came an immediate cropper. It started a hubbub of shouting from all officials on the platform. Quite a sensation and I think my father was notified of my misdeed. I had certainly learnt my lesson.

Les Sayers tells us that Marston Magna Station was opened on 1st September 1856, half a mile east of the village. It was a single line and did not have a passing loop. A second track was added in 1881, providing the up-line to Castle Cary and Bristol and the down-line to Yeovil, Dorchester and Weymouth. The 1904 survey shows a crane on a dock, which could lift 30cwt and would have been essential to deal with the commercial activity. There was a Station Master's Office and even porters to help people with their luggage. There were sidings for goods and cattle pens. All Marston's needs would come through the station: coal, corn, cattle, feeds, horses and, of course, the mail.

Brenda Darch moved to Marston with her parents in April 1937 because her father worked for the railway and had been promoted to Second Man at Marston. She adds that some trains went direct to Bristol and others to Paddington. The journey to Paddington took approximately 3 hours, which meant a day trip to London was possible. She also says that there were two covered areas where you could wait in the dry. One was open ended having walls on three sides and just a long seat at the back, and the other housed the ticket office, waiting rooms and toilets. The waiting room had a grate and during the cold weather it was nice to sit by the fire waiting for the arrival of the train. Many Marstonians and Rimpton inhabitants caught the 8.10am to Yeovil each day to get to work, but during the war it was nothing for the train to be an hour or more late, usually because of bombing the night before in Bristol or Bath.

There was also a Signal Box on the up-side and concrete steps from the bridge down to the platform. For many years there was a Milk Factory on this side and there was a gate from the Milk Factory on to the platform, so that they could wheel the churns right up to the train to load. From where this gate came through right up to the signal box, which was at the opposite end of the platform, there were strips of garden approximately 20 feet wide and the men who worked on the railways had sections of this to cultivate. During the war everyone was told to "Dig for Victory" and all patches like this were turned into vegetable patches.

The men worked long hours anyway, but could be seen cycling back up the station in the evening to tend their patch. After the war little patches of garden with stones around them were placed at the back of the up-platform and flowers bloomed profusely, tended by the station staff. Everything was always kept immaculately clean with shining brass. Marston won the prize for the "Best Kept Station" a good many times.

It is thought that as many as five or six men looked after the track from Sutton Bridge to Hummer Bridge. Brenda's father moved before long to Yeovil Pen Mill, where he was responsible for 8 men and the railway track from Hummer Bridge to the other side of Yeovil, almost into Yetminster.

The banks were cut by hand using sickle, hook, bandy and scythe. There were huts on the side of the railway where the men had their meals.

The Station Masters traced through Kelly's Directories are listed below:

1902 Charles Gilbey - Station Master
1906 William Henry Shord Station Master
1910-1927 James W A Davis Station Master - his wife was Thirza Davis

Bill Squibb worked for GWR railway 1932-1982. He started as a porter at Weymouth and worked his way up to become Station Master at Marston Magna.

Railway staff.

Mrs Davis writes:

In Mr Gilbey's time there was no house on the left, it was built for a Mr. Shord from Evershot who had a wife and two little girls. When he moved, Mr J.W.A. Davis came and I married his son Arthur.

The following set of statistics make interesting reading:

MARSTON MAGNA	1903	1913	1923	1933
Passenger Tickets Issued	8785	7836	6637	4286
Season Tickets Issued	_	_	15	13
Parcels forwarded	11387	15332	5336	5628
General goods forwarded (tons)	725	1567	767	206
Coal/Coke received (tons)	1176	1165	1017	260
Other minerals received (tons)	1771	1967	3122	2322
General goods received (tons)	1332	1622	1943	725
Trucks of livestock handled	87	75	39	15

The Station was closed on 3rd October 1966, but the line remained open.

The Roads

For the first quarter century all the roads in the village were dirt roads and for the most part it was horses and horse pulled vehicles that used them. Jack Noyce recalled the road scraper in use to clean the roads in the early 1920s. It was a board arrangement on two iron wheels, lowered and dragged back by men. It must have been mighty hard work as the roads were very muddy at that time.

The roads leading in and out of the village were wide and rutted to accommodate the carts and wagons, but narrowed down to single lane where there was housing. At that time the route connecting Marston Magna and Queen Camel passed directly in front of Lambrook Cottage, and you can judge the width at that point by the size of the bridge which spans the brook which leads to and skirts the house.

Les Sayers tells us that by the end of the 1920s, a steam engine and steam roller were employed for making the roads, and that the stream in front of the church would be used to fill up with water. Horses hauled all the road making materials. A horse drawn water cart sprayed the road in front of the road roller.

When the tarmac process came into effect there were unused side strips on some stretches of road which people quickly laid claim to.

Children would often avoid using the road and walked across the fields. A former resident of the village spoke of this when explaining how she used to deliver her father's lunch when walking from one end of the village to the other, going from West End to Cooper's Farm.

The turning off Camel Street, which leads past, the Station to Sandford Orcas and Rimpton was always known as Station Road. It was reported in the December 1976 Parish Magazine that the Clerk of the Parish Council informed that to save confusion at the Post Office with Postal Codes, the old Station Road had now been officially named Rimpton Road. Many of the older village inhabitants were highly incensed at this decision and thought that it had been taken without any consultation.

In the 1970s application was made to the Church authorities for them to cede a portion of the Glebe Field for the purpose of road widening. The application did not receive any encouragement. Subsequently, the matter was taken up at County level and the Divisional Highway Surveyor prepared a scheme for the widening of the road, taking in a piece of the Glebe Field, and rebuilding the wall. This scheme was rejected at County level on financial grounds, there being insufficient funds for maintenance in rural areas, let alone improvements.

1980 heralded major work to the A359 through the village as part of a flood prevention scheme. The height of the road was increased on the garage corner (where a lake always appeared after heavy rain) and also past the Church. This necessitated raising the bridge on the village green in front of the Manor House and also raising the wall that runs beside the stream. Garston Lane was brought into use for access purposes while the work was carried out.

Residents enjoyed this contribution to the magazine published in October 1980:

Lament for the new bridge
What have the council in Marston been doing?
Rebuilt the bridge? It's a picturesque ruin.
The character of the Village has gone for good,
It's the centre where many of our ancestors stood.
In this lovely old Village, I no longer reside,
To see money so wasted, I couldn't abide.
The pavements they've narrowed, no room to walk,
Have the Villagers not been allowed to talk?
Alteration! Which is not going to stop Marston from flood,
So the money they've spent will be lost in the mud.

An Old Marstonian.

Sewerage

A recent W.I. publication states:

Two of the biggest issues facing the countryside were only too familiar to WI members, those of housing and sanitation. A WI survey from 3,500 institutes, published in 1944, revealed that just under a third of rural parishes still had no piped water supplies; half were without sewerage, while fewer than 10% of agricultural workers' homes had electricity.

Julian Noyce, living in Camel Street, remembers that the sewers were dug in the road during the period 1969-1970. This must have caused considerable disruption although the road always remained open. Traist House in Camel Street was built in the early 1960s with a cesspit, but Greystones next door, built later in that decade, was connected to the sewerage system. Outlying houses would of course continue to use cesspits.

Street Lighting

Items on the 19th Parish Agenda in 1902 included "What steps (if any) should be adopted to commemorate the Coronation of King Edward VII" and "To present the result of the Voluntary subscription towards lighting the 2 Parish Lamps". The sum of £1/16/0d. had been collected by voluntary subscription and after paying the oil account there was a balance in hand of 15/9d. Mr. E.D. Marden (chairman) said that although Whittle had kindly offered to light the lamps for the past winter free of charge, he considered that he (Whittle) should be given something for his trouble, as it certainly could not have been a very pleasant job. It was proposed and carried that the 15/9d on hand should be given to Whittle.

John Peppin, who recalls life in the village at this time, reports that there were two communal street oil lamps, one at the junction of Station Road and Camel Street (which in his experience was hardly ever lit) and the other at the entrance to the churchyard on the edge of the Green. This was sometimes lit in winter on Sundays for those going to Evensong. He further said that if one went out at night in mid winter, one lit a candle in a small red lantern. It gave uncertain light and if there was a wind blowing, the chances were that it would blow out before one's destination was reached.

In 1911, during its first year in office, the Parish Council were discussing the possibility of lighting the village by electricity, this at a time when there was little or no supply to houses. However, by 1912 the Parish Council accepted a tender by local tradesman Mr A.C. Newberry (the blacksmith) to erect 10 oil lamps with raisers, extinguishers, posts and fittings for the sum of £24/14/-. The following month Mr W. Milverton was appointed to light, clean and extinguish the lamps at a salary of eight shillings per week of seven days, and an additional sum of five shillings to be paid for putting lamps in place and removing to store at the end of season. It was agreed that the lamps be used for the first time this season on 6th October 1912.

The Parish Council Meeting of 15th April 1915 recorded a hearty vote of thanks to Mrs Noyce for her kindness in allowing the village lamps to be stored on her premises (The Marston Inn) during the summer months. Later that year, 5th October 1915, the Parish Council passed a resolution 'That on account of the War and the high prices of the required material, the Council do not consider it advisable to light the Parish lamps this winter'.

Mr Jack Noyce remembers that before the council estate was ready for any occupation in 1921 that there were about six oil lamps, and that Mr Ern March used to light and extinguish them. He remarked that it used to take a box of matches to light the lamps on a windy day.

Les Sayers says there was an oil lamp outside St. Mary's Church and there is still a street light bracket fixed to the corner wall of No 2 Cottage Camel Street, beside Fowkes. He also says there was a street oil lamp in

Rimpton Road which probably refers to the one outside Garston Farm, at the point where the pavement from the Railway Station crossed from one side of the road to the other. The last man to light the streetlights was Mr F. Cannon in about 1929.

Moving on towards the end of the 20th century, the Parish Council AGM for 1986 reported the present position with regard to street lighting:

If a satisfactory system of street lighting is installed on the A359, a speed limit could be imposed. This limit could be 30, 40 or de-restricted to 60mph as it is at present.

The County Council will only take over a newly installed street lighting system, if it is free of any loan. This means quite simply that we have to raise the money ourselves – not from the Rates because that would be raising a loan.

After discussion by the Council it was agreed that rather than a Referendum, which has political connotations, a Street Lighting Questionnaire would be prepared so see if street lighting is the wish of the parish. In addition, as we all have to raise the money, everybody will be asked if they would be willing to provide money towards the street lighting project, and how much. Marston Inn along the A359 to Cooper's Farm and Little Marston Road is estimated at £16,554 + 15% VAT.

Seven years later in 1993, the subject was still being fought, when Marston Magna Parish Council printed the following statement:

There has been a great deal of misinformation circulating in letters and the Press. The scheme would consist of 70-watt side entry lanterns. In no way would they resemble Mudford, Yeovil or indeed "Spaghetti Junction". The Somerset Council still has to satisfy the Parish Council as to the precise details of proposed lanterns. A further scheme for Rimpton Road and Little Marston Road could be considered in the future.

Both Councils would give a total of 50% grants and the rest would be raised by loan spread over 10, 20 or 25 years. National Association of Local Councils advocate that anything that has a long shelf life and would benefit future generations should be spread over 25 years, thereby more people will be paying a contribution.

Running costs, maintenance, broken bulbs, bent poles etc would be paid for by Somerset County Council. Through our Council Tax we are already paying for everyone else's lights in the County.

The Parish Council meeting held in November 1993 voted to proceed with Street Lighting on the A359 in the more decorative style as at Queen Camel, rather than the plainer type as at Mudford. It was a unanimous vote, with the exception of the Council Chairman who did not attend but sent in a letter drawing members' attention to the desirability of regarding previously expressed views.

The Chairman subsequently tendered her resignation; citing decisions taken at the meeting had made her position as Chairman untenable.

In January 1994, the Parish Council reported that Council Minutes for several years back had been examined by a very senior Local Government Officer, who confirmed that the decision to go ahead with street lighting reached at the November meeting was legally in order. It was reported that whilst there were some problems with grants and loans and with the tender validity, it was thought that these could be resolved, with work to commence in the late spring. Questions were admitted from the public at this stage and a petition was presented, signed by 111 residents opposed to the scheme. The Council would consider the petition at its next meeting.

A coffee morning was held in February 1994 in aid of funds for the "Action Committee Against Street Lights" to pay for paper, posters and any legal costs for the forthcoming referendum. Any excess funds after costs would be donated to the New Village Hall Fund.

A referendum was held in Marston Magna on 17th February 1994 asking the 374 electors if they supported the scheme proposed by the Parish Council at their meeting of 15th November 1993.

The full results are listed below, with the areas covered by each ballot box indicated to give an idea of the feeling in each part of the village.

	YES	NO	SPOILT
Centre, Court, outlying parts & postal	14	56	1
West End	16	10	1
Camel Street	31	50	1
Rimpton Road	4	50	1
Townsend & Little Marston Road	10	55	
Yeovil Road	15	17	
	90	238	4

24% of the total electors in favour of the scheme
63.6% of the total electors against the scheme as proposed
88.7% of the electorate voted

At the Annual Parish Meeting held in May of that year, it was noted that the street lighting scheme, which had provoked some local controversy, had been deferred in implementation until May 1995, though in practice could not be earlier than April 1996.

Finally, in June 1995, it was proposed by Marston Magna Parish Council that the Street Lighting Scheme be dropped and the minute of 8 November 1993 be rescinded. The motion was carried by 4 votes to 2 and Councillors Sayers and Hooper requested the recording of their contrary votes.

The Telephone Exchange

The plot of land bordering Camel Street was sold by Percy Aldridge to HMPG (His Majesty's Postmaster General) in 1933 for £25 and the Exchange building and a separate small store were erected.

In 1951 the plot of land to the rear was also purchased by HMPG and on this occasion the vendor was C.W.Hockey.

In 1974 planning approval was given to erect a new Telephone Exchange behind the old one. The Annual Parish Meeting in 1979 notes that the new Marston telephone exchange was ready for opening but was held up owing to a shortage of equipment at the Yeovil end. It was expected to be ready in May when the village becomes 'ten-numbered' and that the 53 prospective and waiting subscribers will be connected.

In 1995 BT put the original two buildings on the roadside up for tender, as they were no longer required for telephone operations.

The sign caught the eye of Nicholas Rheinberg, who as Coroner for East Somerset travelled regularly through Marston Magna to attend inquests in Yeovil Magistrates Court. He had always liked Marston Magna and on a complete whim he put in a sealed bid at a ridiculously low price of £29,300. To his surprise it was accepted. He thought it would be a good idea to convert the buildings for use by Solicitors but primarily to use it as a Coroner's Office. The Coroner's colleagues were less keen on the idea and having been granted permission for office use, a second application was subsequently made for domestic usage. The planning committee refused this, on the grounds that they wished it to remain a commercial property.

A site meeting was convened and a compromise reached. All rooms were granted domestic use except the loft (which is large with concrete trusses), which should retain business use.

The smaller of the two buildings was demolished, as it was impossible to integrate it into the larger building. A large cherry tree nearby had undermined the drains and foundations. The Coroner transferred his design for a dwelling into Lego format and presented it to his appointed architect. The Exchange building was extended, adding an additional 3 rooms with a bedroom created in the new roof space.

Nicholas Rheinberg never lived in The Old Exchange but placed the newly developed property on the market immediately the conversion had been completed.

Both the old and the new Exchanges feature automatic equipment and as such never had an operator working inside. The Exchange acts as a receptor for all calls in the near vicinity. It gathers them up and transmits them to Exeter Exchange where they are forwarded to your chosen exchange number.

As this is written in 2015 the village is eagerly awaiting the arrival of super fast broadband and also changes in communication technology mean the requirement for the Exchange is likely to terminate very soon.

Wells and Water

At the beginning of the century all water in the village was retrieved via wells. Mrs M. Davis records that the mother of her best friend Annie Sherring would draw water from an unfenced well with a bucket dangled on a rope.

Easton Farm, just along the road from the Sherring home, had a well with a wind pump, which provided water for the Creamery and the Cider Factory. That well is still in use at the time of writing, but is now powered by an electric pump.

This well was not meeting the needs of the factories, so in 1916 Mr E.D.Marden hired a water diviner from Sparrows at Martock and found an almost inexhaustible supply of water in the vicinity of Slade Farm on Rimpton Hill. Edwin purchased the piece of land, which was fortuitously owned by his brother Walter. A reservoir was constructed which can still be seen today and Bert Connick was hired to manage it. Les Sayers remembers walking along Slade Lane as a boy and calling in for a drink of nice cool water.

John Peppin remembers:

Until that time all houses had their own wells, which entailed quite a lot of work and might dry up in droughts. When the reservoir was established all potential takers were circularised with the glad news together with the cost of being put on mains water. The water rate for the first year was £1. I remember that my father, who always lived from hand to mouth thought it very expensive, but being the Rectory it was almost obligatory for us to be at least on equal terms with the 'quality' of the village. So it came about that we had piped water - and very good water it was. The well in the garden fell into disuse. But then came 1914, that great watershed, as a result of which, everyone's life was changed and the Victorian and Edwardian ages passed away to return only in the memories of the old. Until the war, the peasants touched their caps when one met one in the road and called me 'Master John'. But in the face of war with Germany there had to be some collaboration between the peasants and the gentry. German spies were everywhere or so we imagined and if everywhere, then why not in Marston Magna? And what would they attack first? The station? The Cider Factory? Why bother, if they could poison the water supply? Our population could be wiped out that way and obviously it was just the sort of mean, dastardly act that only Huns would think of putting into practice. We Marstonians were not to be wiped out so easily and a rota of semi able bodied men was drawn up to protect the little red brick shed under which our spring was sited. I was only ten at the time and I do not remember how many hours were spent at the spring by each custodian. But I do remember being taken to the spot and seeing my father sitting on the grass in front of the shed with a shot gun across his knees. Whether he knew how to use it, I am not sure, as I never in my life saw him fire at any living creature. In fact, we did not possess a gun of any kind, and no doubt there was just the one gun, which was passed on to each custodian for his turn of duty.

Whatever the reason, defence of the waterworks was gradually abandoned.

Mr.E.D.Marden sat on the Rural District Council and in preliminary investigations at Marston samples of water were taken from six existing wells in the village. Five were condemned as impure and the other doubtful! The most frequent cause of contamination was poor practice from the cattle farmers and the abattoirs, which featured in nearly every village. The water samples were taken by Sanitary Inspector Mr N.G. Fish! Water from the reservoir was subsequently piped into the big houses, which certainly the inhabitants found more convenient but it was available only to those that could afford it.

The reservoir is still in existence. It was sold to Yeovil District Council in 1937 and is currently under the control of Wessex Water. It is maintained for emergency purposes only.

Gradually, mains water was introduced to the rest of the houses in the village. As a house was condemned and either modernised or pulled down and rebuilt, so mains water supply would be introduced, but this life changing innovation did not reach completion until after the end of World War 2.

The following well locations have been identified. This is almost certainly not an exhaustive list.

Almshouses (demolished)	Communal pump in front garden (Parish Mag Mrs Davis Aug 77)
Braggcroft	Front Garden (filled in)
Bridge Cottages No 4	Rear garden
Chartwell House (station)	Reformed to Septic Tank
Demolished cottage by rail track	
Fir Villa	At front of building now covered by 1970's extension
The Old Forge	Front Garden
Garston Farm	One in Yard and one inside house In Farm Buildings In field
Jasmine Cottage (Red Lion)	Rear garden, probably served all the building
Marston Inn	In the courtyard (Parish Mag HT May 77)
Marston House	
Michaelmas Cottage	Inside gateway to back garden
Mill	Preserved in good condition at the front of the Mill
Millbrook House	Under rear extension
Old Marston House	Reportedly at the rear of the house
Portway Farm	One by backdoor and three in fields
Potters Well	One filled in
Rosewell	In garden
Sunnyside (Old Butchers Shop)	Reportedly in driveway now filled in
Tippling Ho. (Shaddiloes)	One inside house and one outside
The Rectory	Side of the stable (filled in)
The Old Stables	Garston Lane
Vine Farm (demolished)	At entrance to extension of Church Lane
West End Farm	
White House	Front Garden
Wickham Farm	Inside House In farm buildings In field
Wyndhams	Under patio

House building in The Twentieth Century

1900's

Chartwell House (Station)	Rimpton Road

1920's

West End Nos 1-12
Marston Court (alterations)
The Manor House Rear Extension

1930's

Casa Mdena (The Bungalow)	Camel Street

1940's

Lambrook Cottage

1940's - 50's

Townsend Nos 1-26

1950's

Ashe Cottage	Rimpton Road
Clover Cottage	Lit Marston Rd
Courtside	Yeovil Road
Ginaville	Camel Street
Fairways	Camel Street
Homemead	Rimpton Road
Lambrook Farm House	Camel Street
Standlemead	Camel Street
The Firs converted from 2 into 1	Garston Lane
The Police House	Camel Street

1960's

Carrick	Camel Street
Curracloe	Yeovil Road
Greystones	Camel Street
Home Lea Nos 1-4	Yeovil Road
Kyle	Church Lane
Merryfield (Eyewell)	Camel Street
Old Orchard	Yeovil Road
Saffron Hill	Rimpton Road
St Lawrence	Camel Street
Staddlecote (now the Rectory)	Camel Street
The Old Forge	Yeovil Road

Traist House	Camel Street
Wavelands	Rimpton Road
West End Nos.13-16	
Wisteria Farm	Fiddle Lane

<u>1970's</u>

Bay Tree Cottage	Rimpton Road
Beech House	off Church Path
Brookfield	Rimpton Road
Brooklands	Yeovil Road
Brookside	Marston Court
Camlann	Camel Street
Cheriton	Church Lane
Chesterton	Lit Marston Rd
Clonmellon	Rimpton Road
Court Gardens Nos.1-5	Rimpton Road
Courtlands	off Church Path
Dunelm	Marston Court
Dyffryn	Lit Marston Rd
Farmside	Camel Street
Glenshire	Lit Marston Rd
Greenacres	Yeovil Road
Grey Cedars	Marston Court
Hawkwind	Lit Marston Rd
Hayling	Lit Marston Rd
Homemead	Camel Street
Hunters Lodge	Yeovil Road
Juniper House	off Church Path
Kynloch	Lit Marston Rd
Lyndhurst	Lit Marston Rd
Marden	Lit Marston Rd
Martella House	Camel Street
Mead End	Rimpton Road
Merstone	Camel Street
Orchard House	Camel Street
Orchardlea	Rimpton Road
Ottersey	Rimpton Road
Park Cottage (conversion)	Park Farm
Pinfold	Lit Marston Rd
Rossall	Camel Street
Sandwell	Marston Court

Sharps and Flats	Yeovil Road
Stocklynch	Lit Marston Rd
Sunnybank	Rimpton Road
The Bungalow	Thorney Lane
The Ridings	off Church Path
Tralee	Dampier Lane
Willow End	Lit Marston Rd
Wychways	Camel Street
Wyle Cop	Camel Street

1980's

The Barn (conversion)	Park Farm
Beechwood (conversion)	Park Farm
Coopers Barn (conversion)	Camel Street
Corton View	Camel Street
Dryburn	Camel Street
Portelet	Camel Street

1990's

Mayfield	Camel Street
The Oaks	Yeovil Road
Parkway Mushrooms	Park Farm
Stable Cottage	Camel Street
The Old Exchange (conversion)	Camel Street
The Owl House, Fir Villa	Camel Street

Listed buildings In Marston Magna

2, Church Walk Grade: II Date Listed: 19 April 1961
(Previously listed as- "The Old Rectory")
English Heritage Building ID: 262682
Church Walk, Marston Magna, Somerset BA22 8DQ
Listing NGR: ST592732232

Ashe House Grade: II Date Listed: 19 April 1961
English Heritage Building ID: 262686
Rimpton Road (North side) BA22 8DH
Listing NGR: ST5942822393

Camelot Grade: II Date Listed: 16 August 1984
English Heritage Building ID: 262677
A359, Marston Magna, Somerset BA22 8DB
MARSTON MAGNA CP CAMEL STREET (East side)
No 3 (Camelot) and No 4
Listing NGR: ST5940222583

Church of St Mary Grade: I Date Listed: 19 April 1961
English Heritage Building ID: 262672
Location: Little Marston Road, Marston Magna, Somerset BA22 8DG
Listing NGR: ST5934122341

Collins Higdon Tomb 3 Metres East of the South East Corner of Church of St Mary
Grade: II Date Listed: 16 August 1984
English Heritage Building ID: 262674
Location: Court Gardens, Marston Magna, Somerset BA22 8DE
Listing NGR: ST5936122340

Court House (The North Wing of Marston Court) Grade: II Date Listed: 19 April 1961
English Heritage Building ID: 262683
Location: Garston Lane, Marston Magna, Somerset BA22 8DN
Listing NGR: ST5929422222

Fir Villa Grade: DL Date Listed: 16 August 1984 Date Delisted: 21 September 2009
English Heritage Building ID: 262678
Location: A359, Marston Magna, Somerset BA22 8DB Camel Street (East Side)

Former School House, Grade: II
Date Listed: 16 August 1984
English Heritage Building ID: 262679
Camel Street (West side) BA22 8DD
10 metres N of Rimpton Road Junction
Listing NGR: ST5935022400

Garston Farm House Grade: II
Date Listed: 16 August 1984
English Heritage Building ID: 262689
Rimpton Road, (North Side) Marston Magna, Somerset BA22 8DH
Listing NGR: ST5963022421

Kingsland House Grade: II Date Listed: 19 April 1961
English Heritage Building ID: 262687
Rimpton Road, (North Side) Marston Magna, Somerset BA22 8DH
Listing NGR: ST5947822402

Manor House Grade: II* Date Listed: 19 April 1961
English Heritage Building ID: 262680
Church Green, Garston Lane, Marston Magna, Somerset BA22 8DW
Listing NGR: ST5930322306

Marston House Grade: II Date Listed: 19 April 1961
English Heritage Building ID: 262690
Rimpton Road (South side) Marston Magna BA22 8DH
Listing NGR: ST5987622463

Marston Inn Grade: II Date Listed: 16 August 1984
English Heritage Building ID: 262691
Rimpton Road,(South side) Marston Magna, Somerset BA22 8DL
Listing NGR: ST5987822459

No 1 with East Front Boundary Railings Grade II Date Listed: 19 April 1961
Church Walk, Marston Magna
English Heritage Building ID: 262681
Church Walk, Marston Magna, Somerset BA22 8DQ
Listing NGR: ST5927922325

Park Farmhouse Grade: II Date Listed: 16 August 1984
English Heritage Building ID: 262692
B3148. Sherborne Rd, (East side) Marston Magna, Somerset BA22 8AX
Listing NGR: ST5988121502

Shadiloes Grade: II Date Listed: 16 August 1984
English Heritage Building ID: 262688
Rimpton Road (North side) Marston Magna, Somerset BA22 8DH
Listing NGR: ST5957422419

Taylor-Parsons Tomb 6 Metres South East of South East Corner of South Porch of Church of St Mary Grade: II Date Listed: 16 August 1984
English Heritage Building ID: 262673
Garston Lane, Marston Magna, Somerset BA22 8DG
Listing NGR: ST5934222331

The Mill House Grade: II Date Listed: 19 January 1989
English Heritage Building ID: 262804
Rimpton Road (South Side) Marston Magna, Somerset BA22 8DH
Listing NGR: ST5955822340

The Old Smoke House Grade: II Date Listed: 16 August 1984
English Heritage Building ID: 262675

Camel Street (East side) Marston Magna BA228DB
Listing NGR: ST5940622661

The Rectory Grade: II Date Listed: 19 April 1961
English Heritage Building ID: 262685
Little Marston Road, Marston Magna, Somerset BA22 8DT
Listing NGR: ST5929922384

Wickham Farmhouse Grade: II
Date Listed: 19 April 1961
English Heritage Building ID: 262684
Little Marston Road, Marston Magna, Somerset BA22 8DJ
Listing NGR: ST5919322424

Wyndhams, with Roadside Boundary Railings Grade: II Date Listed: 19 April 1961
English Heritage Building ID: 262676
Camel Street (East side) Marston Magna BA22 8DB
Listing NGR: ST5940622641

Source: EnglishHeritage (now Historic England)

http://www.britishlistedbuildings.co.uk/england/somerset/marston+magna

Post 2000
Note "Shadiloes" has been renamed "Tippling House"

Properties known to have existed during the 20th century but now gone

The Almshouses	Yeovil Road
Mill Cottages	Rimpton Road
3 cottages beside railway bridge	Rimpton Rd
The Forge	Yeovil Road
(small part remaining at The Old Forge).	
The Garage	Yeovil Road
The Foresters Hall	Yeovil Road
Thatched barn beside Studley's Farm,	Rimpton Road.
The Slaughterhouse	Camel Street
Northover Cottage	Camel Street
Vine Farm	Church Lane
Telephone Exchange Store	Camel Street

Notes: Portway Farm was two cottages for agricultural workers in 1900. The buildings still exist as Portway Farm, but it is now one home.

Rosewell was once two cottages, which may have been known as Wickham Cottages.

Conservation Area in Marston Magna

A designated Conservation Area was drawn up in March 1987. The details are readily available on the South Somerset District website. The Area Ref number is 57.

The Mill

Marston Mill, in Rimpton Road, was part of the estate of the Genge-Andrews of Rimpton. It was sold in 1924, six years after the family had left that village. During the 1920s the Mill had a bakehouse, and was worked by a water-powered turbine. The equipment included Peak and French stones, an oat bruiser, and a bean kibbler. (This is a kibbling machine or grinding equipment for beans, corn, for example).

Les Sayers wrote about the Mill in his memoirs. He said that it was used for grinding cattle food, and was a flour mill in the late 1800's. As a boy, he used to play with the Miller's son:

> *The water was controlled in the mill pond by the hatches which were very deep...I can still remember the big West of England sacks containing 2.25 cwts. of flour. With our airguns we would always find a rat or a sparrow to shoot.*

At one time the Mill was owned by dairy farmer P.E. Davis of Wickham Farm.

Milling seems to have ceased soon after 1924.

The Almshouses

The Almshouses stood on 0.284 of an acre of land, having a frontage opposite to the site of the telephone box on the Yeovil Road. The river ran alongside. Three cottages, sometimes referred to as 'Brook Cottages', stood on the plot. These Almshouses had been left by the Revd. J. Williams in the 19th century, together with £100 Stock for the purpose of repairs. His daughter, Mrs Frances Cox, gave stock of £108 16s 11d, the interest of which was to be distributed to the inhabitants of the Almshouses in coals during the months of November through to March.

At the beginning of the 20th century there were four people living in the Almshouses. They were all over 70 years of age.

In November 1981 Mrs Davis described the Almshouses, which she remembered from her childhood:

> *They were pleasant homes, each with a long garden in front, which was gay with flowers near the front door and plenty of room for vegetables. A tall pump stood in the centre of the plot. It must have been about six feet high, cased in wood, with a long iron handle ending in a large round knob.*
>
> *During the winter the pump was swathed in sacking and straw to prevent freezing; if there happened to be a drought in summer the water sometimes would not 'come' and had to be 'fetched'. This meant getting a bucket of water from the brook, pouring it in to the top of the pump, and then working the handle vigorously – this actually succeeded in 'bringing' the water. As a child I found this operation a great mystery.*
>
> *Each cottage had two rooms and a 'back house'.*

Mrs Davis recollects the lady who lived in the Almshouse nearest to the brook as being Mrs Charlotte Biddiscombe, referred to as 'Little Charlotte' to distinguish her from another villager of the same name.

> *She was a little round tubby person who always had a smile for children as she stood by her garden gate. I remember her buttoned up to her chin, wearing a whale-boned bodice fitted over her long black skirt, and a shawl over her shoulders. It was rumoured that she was a witch but she wasn't in the least like any witches in my fairy-tale books. She had white hair, on which she wore a bonnet-shaped cap, trimmed with ribbon and black sequins, brightened by a flower – a daisy or a violet perhaps. This was the headgear that was usually worn by elderly ladies, although some wore a thick black net which held their hair in a loose bag.*

Mrs Davis also remembered an elderly gentleman who lived in the middle house although not his name:

I remember him in shirt and corduroy trousers, the shirtsleeves rolled up and the trousers tied below the knee with a leather bootlace, digging the trench to plant his potatoes.

The third Almshouse was home to her great-aunt, Mary Ann Bush, widow of John Bush, formerly the parish clerk. Mrs Davis visited the house:

My mother sometimes sent me with small offerings - rock cakes or a small pudding. There was a little square window in the sitting room and there was always a cheerful fire in the grate and a kettle on the trivet. All the cooking was done in this fire and in the oven at the side. The walls were covered with framed pictures and photographs, including memorial cards, six or seven in a frame, such as were sent to friends and relatives after a funeral. But I never stayed long – I had to go straight home – so I never heard the stories she might have told me had I known what to ask.

People often moved house around the village during their working life. On retirement, some moved into the Almshouses, although a few people remained in employment whilst they were living there. In 1918 Charlotte Biddiscombe was still living at the Almshouses. John Linthorne was resident in one of the others, and Charles Miller in the third. Sarah March lived in Rimpton Road in 1918 but by 1926 she was living in the Almshouses. Elizabeth Sibley was an occupant in 1926 whereas she had lived in Mill Cottage in 1918. George Jesty was resident there too in 1926 and still there in 1939. In 1948 George Foote had moved into the Almshouses after living in Camel Street for many years.

By 1955, the Almshouses had become 3 condemned uninhabited residences. The people living there had been rehoused by the council. In 1956 there was an order for the demolition of the Almshouses. The land was put up for sale in the late 1950s. Mr Aplin made enquiry about the purchase of the plot, but in 1960 there was a Compulsory Purchase Order made by Yeovil R.D.C. Compensation of £400 was paid to the Revd. Williams Charity.

On 28th February 1982 Henry Trim, in his capacity as Churchwarden, was in correspondence with the Charity Commissioners about the Revd. Williams Charity. Now that the Almshouses were no longer in existence the original terms of the Trust could no longer be carried out.

In the ensuing earlier years the Rector and the Churchwardens arranged for the distribution of coal to Senior Citizens and needy cases.

The rising cost of coal and the small amount of income available made this practice impractible, and so distributions of cash contributions towards heating were now made whenever there are sufficient funds available.

On 27th February 1982 the distribution of £3 each to 30 households was made at the cost of £90 plus envelopes for 50p from W.H.Smith. A very small balance was carried forward at that time. The remaining balance from the fund was held in a bank account. Under the incumbency of Revd. Peter Wood the decision was taken to donate the small amount of remaining money to Water Aid.

Court Garden

Court Garden, nowadays often called the Moat Field, lies behind St. Mary's Church.

It is often used by walkers, dog walkers, and families and it may be of interest to include some of its history here, even though we will begin by going back a little further than the beginning of the 20th Century!

The entrance gate is at right angles to the churchyard wall, in Garston Lane, the western side of the field. To the south, it is bordered by a field clearly showing the original ridge and furrow system of agriculture used from medieval times. The old millstream marks the eastern edge of the field and, since 1971, the northern edge has been bordered by the houses and gardens of the short road called Court Gardens.

In "Phelp's History of Somerset" (1836) Court Garden is described:

On the south east of the church is a square piece of land, containing about an acre, moated round, and exhibiting traces of ruined buildings overgrown with grass. At a short distance on the east is a raised terrace walk, which extended into the adjoining fields. No tradition exists as to this building or to whom it belonged. The most probable supposition is, that it was the mansion of the Barons Beauchamp, to whom the manor belonged in the time of Edward III. (1327-1377).

Nowadays there is little trace of these "ruined buildings" apart from grassy mounds. It is thought that at one time the island within the moat contained various buildings, possibly stables, barns, kitchens and the manor house; and, around the moat, there are traces of paddocks, gardens and other buildings.

The moat may have been a defensive ditch or possibly just a status symbol. The south side is very wide and linked at the southwest corner to a rectangular hollow, which was possibly a fishpond. The date of the moat is not known but it was probably dug in the 13th or 14th century and was considerably deeper than it is today, even within the memory of older villagers still living here.

Kelly's Directory of Somerset 1861 states:

Here are the remains of some ancient building, with a moat and fishponds; it is now called Court garden.

In 1924, the Revd. G.F.C. Peppin, in his booklet "Marston Magna and its Church", makes a connection between Court Garden and Court House (adjacent to Marston Court) as follows:

There is a field known as the Court Garden and the two (i.e. the Court House and Court Garden), local tradition says, are connected by an underground passage. The old folk say that a monastery or convent once existed on the site of the Court gardens, but there is no evidence to support this tradition. The remains of the quadrangular moat, which are very complete, evidently point to the existence of a moated grange in former days, and traces of one or more drawbridges still exist.

Later in his booklet he quotes from Collinson's History of Somerset:

The manor was held by the Barons Beauchamp of Hatch and continued in that name til the time of Edward III when it passed by the co-heiress of John de Beauchamp of Sir John Meriet. In the time of Henry V it was in the Stourton family and in the reign of Edward IV was in the possession of Humphrey Stafford, Earl of Devon. In 1690 Lennard Lord Dacoe did seized of it; and has now for its possessor Humphrey Sydenham of Dulverton, Esq. who inherits it from Sir John St. Barbe. Since that time the property has been purchased by the Governors of Winchester College who are now the owners.

In 1927 the Warden and Scholars Clerks of St. Mary College of Winchester sold 138 acres of land, (including Court Garden) and farm buildings in Marston Magna to Samuel Pitman. At that time he lived at Vine Farm, originally to the west of the Manor House, but long since demolished to make way for four new houses built in the 1970s. (Church Walk). Samuel Pitman subsequently moved to Park Farm.

Samuel Pitman died in December 1966, and in 1968 a small part of the land known as Court Garden, approximately 2.2 acres, was sold to Peter Jones, one time owner of Marston Garage, who planned to develop it.

On the north eastern corner of this land were three cottages, built alongside the stream, approached from over the mill bridge. Mrs. Davis, in her book about the village in 1900, describes how a paved path led to the front doors on the south side of the cottages. There was a well nearby and an outdoor wooden privy. These cottages were occupied until the

1930s when the first council houses were built. Les Sayers (see chapter: A Century of Childhood) lived in one of the cottages as a boy.

The cottages were possibly used for storage by the farmer for some years, but were derelict by the time the land was sold for development in 1968.

Five houses were built between 1971 and 1972, ten feet above the stream. The developer and the Yeovil planning department came to an agreement to call the new houses "Court Gardens." When the new access road was taken over by the council, they insisted on regulation street lighting, which was not universally popular in the village!

In 1986 Ian Burrow, the Field Archaeologist from Somerset County Council, published a report on The Moated Manor House in the Parish magazine:

> *In December 1985 Somerset County Council bought the moat field next to the church. This was done to make sure that the ancient monument in the field is preserved for all time, and to give the village a freely accessible open space. ... the purchase would not have been made possible without the extremely generous contribution of £2000 from twenty-four individuals in the village. The total cost of the 5-acre field was £13,000.*
>
> *...the site is a very good example of the type of establishment built by lesser lords and gentry in the Middle Ages....*
>
> *Finally, a legal note. The site is protected by law as a Scheduled Ancient Monument. It is sad to say that nationally important sites of this sort are often a target for treasure hunters these days. If you see anyone digging on the site or using a metal detector on it they are breaking the law and should be reported to the police. The best protection such a site can have is the sympathy and interest of the people living near it. I am sure the moat has this, and that its future is secure.*

THE MANOR HOUSE AND MARSTON COURT

The Manor House

The Manor House is situated south west of the church. It is a long low seventeenth century house, with mullioned windows grouped together in twos and threes with hood-moulds. The doorway has a cambered head. On the wall at the back of the house is a sundial, which has this inscription above it: "As shadows so man's life doth goe"

It was owned in 1867 by Charles Parsons, who passed it on to Samuel Parsons. In 1905 the Manor was sold to William Roberts. Meanwhile, living at the Manor in 1900, were Mr and Mrs Lane and their daughter, Ada. Mr Lane farmed there, as M.I Davis writes in her history of Marston Magna. They kept dairy cows, hens and ducks. The butter was made in the cool dairy at the back of the house and sold to the villagers. The hens and ducks produced eggs, also sold to the village inhabitants. As well as farming Mr Lane was a gardener at the Court.

In 1901 the Fête was held in the Glebe Field between Wickham Farm and the Rectory. The schoolgirls danced around the maypole and Ada Lane was chosen to be May Queen.

Mr Roberts restored the Manor in 1910. It is during this restoration that a bullock's heart containing pins was found in a chimney and a body of a baby bricked up near a fireplace. John Linthorne, who was the Parish Clerk, overheard that the lady at the Manor House would like to hear of the history of the bullock's heart—"well it was put there in the year 1849 by a Miss Mary Parsons, who was supposed to be bewitched at that time and she was told to get this heart and buy an ounce of pins and stick it with them and hang it up in the chimney and when this heart would drop all would be well."

John Linthorne was working at the self same time as this happened:

> *My wife was a servant there at the same time and know it to be correct and my wife and I know it well to be true.*

The restored Manor was put up for sale by auction on 6 June 1913 as recorded in the magazine, *Country Life*. It was bought by Mrs M.A. Stroud, who sold it on to Mr Chichester.

The Chichester family lived in the Manor until 1917.

A MEMORY OF THE PAST: MARSTON MAGNA MANOR

1913 - 1917

By Michael Chichester.

In December 1913 my family bought Marston Manor. Since their marriage in April 1905 my parents had lived in rented houses in places convenient for my father's naval appointments. Marston Manor was their first real home and they were delighted with it.

At the time of the move to Marston there were three children in the family, Charles (7), Hugh (6), and Anne (3). My father, a Commander R.N., was in command of a destroyer, H.M.S. HORNET in the Harwich Force.

At that time some three centuries old the Manor was a house of history and legend. Soon after her arrival my mother received from the author, Tom Cobbleigh, a copy of his delightful tale of Somerset folk and village life in the 1820s, "Gentleman Upcott's Daughter". Here the Manor is immortalised as the home of Gentleman Upcott and can be recognised by the description of his family's arrival there:

> *Thus they crossed the little footbridge by the ford, passed the pound and the village stocks, and entered the old farmhouse, somewhat retired from but facing the high road.*

My father was on leave for the family's first Christmas and New Year at Marston. Calls were exchanged with neighbours and many new friends made. The Goodfords at Chilton Cantelo and the Medleycotts at Sandford Orcas were some of the nearest neighbours. Across the road at the Rectory the Revd. and Mrs. Peppin were kind and helpful to the new arrivals and their three sons, Tom, John, and Phil, who often came over to play with Charles and Hugh.

In the garden there was a seesaw, a swing and a yew tree, which the boys enjoyed climbing. The lawn was large enough for games. In the summer of 1914 my mother wrote – "The children all so well and happy here." A favourite outing was a drive in the pony cart for a family picnic on Corton Beacon. Relations and old friends came to stay and there were children's parties for the neighbouring families. Charles and Hugh started their education with an excellent governess, Miss Hole, who cycled over every day from West Camel where her family lived.

But dark clouds were gathering during that first happy summer and war was declared on Germany on Aug. 4th 1914. My mother was left alone with the children to cope with the worries and difficulties of life in a nation at war.

H.M.S. HORNET was soon engaged in North Sea actions. My father was at sea on active service until July 1918 with only the occasional brief spells of leave at home throughout all these years. In June 1915 he left H.M.S. HORNET and took command of the patrol cruiser, H.M.S. Forward, which was ordered soon after to the Aegean Sea, where she remained for the rest of the war.

At Marston my mother organised a "Ladies Working Party, to make garments for the hospital ships." In the summer of 1916 a local newspaper reported the last meeting of the Working Party for that season when: -

Mrs. Chichester, in a neat little speech, thanked Mrs. Ketley for so kindly cutting out all the garments, and all those who helped to make them. Twelve parcels were sent to the hospital ships containing 269 articles, including sleeping suits, bed jackets, surgical shirts etc.. For so small a village this result is highly satisfactory and a credit to all concerned. Mrs. Chichester and Mrs Chatterton kindly provided tea for the workers at each meeting.

In the summer my mother invited all the village school children to tea in the Manor garden. There were games on the lawn and Hugh always enjoyed these parties and talking to the "big boys."

In May 1915 Charles started at his preparatory school, St. Aubyn's, Rottingdean near Brighton, and Hugh followed him there in September 1916. Anne began lessons at home. My mother stayed with friends in Brighton for visits to the school for half term, sports days and concerts. Both boys enjoyed school and were happy there.

My mother was a kind, gentle and religious person. As a girl she had taught children at Sunday school in the chapel near her home in Yorkshire and at Marston Magna, the family were regular churchgoers. At home on Sunday evenings there were family hymns sung to my mother's piano accompaniment and daily Bible reading after evening prayers.

During the wartime years of constant worry and anxiety for those on active service, prayers for their survival were a much-needed source of comfort and hope. Every village suffered losses of its men folk as the war memorials record, and Marston Magna was no exception.

Within the first year of the war my mother suffered grievously. She lost a nephew on Oct. 26th 1914 and his brother on Feb. 8th 1915 both killed in France. On Nov. 12th 1914 my father's first cousin, Guy a great favourite of the family after whom I am named, was also killed in France. And on May 27th 1915 my mother lost her dear naval brother, Humphrey, who died when his ship, H.M.S. PRINCESS IRENE blew up with the loss of all hands in Sheerness Harbour. As she put in her diary it had been "a terrible six months of war."

The winter of 1916 – 1917 passed without further misfortunes but this calm was not to last. In March 1917 Charles became ill at school with tonsillitis and despite the subsequent operation complications set in and he was unwell for several weeks. My mother went to Rottingdean to be near him and contracted chicken pox whilst staying with the Headmaster and his wife. At the same time Hugh became very ill. He died suddenly of meningitis in the school sanatorium on March 31st 1917 and was buried at Rottingdean.

My mother was heartbroken. With his equable affectionate and happy nature Hugh had become her favourite in many ways. She saw in him more of a kindred spirit than she did in his brother and sister, both of whom were more difficult in character, harder to bring up and who suffered more from the prolonged absences of their father.

By a stroke of good fortune in March my father had been able to return home from Malta for two weeks leave whilst his ship was refitting there. Hugh had died the day after he had left Malta for the long overland journey home from Brindisi.

As soon as he reached London he went down to Rottingdean to bring strength and comfort to all in their adversity and to help with all the sad tasks which fall to a bereaved family.

After the funeral my parents returned to Marston with Charles, who then underwent his second operation. After his leave my father left for Malta and did not return to England until July 1918.

Left alone once more my mother felt unable to remain at Marston. The memories of the happy years there in the first family home were too hard to bear. On June 1st she sold the Manor House to Mr Coote for £1,700 and took Charles and Anne to Woolacombe for the sea air Charles needed after his long illness. Later she moved to Denham in Buckinghamshire, where she had been lent a house by her cousin, Colonel Ben Way of Denham Place.

More compensation for the family's misfortunes was to come. On December 22nd 1917 I was born at Hill House, Denham. Family morale was restored and the sadness of Hugh's death was somewhat diminished but never forgotten.

During those last weeks at Marston it must have been almost unbearable for my mother to pray in the church sitting in the familiar pew with an empty place beside her. She wished that Hugh could be remembered there so before leaving she gave to the church the picture of "Suffer little children to come unto Me," with its inscription:

> *Placed in Marston Magna church to the glory of God and in ever loving memory of Hugh Chichester. Born November 26th 1907 – passed away March 31st 1917.*

This picture that hangs in the Lady Chapel and his grave at Rottingdean are the memorials to an innocent, happy and lovable child.

John Peppin wrote this memory of the Chichester boys:

> *The two sons were away at school most of the time, but we did play with them very occasionally. They had much more elaborate toys than ours, and in particular, they had a layout of rails and steam engines, which put our German 5/- engine, and one circle of rails, to shame.*

The next owners and occupants were John Coote and his wife Norah, who bought the Manor on 1st June 1917 for £1,700 from the Chichester family. John Coote was a Lieutenant Commander R.N. and during the Great War he was in the R.N.V.R. (the Royal Naval Volunteer Reserve). Men who were not required at sea, fought on land alongside the army during World War I.

The Manor changed hands again in 1920, when John Coote sold it to Mr Thomas Stanford-Booth, who is recorded by Kelly's Directory to be living at the Manor in 1923. He sold it in 1929 to the Chichester family, who had lived there before.

Captain Cecil George Chichester D.S.O., another member of the Chichester family, earned his decoration in April 1918:

> *In recognition of the energy, good judgment and coolness under fire with which he organised and executed the evacuation of the Aerodrome at Thermi, on the 9th to 15th October, 1917. The evacuation of the Aerodrome was carried out under continuous bombardment by the enemy, and was effected entirely without casualties and without loss of stores.*

Mrs. Chichester sold the Manor in November 1932 to three buyers, who were Mrs Louise Forbes Robertson, George Victor Wallender, and Walter Stanley Rigby.

Lt. Col. Walter Rigby D.S.O. has a service record, held at Kew. He left Ireland at the age of 16 with the Royal Irish Rifles to fight in the first Boer war. He was made a captain when serving with the King's African Rifles and a Major while serving with the East African Police, and a Lieutenant Colonel while serving in the Durham light Infantry, in which he served until the armistice.

In May 1933 Captain John Geoffrey Frere bought the Manor and lived there with his wife, Violet Ivy, until 1938, when it was sold to Mr Charles Henry Hardcastle, who lived there with his wife Hazel Isobel. Gertrude Lawson also lived there at this time.

During the war the Manor was taken over by the British Forces, and later by the Americans. (See chapter on WAR).

During the war young women who served in the WRNS were billeted in the Manor. Each day they cycled to the Fleet Air Arm base at Yeovilton and returned in the evening.

After the war, Philip H.C. Illingworth R.N. bought the Manor in 1945 and lived there with his wife Dorothy and family. His daughter, Sally, says he bought it for a song. She says £1000 was deducted because of the ghost and a further £1000 chopped off because of church bells. She doesn't remember the ghost being green, however, she is sure it was grey!

Most of the Illingworth children were born while living at the Manor: Gay, Sally, Richard, Michael, Norman and Sophie.

P.H.C. Illingworth served on H.M.S. Warspite to 16th September 1937 and the next two years from 16th April 1939 on H.M.S. Indomitable. During the war he rose from Commander to Captain. On 7th January 1967 he was appointed a Naval Aide to the Queen. He later became appointed to the rank of Rear Admiral.

While living in the village he was a member of the Parochial Church Council and the Parish Council. He organised the planting of Silver Birch Trees in front of the church to mark the Silver Jubilee of the Queen in 1977. In September 1979 Admiral Illingworth approached the Archdeacon regarding the erection of a Village Silver Jubilee Weather Vane on the tower. In 1980 permission was granted and the Weather Vane was put in place. He also organised the purchase of a new flagpole, as the old one had split in half during winter storms.

Rear Admiral Illingworth died in May 1987. On May 22nd a Quarter Peel was rung following interment of ashes on that day. The family arranged a Thanksgiving Service for his life at Wells Cathedral on 22nd May, and Peter Clarke organised a coach to take villagers from Marston Magna and Rimpton to the Cathedral.

His wife, Dorothy Jean (Dottie) died on 10th July 2007 while living in Sherborne. She was a devoted grandmother and great- grandmother to their many children, and took an active part in village life. The funeral and thanksgiving service was held on 27th July.

The Manor was sold in 1987 to Mr. Hugh Privett and his wife Jane. They have four children. Hugh Privett is Treasurer of the PCC and organist at St Mary's Church. Hugh and Jane have organised and hosted many Church Garden Parties in their garden, to raise much-needed funds for the church, and Hugh takes responsibility for mowing the village green and makes sure that the church clock keeps good time!

Marston Court

Mrs Davis describes how Marston Court appeared in her childhood:

The entrance to Marston Court from Yeovil Road was open and treeless behind its big gates and apart from wandering down Garston Lane past the back way in, this was unknown country to most of us. Mr. Roberts lived there then. They had a little pew in the chancel at St Mary's and always came into church through the little priest door in the south wall.

William Chatterton and his wife, Ethel Mary, lived at Marston Court during WW1 and Mrs Chatterton continued to reside there in the early 1920s.

Then Lt-General Sir William Rayne Marshall G.C. M.G., K.C.B., K.C.S.I. was resident at Marston Court. Sir William Rayne Marshall (1865-1939) saw service in WW1. By 1917 he was Commander-in-Chief on the Mesopotamian Front. After the war he returned to service in India before retiring in 1924.

Mr Herbert Ashworth Hope (1880-1962) and his wife Mary Letitia retired to Marston Court, which they enlarged in 1927. Mrs Ashworth Hope was a keen rider. They kept two grooms and a gardener.

Herbert Ashworth Hope had a music room at the Court with a theatre organ and held musical evenings. BBC in the West recorded some concerts there. Some people in the village were invited to sing in a choir at Marston Court and they also went to Wells to sing with the choir.

Mr. and Mrs. Ashworth Hope in hunting dress.

Mr Ashworth Hope was a composer. One of his compositions, which became well known to the public, was "Barnacle Bill", used for many years at the start of the Blue Peter television programme. It is interesting to note that Boosey and Hawkes still have 25 of his compositions of his light music on their sheet music list, including "Song of the Blackmore Vale" and "In Grandma's Day".

Herbert Ashworth Hope's musical skill was in addition to his other occupations. He studied at Trinity College, Cambridge, and then became a solicitor in the North West of England. He had numerous business interests, including tin and rubber. Some of his working life was spent overseas. He was a founder member of Gibb and Co., one of the oldest solicitors' firms in Malaysia. He came to Marston Magna to retire, but he was chairman of Malayan Tin Dredging Limited and Southern Malayan Tin Dredging Limited, high profile companies in the 1930s-1950s.

Herbert Ashworth Hope and his wife had 3 children. Their daughter Iris was married at St. Mary's Church. Mr. and Mrs. Ashworth Hope gave the fourteen Stations of the Cross placed around the nave of Marston Magna Church, in memory of their son, Herbert Ebdon Ashworth Hope, who died in 1946, from wounds sustained during World War 2. Like his father, the younger son Eustace Victor Hope (1914-1982) studied at Trinity College before entering the medical world, qualifying at St Thomas' Hospital in 1940. He served in the RAF medical Service 1945-7. He was a surgeon working at London Hospitals until 1951 when he moved to Paignton, Devon and served as both a GP and surgeon at the local hospital for 26 years.

Marston Court was split in 1954.

Mr. and Mrs. D. Innes lived at Marston Court from 1955 with their three children, Elizabeth, Jessica and John. Mr. Innes was a member of the British Legion, and his wife Mary took an active part in village life. Derrick died suddenly just after they had left Marston Court in 1966 to move to Dorset. However, his widow, Mary, missed the village so much that she decided to move back to Marston Magna and arranged to have Traist House built in Camel Street. She was a keen and knowledgeable gardener, and at one time a trustee of the Village Hall.

Following her death, her daughter Elizabeth wrote in the Village Magazine:

> *The family moved to Marston Magna in 1955. Mother immediately joined in the life of the village. She joined the W.I. first and was then asked to do church cleaning by the late Sallie Brown. She became a member of the PCC, and then Secretary. Later on she became Church Electoral secretary. She was also a member of the Parish Council for many years.*
>
> *Her first love was the W.I. and she was at different times Secretary, President and for one year only, Treasurer! (I think Father did most of the work).*
>
> *In early 1996 she moved to Fir Villa, where she lived out the remainder of her days. Mother used to do "meals on wheels". She told me that if she had only realised at the time how much the ladies and gentlemen relied on her, and for the bits of chat about the village, she would have tried to stay longer.*

Following the church service after her mother's death in 1998 Elizabeth wrote that:

> *...the family had felt supported by the love and affection the village had for her...she is at peace among friends.*

On the electoral roll of 1974, Judith A Wheeldon and Peter G. Wheeldon are listed as living at Marston Court. They may have left by 1980.

James D Hickman is listed as living there at same time as the Wheeldons, but not for as long and not in 1974 or 1975.

By 1980 Mr. and Mrs. Martin Gee were living at the Court, with their children Caroline, Sarah and Wilfred. The Parish Magazine of May 1980 stated:

The Garden Party will be held at Marston Court this year on July 19th by kind invitation of Mr. and Mrs. Martin Gee.

Martin and Pat Gee were both active members of the Choir at St Mary's Church.

In 1985 Marston Court was inhabited by Mr and Mrs J.N.B. Jacobsen, Elizabeth and John.

By 1988 Major General Eric Mackay and his wife came from London to live at Marston Court. Major Mackay was awarded medals: Commander of the Most Excellent Order of the British Empire, Distinguished Service Cross.

The Vicar wrote in the Parish Magazine of June 1998:

A most welcome gift to the church at Marston Magna is that of a St George's flag, given in proud memory of Major General Eric MacKay by his wife and dedicated on Sunday 10th May. You will know I am sure, the exciting story of his leadership, ultimate capture and daring escape following the Arnhem landings of 1944. At one stage he was half-buried beneath a pile of bricks, at another one enemy bullet shattered the binoculars slung around his neck, whilst another pierced his helmet!

Ultimately a bayonet thrust into his thigh forced him to surrender, but his second attempt to escape, using a rudderless boat and only one oar to carry him downstream to the allied lines at Nijmegen was successful, all within one week after the initial parachute landing. Later in life he was chief engineer of four armies before retiring from the army in 1976. Thereafter he was primarily engaged in large-scale construction projects abroad. Sadly he came to Marston Court all too late in life. He loved it here and looked forward to taking a full part in village life. This is the man in whose memory the new St. George's flag will fly over the village. How thankful we should all be as we approach the Millennium that men and women such as he served our country in its hour of need.

Mrs.Mackay was a great character and very supportive of village events, such as the Harvest Supper, and the Fête. Hadders, as she was known, kept several dogs, from a standard poodle to small dachshunds, which she would exercise in the fields of the village, always wearing a lovely hat! The dogs were very well behaved when out, and followed her everywhere. She lived here until a few years after the Millennium.

Post 2000

Post 2000, time has not stood still and neither has Marston Magna! We offer a list of innovations and changes that have taken place up to this publication in 2015 and invite you, some unknown and probably yet unborn Marstonian, to take up the challenge to record the next century in the life of "Our Village".

2000	Millennium Celebrations
2002	New Doctor's surgery built at Queen Camel
2002	Welcome Pack for new arrivals was initiated
2000-2004	New playground equipment installed beside the Village Hall
2007	Revd. Michael Hayes (vicar) and Mrs Hilary Hayes (lay reader) arrived in the village.
2008	The Village Café opened for the first time by Mrs. Hilary Hayes in March
	The Introduction of a speed indicator device sponsored by Perrys and the formation of a volunteer speed watch team
2009	A fire at Perrys
2010	Closure of The Red Lion Public House
2012	Jubilee Stone laid on village green
2014	First woman vicar - Revd. Barbara Stanton
2015	Introduction of Superfast Broadband
	Marston Magna W.I. 90th Anniversary

New Builds

Homefield Court development, corner of Little Marston Road.
Holly Cottage, Rimpton Road
Millstone House , Rimpton Road
The Garden House, Church Walk
Bungalow in Little Marston Road

Population

In the 1901 census it was evident that the constituents of households varied. There were households made up of parents and children but quite often a variety of family members resided together. Nephews, nieces, sister-in- laws, and sisters were frequently listed. For the most part these family members were younger than the head of the household. There was an instance of a father-in-law residing with a family but he was still in employment. One household had an aged uncle living with a widowed nephew and his sister. One family of children lived with a grandparent. The occasional household had a lodger. The dynamics of households changed as the century progressed, families were smaller and households less diverse. Later in the century the additional family members joining a household seemed to be of the elder generation, often parents moving to live with their children.

Post 2000

There has again been a change in households as children are often living with their parents for longer than previously due to challenging economic circumstances.

Date	Population	Male	Female	Total Households
1901	272			73
1911	311	147	164	73
1921	308	152	156	73
1931	336	166	170	87
1951	295	155	140	96
1961	337	174	163	114
1971	390	195	195	
1977	485			175
1981	484			169
1991	473	223	240	184

Acknowledgements

We would like to thank all those people who have kindly helped us by giving information and time to talk to us. We cannot mention them all, but would like to include the following:

The Marden Family - Jim Nowell and Muriel Marden, the Noyce Family - Andy, Geoff, Dean and Lorna, the Chainey Family - Ron, Michael and Kath, Bernie Darch, Judith Taylor and Geoff Biggins, Les Dewey, Ann Hayward, Biddy Peppin and Jinny Fisher, Mark Willis, Tom and Jill Martin, Peter Clarke, Betty Lashmar and Joan Sheen, Charles Lodge, Tony and Nigel Penn, Brian Perry, Suzanne Pitman, Dilys Jagelman, Ricky Gibbs, Norman Holt, David Crabb, Chris Dennett, Stella Highmore, the late Gladys Bond, Maureen Ashman (née Trim), Liz Grant, Archivist, Somerset Heritage Centre, Debra Mallett, Somerset Library Information Service.

Finally, we did not speak with them but they spoke to us, and without them many of these memories and much of this book would have been lost…

Marian Davis, John Peppin, Les Sayers, Henry Trim, and Brenda Darch.

Sources of Reference

Abbreviation: S.H.C. - Somerset Heritage Centre

The Churches:

http://www.flightglobal.com/pdfarchive/view/1961/1961%20-%201750.html
Date Accessed: 3rd February 2015
S.H.C. D/P/mar.m/23/12 1951-1994 Visitors Book
St Marys Church Visitors Book 1994-to date
The Methodist Church. Marston Magna. Personal Papers of Mrs E. Robinson
Parish Magazine April 1979
S.H.C. D\N\yeo/4/1/4 Marston Magna trustee documents 1914-1966
S.H.C. D\N\yeo/4/2/34 Marston Magna Methodist Church Council Meeting minute book

The Parish Council:

http://www.british-history.ac.uk/vch/som/vol7/pp131-138#h3-0006
Date Accessed: 20th January 2015
http://www.legislation.gov.uk/ukpga/1972/70/section/9
Date Accessed: 17th June 2015
http://www.legislation.gov.uk/ukpga/Vict/56-57/73/section/6
Date Accessed: 17th June 2015

Farming:

Kelly's Directory of Somerset and the City of Bristol, 1919 pp.326-7
http://www.yeovilhistory.info/aplin%20and%20barrett.htm
Date Accessed: 26th June2015
Parish Magazine June 1978
http://www.history.co.uk/shows/the-real-war-horse/articles/history-of-horses-during-wwi Date Accessed: 26th June 2015
http://www.nfuonline.com/about-us/history/farming-and-the-first-world-war/
Date Accessed: 26th June 2015
International Journal of Dairy Technology Volume 51, Issue 3, p. 77 August 1998
British Agriculture in the First World War (RLE The First World War) by Peter Dewey. Routledge, 2014

http://timewitnesses.org/english/food/Rations.html
Date Accessed: 10th July 2015
http://www.tbfreeengland.co.uk/assets/4148 Date Accessed: 10th July 2015
http://researchbriefings.files.parliament.uk/documents/SN03339/SN03339.pdf
Date Accessed: 10th July 2015
http://www.google.co.uk/?gwsrd=ssl#q=Outbreaks+of+foot+and+mouth+in+Somerset+in+1916
Date Accessed: 26th June 2015
http://hansard.millbanksystems.com/lords/1933/nov/16/foot-and-mouth-disease-in-somerset Date Accessed: 26th June 2015
http://hansard.millbanksystems.com/lords/2001/may/03/foot-and-mouth-disease Date Accessed: 26th June 2015
http://www.somerset.gov.uk/business-and-economy/do-business-with-the-council/county-farms/Somerset Date Accessed: 10th July 2015
Parish Magazine March 1979

Social Life

Marston Magna at the turn of the century by M.I.Davis sometime of this parish. Alpahbooks. 1984
Memoirs of John Peppin (1904 -1987) Personal papers of the Peppin family
Parish Magazine May 1977
Recollections of Brenda Darch (1930- 2002) Personal papers of the Darch family
Minutes of Committee 1926-1929 re. catering for The Ancient Order of Foresters' social events.
Kelly's Directory of Somerset, 1939. p.306
http://www.forestersfriendlysociety.co.uk/about-us/history/
Date Accessed: 13th March 2015
http://www.epsomandewellhistoryexplorer.org.uk/Foresters.html
Date Accessed: 13th March 2015
S.H.C. A\BTW/1/1 Minutes of the Marston Magna and District Branch 1955-78
S.H.C. A\BTW/1/2 Minutes of the Marston Magna and District Branch 1979-88
S.H.C. A\BTW/3/1 Register of members of the Marston Magna and District Branch 1955-1967
S.H.C. A\BTW/3/2 Register of members of the Marston Magna and District Branch 1967-1977
S.H.C. A\BTW/3/3 Register of members of the Marston Magna and District Branch 1977-1989
Marston Magna Women's Institute 1925-2005 by Agneta Hickley
Parish Magazine September 1981
S.H.C. C/E/4/196/1 Log Book 1904-1927

Employment:

1901 census. Microfilm. Yeovil Library, Somerset. RG 13/ 2300 Subdistrict: Yeovil Civil Parish. Marston Magna
S.H.C. Q/RER/18/1 Register of Electors for Yeovil Constituency 1918
Parish Magazine March 1979. Story of the rabbits taken from 'The Blacksmith'
Kelly's Directory of Somerset, 1902 pp.432-3
Kelly's Directory of Somerset, 1906 pp.327-8
Kelly's Directory of Somerset, 1910 p.327
Kelly's Directory of Somerset, 1914 pp.342-3
Kelly's Directory of Somerset, 1923 pp.339-40
Marston Magna at the turn of the century, by M.I.Davis sometime of this parish. Alpahbooks, 1984
Register of Electors. (Qualifying date, 10 October, 1960) In Force 16th February, 1961, to 15th February, 1962
Queen Camel , Our Royal Heritage, by Gordon Moore. Queen Camel PCC, 1983
http://list.historicengland.org.uk/resultsingle.aspx?uid=1273442
Date Accessed: 10th July 2015
Re: House between Morven and Camelot, High Street, Queen Camel
Kelly's Directory of Somerset, 1923 p. 395
Kelly's Directory of Somerset, 1931 pp.383-4
Kelly's Directory of Somerset, 1935 p.362
Parish magazine September 1977. Mrs M. Davis' information re Christmas post in 1900
http://www.aim25.ac.uk/cgi-bin/vcdf/detail?coll_id=17230&inst_id=124&nv1=search&nv2= Date Accessed: 3rd March 2015
Re: Post Office; Inland Mail Services: Money Orders and Postal Orders
Extract from Birchfield School Domesday Survey. 1985

The School

Parish Magazine April 2006. The Sir John St. Barbe Foundation
http://www.british-history.ac.uk/vch/som/vol7/pp131-138#fnn20
Date Accessed: 22nd January 2015
Gillard D (2011) *Education in England: a brief history*
www.educationengland.org.uk/history Date Accessed: 22nd January 2015
Parish Magazines May 1977, September 1978, December 1977
S.H.C. C/E/4/196/1 Log Book 1904-1927
S.H.C. C/E/4/196/2 Log Book 1928-1951
S.H.C. D\P\mar.m/18/8 Reports on school buildings, plans, estimates, specifications; accounts and vouchers relating to buildings and their repair

S.H.C. D\P\mar.m/18/8/1 Correspondence concerning the installation of School Lighting
Correspondence. A.R. McMillan to Revd. A.J.Bartlett. (22nd July 1949)
Correspondence. Revd.A.J. Bartlett to A.R.McMillan. (25th July 1949)
Correspondence. Lieutenant Colonel Russell Anderson to Mrs.P. Goodwin (18th September 2007).

Families

http://www.yeovilhistory.in fo/workhouse-2.htm Date Accessed: 14th July 2015
Re: A-Z of Yeovil's History by Bob Osborn, See: The need for Victorian Improvements

Personalities

Parish Magazine December 1988 The Late Mrs. Sallie Brown - A Tribute by the Revd. Peter Clarke
Walter Raymond : The man, his work and letters by Evelyn V. Clark *and Somerset and her Folk Movement* by Walter Raymond. Dent, 1933

A Century of Childhood

Memoirs of John Peppin (1904 -1987) Personal papers of the Peppin family
Down the Lane by - *a childhood memory* Mrs.M.I.Davis first appeared in the Parish Magazine of October 1978
Now and Then Marston Magna L.H.Sayers *in a reminiscent mood of Marston Magna* P.P .n.d. Tite Collection, Yeovil Library

Extreme Weather

S.H.C. C/E/4/196/1 Log Book 1904-1927
S.H.C. C/E/4/196/2 Log Book 1928-1951
Parish Magazines 1978, 1979

The Wars

S.H.C. Q/RER/18/1 Register of Electors for Yeovil Constituency 1918
S.H.C. C/EW/8/3 WW1 (Marston Magna entry)
Memoirs of John Peppin (1904-1987) Personal papers of the Peppin family
Recollections of Brenda Darch (1930-2002) Personal papers of the Darch family
http://somersetremembers.com/content/storys/the-home-front/marston-magna-where-the-cider-apples-grow.ashx

Date Accessed: 13th February 2015
http://www.1914-1918.net/derbyscheme.html Date Accessed: 13th February 2015
http://webapp1.somerset.gov.uk/her/details.asp?prn=14641
Date Accessed: 28th August 2015 Re. Second World War ammunition dumps, Marston Magna
Marston Magna Women's Institute 1925-2005 by Agneta Hickley.

Services

Marston Magna at the turn of the century, by M.I.Davis sometime of this parish. Alpahbooks. 1984
Now and Then Marston Magna L.H.Sayers *in a reminiscent mood of Marston Magna* P.P.n.d. Tite Collection, Yeovil Library
Memoirs of John Peppin (1904 -1987) Personal papers of the Peppin family
Recollections of Brenda Darch (1930-2002) Personal papers of the Darch family
http://www.engineering-timelines.com/how/electricity/electricity_07.asp
Date Accessed: 3rd July 2015
S.H.C. D\P\mar.m/6/2/2 Papers relating to the Silver Jubilee memorial fund for electric lighting
S.H.C. D\P\mar.m/18/8/1 School Lighting
Kelly's Directory of Somerset, 1902 pp.319-20
Kelly's Directory of *Somerset,* 1906 pp.327-8
Kelly's Directory of Somerset, 1910 p.327
http://www.nrm.org.uk/RailwayStories/railwayvoices/billsquibb.aspx
Date Accessed: 16th February 2015
Branch Lines around Chard and Yeovil from Taunton, Durston and Castle Cary by Vic Mitchell and Keith Smith. Middleton Press, 1999
The WI Cookbook.The first 100 years by Mary Gwynn. Ebury Press, 2015 p.82
Cider and Cider-making A Visit to Marston Magna by W.A.Perkins The Somerset Year Book,1924 p.56
Rimpton In Somerset A thousand years of Village History 938-1939 by Annette Sandison. The Abbey Press, 1983, p.28

Houses

http://www.britishlistedbuildings.co.uk/#VaEtXY1waig
Date Accessed: 10th July 2015
https://historicengland.org.uk/listing/the-list/
Date Accessed: 10th July 2015
S.H.C. D\P\mar.m/17/2/3 Deeds of foundation and settlement of money on Almshouses, sale of stock and accounts.

S.H.C. D\P\mar.m/17/2/2 Sale of Almshouses
S.H.C. Q/RER/18/1 Register of Electors for Yeovil Constituency 1918
S.H.C. Q/RER/18/19 Register of Electors for Yeovil Constituency 1926
S.H.C. Q/RER/18/32 Register of Electors for Yeovil Constituency 1939-40
S.H.C. Q/RER/18/38 Register of Electors for Yeovil Constituency 1948
History and Antiquities of Somersetshire by William Phelps Vol.1 1 J.B.Nichols and Son, London 1836 p.361
Kelly's Directory of Somerset, 1861 p.388
Marston Magna and its Church by Revd. G.F.C. Peppin 1924
The history and antiquities of the county of Somerset, collected from authentick records Vol 2 by John Collinson. Bath, 1791 pp.374-5

The Manor House and Marston Court

South and West Somerset: The Buildings of England by Niklaus Pevsner. Penguin, 1958 p.31
Parish Magazine June 2001 *A Memory of The Past - Marston Magna Manor 1913-17* by Michael Chichester.
Reference made to *Gentleman Upcott's Daughter* by Tom Cobbleigh. Fisher Unwin, 1892
Tom Cobbleigh was pseudonym of Walter Raymond
Kelly's Directory of Somerset, 1923 pp.339-40
http://www.mocavo.co.uk/The-Inns-of-Court-Officers-Training-Corps-During-the-Great-War/231772/144
Date Accessed: 4th July 2015 Re: John Coote
https://livesofthefirstworldwar.org/lifestory/6101032 Date Accessed: 4th July 2015
Kelly's Directory of Somerset, 1923 pp.339-40
Kelly's Directory of Somerset, 1927 p.344
http://discovery.nationalarchives.gov.uk/details/r/C1062659
Date Accessed: 4th July 2015
http://www.forcesreunited.org.uk/forum/54781/1/Col_Walter_Rigby_WW1
Date Accessed: 4th July 2015
Kelly's Directory of Somerset, 1931 pp.326-7
S.H.C. Q/RER/18/32 1939-40 Register of Electors for Yeovil Constituency
Re: P.H.C. Illingworth
http://deriv.nls.uk/dcn30/9270/92703524.30.jpg Date Accessed: 4th July 2015
http://www.flightglobal.com/pdfarchive/view/1958/1958-1-%20-%200055.html Date Accessed: 4th July 2015
https://www.thegazette.co.uk/London/issue/44227/supplement/569/data.pdf
Date Accessed: 4th July 2015
Re: Sir William Rayne Marshall

http://www.firstworldwar.com/bio/marshall_william.htm
Date Accessed: 21st February 2015
http://www.kingscollections.org/catalogues/lhcma/collection/m/ma76-001
Date Accessed: 21st February 2015
Re: Ashworth Hope Family
http://www.robertfarnonsociety.org.uk/index.php/light-music-cds/up-to-december-2013 Date Accessed: 4th July 2015
http://livesonline.rcseng.ac.uk/biogs/E006583b.htm
Date Accessed: 4th July 2015
Register of Electors for Yeovil Constituency (Qualifying date 10th October 1960)
Register of Electors for Yeovil Constituency (Qualifying date 10th October 1974)
Register of Electors for Yeovil Constituency (Qualifying date 10th October 1978)
Register of Electors for Yeovil Constituency (Qualifying date 10th Oct 1982)
Re: Major General Eric Mackay:
Parish Magazine June 1998 Vicar's Letter
http://www.pegasusarchive.org/arnhem/eric_mackay.htm Date Accessed: 21st February 2015

Population

1901-1961 figures from:
http://www.visionofbritain.org.uk/unit/10438068/cube/TOT_POP
GB Historical GIS / University of Portsmouth, Marston Magna AP/CP through time | Population Statistics | Total Population, *A Vision of Britain through Time*. Date Accessed: 20th June 2015
1971-1991 figures from:
1971: From the Census 1971: England and Wales County Report. Somerset Part 1. Office of Population Censuses and Surveys. Published by HMSO, London, 1973.
1977 figures taken from Annual Parish meeting report in Parish Magazine April 1979
1981: from "Persons present" (may include visitors as well as resident population) From the Ward and Civil Parish Monitor 1991 Census Somerset. CEN 91 WCP 36 March 1994
1991 Population figure from:
1991 10% Census Atlas: Information for South Somerset. S.S.D.C. 1993
1981 and 1991 Total Household numbers from:
1991 10% Census Atlas: Information for South Somerset. S.S.D.C. 1993